Routledge Revivals

CONVERSION : CHRISTIAN AND NON-CHRISTIAN

CONVERSION: CHRISTIAN AND NON-CHRISTIAN

A COMPARATIVE AND PSYCHOLOGICAL STUDY

BY
ALFRED CLAIR UNDERWOOD

First published in 1925 by George Allen and Unwin Ltd

This edition first published in 2018 by Routledge
2 Park Square, Milton Park, Abingdon, Oxon, OX14 4RN
and by Routledge
52 Vanderbilt Avenue, New York, NY 10017, USA

Routledge is an imprint of the Taylor & Francis Group, an informa business

© 1925 by Taylor and Francis

All rights reserved. No part of this book may be reprinted or reproduced or utilised in any form or by any electronic, mechanical, or other means, now known or hereafter invented, including photocopying and recording, or in any information storage or retrieval system, without permission in writing from the publishers.

Publisher's Note
The publisher has gone to great lengths to ensure the quality of this reprint but points out that some imperfections in the original copies may be apparent.

Disclaimer
The publisher has made every effort to trace copyright holders and welcomes correspondence from those they have been unable to contact.
A Library of Congress record exists under ISBN:

ISBN 13: 978-0-367-17997-7 (hbk)
ISBN 13: 978-0-367-18000-3 (pbk)
ISBN 13: 978-0-429-05896-7 (ebk)

CONVERSION: CHRISTIAN
AND   NON-CHRISTIAN

CONVERSION: CHRISTIAN AND NON-CHRISTIAN

A COMPARATIVE AND PSYCHOLOGICAL STUDY

BY

ALFRED CLAIR UNDERWOOD

M.A. (Oxon), D.D. (Lond.)

John Clifford Professor and Tutor in the History of Religions in Rawdon College, Leeds; formerly Professor in Serampore College, Bengal

LONDON : GEORGE ALLEN & UNWIN LTD.
RUSKIN HOUSE, 40 MUSEUM STREET, W.C.1

First published in 1925

All rights reserved)

Printed in Great Britain

PREFACE

No apology is needed for a new study of conversion. For some time past the need has been felt of a treatment which would take into account the recent advances in psychology and in the comparative study of religions. In these days it is not possible to separate the Christian from other forms of religious experience. This book is a pioneer attempt to deal with conversion from the comparative as well as the psychological point of view. In a somewhat different form it was approved by the University of London for the Degree of Doctor of Divinity. It is, however, much more than an academic treatise. I have done my best to make the book of practical service to those who are engaged in the ministry of conversion, both at home and abroad.

The work falls into two main parts. In Part I I have thought it desirable to set out at some length the evidence for the fact of conversion in the New Testament and in the non-Christian religions. Part II is mainly psychological. In taking account of the recent advances in psychology, I trust I have not been stampeded by the "latest" theories. I have confined myself to those principles which have won widespread recognition. It has been suggested to me that the general reader and those whose interests are mainly psychological might do well to begin at Part II and then turn back to Part I. Part of the material of the book was delivered in a course of Public Lectures at the University of Leeds in the Spring Term of 1924.

In order to bring down the costs of production it has been found necessary to omit diacritical marks and vowel quantities. If any scholars complain of this omission, which I personally regret, I shall take refuge in the reflection that I may gain the gratitude of many ministers and clergy, who do not find it easy to buy as many books as they would like to do in these days of high prices.

I am indebted to the Rev. Principal H. Wheeler Robinson, M.A., of Regent's Park College, London ; to Professor J. N. Farquhar, D.Litt., of the University of Manchester ; and to my colleague, the Rev. H. C. Rowse, M.A., for serviceable suggestions. My former colleague on the staff of Serampore College, Mr. H. P. Sen Gupta, M.A., was good enough to check my translations from the *Chaitanya Bhagabat* and the *Kadcha* of Govinda Das. Miss Helen Glass, B.A., has rendered similar help in connection with several passages I have cited from French writers. It seemed best to render them into English for the benefit of those who do not read French easily. My greatest debt is to Dr. George Howells, Principal of Serampore College. It is more than ten years since he suggested to me that I should attempt a study of conversion along comparative lines. He has constantly helped me with that stimulus and encouragement he always gives to his junior colleagues. Acting on his suggestion, I have tried in the last chapter to present the case for the supremacy of Christian conversion in such a way as to avoid giving the impression to the non-Christian reader that I am judging the highest type of conversion by what I know will fit in with Christianity. I am deeply grateful to my wife and the Rev. F. Holmes Bedford, of Burnley, for the time and labour they have spent on the proofs.

It only remains to add that the Index is also a Glossary. In it a number of unusual words and phrases are explained.

A. C. UNDERWOOD.

RAWDON,
   December 1924.

CONTENTS

	PAGE
PREFACE	5

INTRODUCTION

CHAPTER
I. THE COMPARATIVE AND PSYCHOLOGICAL METHODS . 11

PART I

HISTORICAL

II.	CONVERSION IN THE OLD TESTAMENT AND LATER JUDAISM	17
III.	CONVERSION IN CLASSIC CHRISTIANITY	23
IV.	CONVERSION IN HINDUISM	46
V.	CONVERSION IN EARLY BUDDHISM	67
VI.	CONVERSION IN ISLAM	80
VII.	CONVERSION IN THE RELIGIONS OF GREECE AND ROME	90
VIII.	CONVERSION IN VARIOUS NON-CHRISTIAN RELIGIONS	95
IX.	THE DRAMATIC REPRESENTATION OF REGENERATION	100

PART II

PSYCHOLOGICAL

X.	CONVERSION AND ADOLESCENCE	116
XI.	EXPERIENCES PRECEDING CONVERSION	132
XII.	TYPES OF CONVERSION	143

8 *Conversion : Christian and Non-Christian*

CHAPTER		PAGE
XIII.	THE IMMEDIATE ACCOMPANIMENTS OF CONVERSION	153
XIV.	THE PSYCHOLOGICAL MECHANISM OF CONVERSION	177
XV.	CONVERSION DURING REVIVALS	197
XVI.	THE FRUITS OF CONVERSION	223
XVII.	THE INDIVIDUAL AND THE SOCIAL	245

PART III

XVIII.	CONVERSION IN ITS COMPARATIVE ASPECTS	258
	INDEX AND GLOSSARY	279

LIST OF ABBREVIATIONS USED

D.A.C.	Hasting's Dictionary of the Apostolic Church.
D.C.G.	Hasting's Dictionary of Christ and the Gospels.
E.R.E.	Encyclopædia of Religion and Ethics.
Farquhar, M.R.M.	Modern Religious Movements in India (N.Y., 1919).
Farquhar, O.R.L.I.	Outline of the Religious Literature of India (Oxford, 1920).
Finney	Charles G. Finney: An Autobiography (London, 1892).
H.D.B.	Hasting's Dictionary of the Bible in five vols.
Hujwiri	The Kashf al-Mahjub of Hujwiri, translated by R. A. Nicholson (London, 1911).
I.C.C.	International Critical Commentaries.
James	Varieties of Religious Experience.
J.R.A.S.	Journal of the Royal Asiatic Society.
Macnicol, P.M.S.	Psalms of the Maratha Saints (Calcutta, 1919).
Sarkar	Chaitanya's Pilgrimages and Teachings, being an English translation of the middle part of the Chaitanya-charita-amrita (Calcutta, 1913).
Sen, H.B.L.L.	History of the Bengali Language and Literature (Calcutta, 1911).
Sen, V.L.	Vaisnava Literature of Mediæval Bengal (Calcutta, 1917).
Sen, V.S.P.	Vanga Sahitya Parichaya, being Selections from Old Bengali Literature (Calcutta, 1914).
Starbuck	Psychology of Religion (London, 1899).
Warneck	The Living Forces of the Gospel (Edin., 1909).

INTRODUCTION

CHAPTER I

THE COMPARATIVE AND PSYCHOLOGICAL METHODS

OF the different methods of studying religion now in vogue, the comparative and the psychological are the two which seem to have the greatest attraction for the modern mind. While the exponents of the psychological method have left no part of the religious life untouched, they have devoted most attention to the phenomenon known as conversion. Investigators like Starbuck, James, Coe and Pratt (to mention only a few names) have provided us with a mass of material relating to conversion which is of the utmost value. The diaries of the saints and many other forms of literature have been ransacked and made to yield their data to the investigator, while by means of the *questionnaire* method living men and women have been induced to relate their own spiritual experiences. One thing, at any rate, has been made clear by these researches. Conversion is not simply a lingering superstition among certain sects, but an undeniable fact, occurring at all periods in the history of the Christian Church.

Professor James and others [1] have further recognized that conversion is not a distinctively Christian phenomenon, but one which is also found in non-Christian religions. As yet, however, no attempt has been made on any adequate scale to investigate the phenomena which the non-Christian religions afford; indeed, most investigators have drawn a very narrow circle, and have, so far, been content to take

[1] James, 402 ff.; Pratt, *The Religious Consciousness*, 128 ff.; Newton H Marshall, *Conversion or the New Birth*, 140 ff.

the bulk of their evidence from Protestant Evangelical circles.[1] The conclusions at which they have arrived are, therefore, based on a narrow range of instances. There seems, then, to be room for a study of conversion which will throw the net wider than has hitherto been done, and which will include non-Christian as well as Christian conversion, for the comparative method of studying religion no longer allows us to isolate the Christian from all other religious experiences.

In the present work such an attempt is made to widen the bases of induction by combining the comparative and the psychological method. It is hoped that the attempt will yield results of value to both methods of study. Too often has the comparative method dealt almost exclusively with the institutions and dogmas of religion, omitting from consideration the personal religious life. It has been in frequent danger of stressing the form rather than the content of religion. Nor is it difficult to see why this should be so. In certain stages of its development, religion possesses such a corporate and social character that the student is apt to ignore the question of its effect on individuals. Even if he desires to face this question fully and frankly, the surviving records often fail to help him, since they are often public and political in character and fail to afford him many glimpses of the soul's inner life. In what follows it is hoped to avoid the above-mentioned danger by making the psychological study of religion the handmaid of the comparative method.

As we proceed the limitations imposed upon us by the available data will often be apparent. Though many sources have been ransacked for information, the details forthcoming are often lamentably sparse and tantalizingly meagre. Nowhere, perhaps, is the scantiness of the psychological material more apparent than in the New Testament writings. No one doubts that the New Testament Church was a Church of converted men and women, but, except in the case of Paul, the materials available for reconstructing their conversions are very slight. This is why exponents of the psychological method have, as a rule, left the New

[1] Starbuck frankly concedes this point; 25.

Comparative and Psychological Methods 13

Testament severely alone. In the present work some attempt is made to repair that neglect by using all the available New Testament material. But here, as elsewhere, nothing has been set down which does not bear the marks of psychological probability. Wherever possible the converts have been allowed to tell their story in their own words. No apology is needed, therefore, for the large number of quotations that follow. It may be thought by some that the religions of India bulk more largely than they have any right to do. The reason for this is twofold. In the first place, in no other country has religion taken so many forms and engaged such numbers of men and women in its passionate quest. Secondly, the writer has had the advantage of several years' residence in India and has thus been able, in some degree, to put himself *en rapport* with the psychological climate of the country.

Before proceeding farther, it is necessary to define the sense in which the term " conversion " is used in the following pages. Even by writers on the psychology of religion the term is differently understood and applied. Some omit entirely any reference to the religious nature of the experience. Pratt, for example, says: " The essential thing about conversion is just the unification of character, the achievement of a new self "; " the inner unity of perfect moral selfhood." [1] In accordance with his definition he takes as a typical case of conversion the processes by which an ardent Roman Catholic priest became a free-thinker. That such counter-conversions do occur is well known, but to call them by the great name conversion is to darken counsel. Starbuck in 1899 offered the following definition: " Conversion is characterized by more or less sudden changes of character from evil to goodness, from sinfulness to righteousness and from indifference to spiritual insight and activity." [2] Many would think the definition improved if the words " more or less sudden " were omitted. Conversion processes are known that have extended over some years, and these can hardly be called sudden. The time factor is stressed by Coe also in his latest work. " When this religious self-realization," he writes, " is

[1] Op. cit. 123, 130.   [2] 21; cf. 156 f.

14 Conversion : Christian and Non-Christian

intense and is attained with some abruptness, the change is called conversion."[1]

Saunders omits any reference to the time factor, but, like Starbuck, makes conversion equivalent to an awakening to the sense of religious values. " Conversion," he says,[2] " is the process by which the ' God-consciousness ' hitherto marginal and vague becomes focal and clearly defined, passing from its former position as an accessory to its new position as the most real and penetrative influence in life." But such a definition of conversion would exclude the experience of Paul on the Damascus road, the conversion of al-Ghazali to Sufism, and the experience of John Wesley at 8.45 p.m. on May 24, 1738. In none of these cases can it be said that the God-consciousness was marginal and vague before their conversion.

All the definitions noticed above will cover a certain number of cases ; the difficulty is to frame a definition that will cover every case we are prepared to recognize as a conversion. James's now famous definition will cover a great number of cases, but not all. According to him, conversion is " the process, gradual or sudden, by which a self hitherto divided and consciously wrong, inferior and unhappy becomes unified and consciously right, superior and happy in consequence of its firmer hold upon religious realities."[3] This definition excludes conversions in which there is no conscious feeling of being wrong, divided, inferior and unhappy. It also extends the conversion process beyond the moment when the subject first gets a grip of religious realities. Thus Bunyan's conversion was not completed when he gave up swearing and lying and adopted the religious mode of life. Unification and happiness came to him some years later, when he was rid of the " terrors of the law " by the discovery of the way of faith. Similarly not all the early Buddhist converts were unified and made happy when they accepted the Dhamma and entered the Sangha. Many of them had to spend years in strenuous self-discipline before they attained inner unity and peace. The value of James's definition lies in the fact

[1] *Psychology of Religion*, 152.
[2] *Adventures of the Christian Soul*, 61.   [3] 189 ; see also 196.

that, while it excludes very few cases that we are prepared to recognize as conversions, it includes both the first awakening to the claims of the religious life and the subsequent experiences that are necessary, in some cases, to bring unification and happiness to the soul. It includes, for example, the religious awakening that John Wesley passed through before he founded the Holy Club as well as the experience of the evening just referred to, which experience Wesley always spoke of as his conversion. In the case of Gotama Buddha, it includes both the Great Awakening and the Great Enlightenment. For the present we may accept James's definition of conversion as sufficient for all practical purposes, though we may find it advisable, as we proceed, to prune away some of his adjectives.

Before we set out the evidence for the fact of conversion in the religions of the world, it may be well to raise the question as to the exact stage in the development of religion at which conversions begin to appear. It is sometimes assumed that they cannot take place before the rise of religious individualism, when men begin to assert for themselves a religious status independent of their standing in the corporate body and also begin to reflect on their own inner life. Such an assumption is, however, mistaken. "Since man has been man, he has lived his own life, his heart knowing its own bitterness, and a stranger intermeddling not with its joy."[1] Thus conversion, in the sense of the unification of the unhappy soul by its obtaining a stronger grip on religious realities, is possible even on the lowest levels of the religious life, for even ritualistic tabus may lay a heavy burden on man's conscience. In the nature of the case, however, records of such experiences are not likely to be forthcoming. The only means we now possess of recapturing the religious experience of these cultural levels is the interrogation by trained anthropologists of people living to-day on those levels, and the less satisfactory method of thinking back from existing beliefs and practices to the religious experience that created them.

Even after the introduction of writing has made possible the survival of records, time will need to elapse before

[1] H. Wheeler Robinson, *Christian Doctrine of Man*, 28

16　*Conversion : Christian and Non-Christian*

men turn their gaze inward and develop any marked powers of introspection, and are thus able to produce documents of any great value to the psychologist. The Christian Church had to wait more than three centuries for the appearance of Augustine before it saw another saint with anything like the introspective powers of Paul.[1] These considerations will go far to explain the absence of clear testimony to the fact of conversion in large tracts of the religious history of mankind.

[1] I am not forgetting Tertullian's *de Anima*. One often reflects on the magnificent opportunity missed by Palladius. In his *Lausiac History*, which he gave to the world in 419–20, he gives accounts of more than seventy monks and nuns who had left the world to live the ascetic life in the deserts of Egypt. Obviously many of them were converted men and women, but Palladius only very rarely gives a hint as to the causes that led them to forsake the world.

PART I.—HISTORICAL

CHAPTER II

CONVERSION IN THE OLD TESTAMENT AND LATER JUDAISM

THE story of Jacob's wrestling with the angel at the Brook Jabbok (Gen. xxxii. 24-30) is treated by Driver as a kind of conversion crisis in the life of the Patriarch. He writes:

> "The struggle at Penuel marks the triumph of the higher over the lower elements in his character. It is the critical moment of his life ... memories of the past return upon him; his conscience smites him, and he is 'greatly afraid.' But God is his real antagonist, not Esau; it is God Whom his sins have offended and Who here comes to contest His right. These thoughts and fears are, as it were, materialized in his dream.... The moment marks a spiritual change in Jacob's character. His carnal weapons are lamed and useless—they fail him in his contest with God. As the result of his struggle his natural self is left behind; he rises from it an altered man ... and his new name symbolized his new nature." [1]

If it be objected that Jacob cannot be regarded as an historical person, but only as the imaginary ancestor of a tribe, it is sufficient to reply that, even if the story is unreliable as history, it is still valuable as evidence for the existence of conversion in Old Testament times. It affords the clearest possible proof that the fact of conversion was known to the Jahwistic writer (J).

It is not unnatural to suppose that the historical kernel of the story of the call of Samuel (1 Sam. iii.) is to be found in the conversion crisis of an adolescent. His early training bore its appropriate fruit in the decision deliberately made at that time to dedicate himself to the service of Yahweh.

[1] H.D.B. ii. 533; see also ii. 529 f.

18 *Conversion : Christian and Non-Christian*

The experiences of some of the prophets, when they received their call to the prophetic ministry, seem to be akin to, if not identical with, the experience of conversion. Particularly does this appear to be the case with Isaiah, who received his call in the vision recorded in chap. vi. Standing one day in the temple, he passed into an ecstasy in which he had a vision of Yahweh exalted in majesty. The account is no doubt coloured by the prophet's later experiences, but it is difficult to rid oneself of the impression that Isaiah has here recorded his conversion experience. His conviction of sin, his repentance, and his sense of divine forgiveness are all the marks of a true conversion, a spiritual change. There came to him at this time, as to Paul in later days, a sense of his vocation. It was the supreme moment of his life, and he records no other such experience in the course of a lifetime of prophetic work. "Temple and seraphim are nothing more than the necessary pictorial clothing of the supreme truth that in this vision his soul met the Infinite and Eternal face to face."[1] The prophet's conversion has all the appearance of being sudden, but it need not necessarily have been so. "We may somewhat safely assume that the vision of Yahweh, bringing with it the sudden apprehension on the prophet's part of Yahweh's purpose concerning him, was the culmination of a larger experience ; not, we may well believe, for the first time on that day he felt his own unworthiness or contrasted the moral uncleanness of his people with the ethical holiness of God."[2]

It is permissible to interpret the calls of Amos, Jeremiah and Ezekiel in the light of what has been said in reference to Isaiah. The two last-named received their call to the prophetic ministry in a vision, and it is worth pointing out that Isaiah, Jeremiah and Ezekiel mark down precisely the moment of their call. This surely points back to a definite historical experience which brought their lives into truer harmony with the divine will, for to this experience they trace their subsequent course of action. After it their lives are based on a truer and broader basis. The

[1] Robertson Smith, *The Prophets of Israel*, 218
[2] G. B. Gray, I.C.C., Isa. i. 101.

individual idiosyncrasies of each affect, of course, both the form and the content of this crucial experience. "A straightforward, direct and simple nature, like that of Amos, feels himself taken from following the flock (Amos vii. 15), quickly rises up and sets forth to carry out Yahweh's command. In Isaiah's case a voluntary and free human resolution goes along with the divine calling; Jeremiah is overmastered only by force (i. 6). . . . Ezekiel, after his call, feels as if he had been smitten to the ground by a mighty blow, and in the agitation of his spirit he sits silent and astonied for seven days (iii. 14 ff.)." [1]

A small point in connection with the call of Jeremiah is worth notice. Jer. i. 6 seems to indicate that the prophet was at that time but a youth, though the words, "I cannot speak, for I am a child," may only give expression to Jeremiah's characteristic humility. But if we are at liberty to infer from them that Jeremiah was an adolescent at the time, our contention that the prophetic call was frequently the accompaniment of a conversion crisis receives further support.

This discussion may also prepare us to see in Moses's experience at Horeb a conversion crisis (Exod. iii. 2 ff.). Exiled from the throbbing life of Egypt, the solitudes of the wilderness spake to him, and after his experience of the burning bush his call to a life-long vocation is unmistakable and clear.

It is, of course, possible to argue that thus to construe the calls of the Old Testament prophets is to read into their narratives more than their words allow. "A call is not the same thing as a conversion. The one is a summons to a new work, the other to a new ideal; the one is merely a change of activity, the other a change of heart. Doubtless the two often go together, but they are separable both in thought and experience." [2] What happened in the case of these prophets was that after a period of intense and baffled interest in some moral and spiritual problem, the moment of illumination came suddenly, and the prophet was provided with his message.

[1] Volz in the *Enc. Bib.*, col. 3868.
[2] Canon Streeter in *Foundations*, 97.

20 Conversion : Christian and Non-Christian

The force of these contentions may be admitted without reserve. The real point at issue is whether there is sufficient evidence to warrant the conclusion that in the above-mentioned cases the call to the prophetic vocation was the accompaniment of a definite spiritual change, and not merely a sudden flash of religious insight. That we must accept the first of these alternatives in the case of Isaiah seems hardly open to doubt. In Isa. vi. we have the record of a "spiritual process which the prophet actually passed through before the opening of his ministry."[1] The documentary evidence is not so decisive in the cases of the other prophets, but it is permissible to read it in the light of the undoubted fact that a sense of vocation is frequently one of the results of the psychological ferment caused by the conversion crisis. Who, after reading Jeremiah's wonderful disclosures of the soul's deepest secrets, can doubt that he was a "twice-born" soul?

That the fact of conversion was well known to the Old Testament writers is further evidenced by the manner in which some of the higher minds in Israel sought the conversion of the heathen. Not all the Old Testament writers adopt the exclusive attitude towards the heathen which characterizes some of the prophets and Ezra-Nehemiah. Their conversion is contemplated in the "Servant" Songs of Isa. xl.-lv., while the allegory contained in the Book of Jonah is a clarion call to the Jews to abandon their policy of exclusiveness and rise to that true universalism which seeks the spiritual conversion of those who sit in darkness. How firmly the author of Jonah believed in the possibility of the conversion of the heathen is seen by the manner in which he makes the whole allegory turn on the reality of the spiritual change undergone by the Ninevites (iii. 5-10).

The prophets desired nothing so much as to produce a change in the moral conduct of their hearers. Apparently they expected sudden conversions to take place under their preaching, and aimed at securing them pretty much in the manner of the evangelical preacher of to-day. And it would be a surprising thing if their expectations were not fulfilled. But when we pass to the later stages in the

[1] G. A. Smith, *The Book of Isaiah*, i. 58.

development of religion in Israel this expectation disappears with the passing of the prophet and the growing influence of the priest and scribe. In the changed atmosphere sudden and explosive conversions would be replaced by conversions of the cultural type. Much care was devoted to the training of the young, and the discipline to which they were subjected was more definitely religious than intellectual (Prov. i. 7). The prevailing belief was that, if the young were trained in the law, their spiritual development was thereby secured. No violent break with the past was to be expected, for early religious training might be relied upon to bear its appropriate fruit.

In so far, then, as the Scribal element became dominant, Judaism became, as Mr. Montefiore says, a religion of the " healthy-minded " and of the " once-born." " For the most part it taught a gradual progress in goodness and knowledge and the love of God." [1] Rabbinic theology, as Mr. Abrahams points out, did not look for a permanent change of character by a single act of repentance. " The renewal of man's nature by repentance, unlike the rebirth by conversion, is continuous and constant. It is a regular process, not a catastrophe." [2] But that rebirth by conversion was not unknown even in a Judaistic *milieu* is shown by the following case :

> " Famous is the tale of R. Eliezer b. Durdaiya (second century), who was so addicted to the sin of unchastity that it was said of him that there was no harlot in the world whom he had not visited. It was recorded of him that, on the occasion of his last sin, the harlot herself said to him that his repentance would never be received.
>
> " Then he went forth, and sat between the hills, and said, ' Ye mountains and hills, seek mercy for me.' But they said, ' Before we seek mercy for you, we must seek it for ourselves. . . .' Then he said, ' Heaven and earth, ask mercy for me.' But they said, ' Before we ask mercy for you, we must ask it for ourselves. . . .' Then he said, ' Sun and moon, ask mercy for me.' But they said, ' Before we ask for you, we must ask for ourselves. . . .' Then he said, ' Planets and stars, ask mercy for me.' But they said,

[1] *Judaism and St. Paul*, 48 and 50.
[2] *Studies in Pharisaism and the Gospels*, 42 f. For the Rabbinic insistence on repeated repentance see Schechter, *Some Aspects of Rabbinic Theology*. Vide index, s.v. " Repentance."

22 Conversion : Christian and Non-Christian

'Before we ask for you, we must ask for ourselves. . . .' Then he said, 'The matter depends wholly upon me.' He sank his head between his knees and cried aloud and wept so long till his soul went forth from him. Then a heavenly voice was heard to say, 'R. Eliezer b. Durdaiya has been appointed to the life of the world to come.' But R. Jehudah I., the Patriarch (Rabbi) (second century), wept and said, 'There are those who acquire the world to come in years upon years; there are those who acquire it in an hour.'"[1]

[1] Montefiore, in *The Beginnings of Christianity*, part i., vol. i., 71 f.

CHAPTER III

CONVERSION IN CLASSIC CHRISTIANITY

ALL four Evangelists trace the beginnings of Christianity to the religious movement set on foot by the preaching of John the Baptist and continued in the preaching and ministry of Jesus. It is to be regretted that their accounts of the Baptist's ministry are so slight, but it did not fall within their purpose to recount the life of the Forerunner. It is, however, certain that conversions took place as a result of his ministry. The words put into the mouth of the angel who appeared to Zacharias, "And many of the children of Israel shall he turn unto the Lord their God" (Luke i. 16), certainly embody a genuine historical reminiscence of the Baptist's ministry. John seems consciously to have adopted the rôle of the Old Testament prophet. With eyes aflame with fire he calls his nation to repentance in view of the near approach of the Kingdom of God, which is even now knocking at the door. A sincere repentance is the only way of escaping the coming doom. This chance to repent will soon, however, be withdrawn, and for the unrepentant there can be only a fearful expectation of judgment. Descent from Abraham confers no security, nor is it sufficient to be plunged into water. Each man must make a true repentance and manifest in his life its fruits.

John stated his message in terms of current Jewish apocalyptic, but in its inmost spirit his teaching was prophetic rather than apocalyptic. He was more akin to Amos than to Zechariah or Daniel. His interest in the apocalyptic hopes of his countrymen was in all probability neither dogmatic nor speculative, but practical. "While he shared in the visionary beliefs which were prevalent in the Jewish world of his time, he sought to employ them

24　Conversion : Christian and Non-Christian

as the motive and dynamic for a practical religious appeal."[1] With a message such as this it is impossible not to believe that John definitely aimed at producing conversions. His stern and terrible words at a time of eschatological expectation, when men's minds were full of thoughts of the cataclysmic end of all things, would strike terror into the hearts of some, as is shown by the numbers of those who sought his baptism. His gloomy eschatological mood must have had its effect on his hearers and instigated some of them to self-examination and change of life, as does the preaching of some modern sects who are obsessed with the idea that the end of the world is imminent. There is direct testimony of Jesus Himself as to the powerful personality of the preacher, who seems especially to have drawn to him those who were dissolute and of ill-repute : " For John came to you in the way of righteousness, and ye believed him not ; but the publicans and harlots believed him " (Matt. xxi. 32 ; cf. Luke vii. 29 and iii. 12). On many of his hearers the impression he created would doubtless be transitory. They would return to their ordinary life, but there is evidence that some were won to definite discipleship. He seems to have gathered around him a group of disciples very much in the manner of Jesus (see such passages as Mark ii. 18, vi. 29 ; Matt. xi. 2 ; Luke vii. 18, xi. 1 ; and John i. 35), and to have set in motion a religious revival, the influence of which reached Ephesus even before Christianity was preached there (Acts xix. 3). Further, if it be granted that John administered baptism only to those who professed repentance, we have in the fact that John received the name " The Baptizer " further evidence as to the number of his converts.

According to Mark i. 14 the imprisonment of the Baptist brought Jesus from His retirement in Galilee to engage in the work of His public ministry. Apparently He took up John's message in almost identical terms, saying : " The time is fulfilled, and the Kingdom of God is at hand ; repent ye " (Mark i. 15). Like John, He used both apocalyptic language and apocalyptic ideas. But Jesus did not merely take over these beliefs ; He transmuted them by placing

[1] E. F. Scott, *The Kingdom and the Messiah*, 68.

frequent emphasis on the inward and present character of the Kingdom, whose near advent He proclaimed.

The rigid eschatologists find no difference between the preaching of Jesus and that of John, but a closer examination of the Synoptic Gospels will reveal a considerable difference in the methods they adopted to win men over to the higher life of righteousness. It is easy to exaggerate this difference and to picture Jesus as almost the very antithesis to John— the one a gloomy and forbidding preacher of repentance; the other a prophet of " sweetness and light," full of a genuine joy in life. But this is to ignore the common eschatological background of their teaching. If we are correct in thinking that John often appealed to men's sense of fear and used the nearness of the coming judgment to sharpen the edge of his appeal for amendment, it is also certain that eschatological considerations gave urgency to Jesus's appeal as well, though we need not believe that the crash of impending doom was so frequently in His ears as Schweitzer would have us believe. Still, there are differences between John and Jesus that cannot be ignored. As far as we can judge, John seems to have relied upon preaching to masses of men to bring back the sinner to the right way. In the earlier part of His ministry Jesus may have followed this plan, but He more usually avoided it and sought out individuals, and by close association with them strove to enable them to overcome their sinful nature. And not merely did He seek out individuals, but individuals of a certain type—the sinful, dissolute and despised. The modern Christian reader of the Gospels brings to them a mind so saturated with the idea that it is of the essence of Christianity to seek and save that which is lost that he often fails to see how unique was the action of Jesus in this regard. But His action is a constant source of wonder to Mr. Montefiore, a modern Liberal Jew, and in his illuminating *Commentary on the Synoptic Gospels* he constantly refers to it. Jesus's concern for those classes from whom the Pharisees and Rabbis kept carefully aloof, and the manner in which He sought them out and shared their meals, Mr. Montefiore feels to be " a new and sublime contribution to the development of religion and morality. . . . To deny the greatness and originality of Jesus in this connection, to deny that He opened a new chapter in men's attitude towards sin and sinners, is, I think, to beat the head against a wall." [1]

When we turn to consider the question how far the ministry of Jesus was successful in securing conversions, we have the advantage of a much fuller record than in the case of John. But even so, the records are meagre enough, and, when the evangelists record what are obviously cases of conversion, they narrate the bare facts and show no interest in those psychological processes which interest the modern investigator. Nor need we be surprised at this, for they had not been trained in introspection, still less were they experimental psychologists. Before we turn to an examination of those incidents recorded in the Synoptic Gospels which *prima facie* have the appearance of conversions, we notice the indirect evidence the Gospels contain for the fact of conversion.

In the parable of the Sower and its explanation (Mark iv. 1-20) our Lord is describing the various effects of His preaching and teaching on the lives of his hearers. " The parable," says Menzies,[2] " gives us, under thin disguise, the experience of Jesus as a preacher." Wellhausen remarks: " Jesus is not so much teaching here as reflecting aloud upon the results of His teaching." [3] In three classes of His hearers His teaching is unproductive, though two of these classes experience some transitory, evanescent change of feeling. But by another class of hearers His preaching is received with whole-hearted acceptance, and they bring forth fruit, thirty, sixty and a hundredfold. Evidently Jesus had seen such abundant yields of moral fruit in the lives of some. Similarly, the parables of the Hidden Treasure and the Pearl (Matt. xiii. 44-46) look like transcripts from experience, the former depicting a conversion of the sudden and the latter of the gradual type.

According to Mark i. 14 f., Jesus began His ministry in Galilee; and one day, when walking along the side of the lake, He came across two fishermen, Simon and his brother

---

[1] 86. See also lxxxiv. f., lxxviii. 573 f., 985 and 1098.
[2] Cty. in loco. [3] *Einleitung*, 94.

Andrew, engaged at their trade, and addressed to them the words: "Come ye after me and I will make you become fishers of men." "And straightway they left their nets and followed Him." A little farther on Jesus came across another pair of brothers, James and John, called them in the same manner, and they responded.

The dramatic suddenness with which Jesus sprang a call so absolute on these men, and the equally dramatic suddenness with which they left their means of livelihood and their father, import, for some minds, an air of unreality into the story. "It is unthinkable," says Schmiedel, "that in this scene no words but these of Jesus should have been spoken, 'Come ye after me and I will make you fishers of men!'"[1] But Schmiedel is convinced that the call of Peter and his comrades is historical. So he assumes that these four disciples had had a previous opportunity of making the acquaintance of Jesus and of conversation with Him. The first two Evangelists, however, had no interest in the psychological processes which resulted in the decision of the four fishermen, so they omitted to mention them, and gave their present colourless narratives.

In discussing the psychological probability of this incident, differences of climate and natural temperament need to be borne in mind. The average Britisher or Teuton is not as the Easterner in these matters. The former requires some inducement to leave the security of a settled calling to face the rigours of a wandering, and, perhaps, homeless, life in an unfriendly climate. But the man of the East lays much less store on this world's goods, and displays at times an almost quixotic tendency to renounce them. His climate and temperament both help to make this possible. "To the Galilean wanderer, whose slight needs were supplied by the hands of friends, and who in a rich and fertile country ever found God's table spread for him, life was easier than to the modern townman, who must put forth all his strength to gain a scanty reward."[2] In the relation between the Hindu *guru* and his *chela* we have something in many respects akin to the relation between

---

[1] *Enc. Bib.*, col. 4573.
[2] Johannes Weiss, quoted by Montefiore, op. cit 544.

28 Conversion : Christian and Non-Christian

Jesus and His disciples, and, above all, it is worthy of notice in the present connection that the *chela* has often forsaken his occupation and followed his *guru* with the same surprising suddenness as that which characterized the response of the first four disciples.

Here, too, the eschatologists come to our aid. If it be a fact that Jesus, the Baptist, and those who responded to their preaching were convinced of the near approach of the Kingdom in a world-embracing catastrophe, it is easier to see why they were willing to forsake their occupations. Again, J. Weiss puts the point picturesquely : " Jesus and His followers had broken the bridges behind them in the convinced consciousness of a near, new world, where everything would be different and everything would be perfect." [1] We conclude, then, that there is nothing intrinsically improbable in the story of the prompt obedience of the four fishermen to the sudden and absolute call of Jesus, and that there is no need to resort to the hypothesis of a previous acquaintance.

Much that we have written in explanation of the sudden obedience of the first disciples applies equally to the call of Levi, though it seems reasonable to suppose that his position at the custom house would afford him some opportunities of seeing Jesus and of hearing current gossip about the new prophet. He may, in fact, have been present at His preaching.

Most commentators take the story of the healing of the paralytic (Mark ii. 1-12 ; cf. Matt. ix. 1-8, Luke v. 18-26) not only as a case of bodily but also of spiritual healing. The sympathy and insight of Jesus saw that the man was troubled about his spiritual state. He Who was capable of reading the inner thoughts of the Pharisees (ii. 8) was equally capable of penetrating the secrets of the paralytic's soul. Doubtless the man shared the current view that the malady from which he was suffering implied previous sin. The first words of Jesus (ii. 5) perhaps warrant the conjecture that He was preaching about repentance and the near Kingdom when the interruption occurred, and that the man's heart had been touched by His words.

[1] Op. cit., loc. cit.

Jesus desired to heal both soul and body, and it is not difficult to see why the proclamation of forgiveness preceded the bodily healing. In the first place, He probably intended the healing as a visible sign of the reality of His forgiveness, for in all probability He, and certainly the paralytic, held the current view as to the connection between sin and sickness, and would have agreed with the Rabbinic saying that a sick man does not arise from his couch till his sins have been forgiven. But, above all, " the forgiveness was assured to him first in order that the man's heart might be encouraged and lightened, and that thus his body as well as his soul might become receptive to the religious and moral power of Jesus."[1] Jesus saw that there was something in the man's mental state that was inhibiting all healthy operations both of mind and body. He could not cure the paralytic's body until He had got rid of that; but once the man's conscience had been unburdened by the declaration that his sins were forgiven, it was possible for Jesus to accomplish the bodily cure. It is a pretty clear case of what in modern psychotherapy is called resolving the mental complex, and we are confirmed in our opinion that the story of the paralytic is an instance of conversion, followed by bodily healing. It was one of those cases in which it is necessary to restore unity to the divided soul before health can be restored to the sick body.

Luke alone gives the story of Zacchæus. He was the chief collector of customs ($\dot{\alpha}\rho\chi\iota\tau\epsilon\lambda\dot{\omega}\nu\eta s$, Luke xix. 2) at Jericho, which was a frontier post. As Jesus was passing through the town Zacchæus climbed a sycamore-tree in order to get a good view of Jesus, for his short stature put him to disadvantage in such a crowd as was then gathered together. Whether it was mere curiosity that drew him or a deeper religious interest, it is impossible to say. Nor do we know how much the tax-gatherer knew about Jesus and His teaching. Jesus saw him and asked whether he would receive Him as a guest at his house—or, rather, He tells Zacchæus that He must abide with him that day. Deeply stirred by the friendliness of Christ, the despised tax-gatherer declared he would give half of his possessions

[1] Montefiore, op. cit. 76.

30 Conversion : Christian and Non-Christian

to the poor and make fourfold restitution to any man he had wronged. The joy of Jesus at such manifest fruits of repentance showed itself in the declaration : " To-day is salvation come to this house, forasmuch as he is a son of Abraham " (Luke xix. 9).

Can we regard this as a genuine case of conversion ? Schweitzer says we cannot, for " Luke tells us nothing whatever about a conversion of Zacchæus, but only that Jesus was invited to his house and graciously accepted the invitation."[1] Such an assertion is much too dogmatic. Some great inward change must have come over the presumably rapacious chief tax-collector for him to have declared his intention of giving away half his possessions to the poor. This looks very like the characteristic altruism of the converted man. And when he expressed his desire to make fourfold restitution to any he had wronged, it looks as if the memory of some wrong he had committed was weighing upon his conscience, and he was anxious to make amends. As Montefiore points out, he regards his wealth as the product of theft, and applies the law of Exod. xxii. 1. And surely the joy of Jesus means something. The joy He manifested and the words He used are exactly typical of Him on those occasions when the lost was found and the sinner saved.

The conjecture is worth hazarding that we have here a case of conversion through gratitude. The despised tax-gatherer was delighted at the way in which Christ brushed aside popular prejudices and treated him no longer as an outcast, but as a man. Jesus asked his hospitality and gained his heart.

In Luke vii. 36–50 (cf. Mark xiv. 3–9, Matt. xxvi. 6–13) we have a graphic story of the conversion of a courtesan. Jesus was dining with a Pharisee named Simon, when the woman introduced herself into the room and fell at His feet in a flood of tears. She washed His feet with her tears, wiped them with her hair, and anointed them with the ointment she had brought. When Simon expressed surprise that his guest allowed such a woman to touch Him, Jesus uttered the parable of the two debtors, and, telling the

[1] *Quest of the Historical Jesus.* 299.

woman her sins were forgiven, sent her away in peace. The historicity of this incident has been challenged by those who see in it nothing more than an adaptation of Mark xiv. 3–9. Montefiore, e.g., speaks of it as "one of the greatest and most famous of Luke's additions to the Gospel store," and thinks Luke has recast and enlarged the incident recorded by Mark at the close of Jesus's ministry, and transferred it to the opening of the ministry.[1] Loisy, on the other hand, thinks there were two separate incidents, and the fact that the *mis-en-scène* was a dinner in both cases led to their amalgamation in the Lucan narrative.

Assuming its historicity, there seem to be two ways of construing the incident. Most Catholic theologians hold that our Lord forgave the woman her sins and sent her away in peace because of her great love for Him. This, they contend, is the clear meaning of verse 47a: "Her sins, which are many, have been forgiven, for she loved much."

There are three main objections to this interpretation: (1) It fails to make the parable fit the story which it is intended to illustrate, for the teaching of the parable clearly is "great love is the outflow of great forgiveness"; (2) it involves the rejection of the last clause of 47b, "To whom little is forgiven the same loveth little"; (3) Protestant scholars urge that it is contrary to the genius of the teaching of Jesus to make the woman's forgiveness the reward of her love—to make her love "la cause méritoire du pardon."

The other interpretation seeks to make the whole of verse 47 consistent with the parable by stressing the perfect tense of the verb (ἀφέωνται), and by making the ὅτι declarative rather than causal. Her forgiveness has already taken place. It is assumed that the woman had already been converted and had repented on some occasion previous to the anointing. Verse 47a, then, becomes an assertion by Jesus that the woman's love is the clearest proof of her conviction that already she has been forgiven. The anointing, then, becomes the loving demonstration of a newly repentant and forgiven heart, overflowing with gratitude to Him who had wrought in it the wondrous change. Her love is proof of the pardon already accorded.

[1] Cty. in loco.

On the whole, the second of these two interpretations seems the better, and it is the one favoured by Plummer, B. Weiss, J. Weiss and Loisy, among others. It finds in Luke's account a description, not of the moment of conversion, but of the psychological effects which immediately, or almost immediately, followed upon it. We do not know what interval of time there was between the anointing and the day when the woman had first been touched by the words of Jesus and had formed the resolve to amend her life. But her tears attest the reality of her penitence, and the manner in which she let down her hair in public (a shameful act according to Jewish sentiment) testifies to her deep desire to humiliate herself before One for whom she showed the deepest reverence by kissing His feet. Indeed, it is difficult to explain her conduct, or even her coming to Jesus at all, except on the supposition that she had decided to change her life.

Both Mark and Matthew tell us that two robbers were crucified with Jesus, and that both of them insulted Him. Luke alone makes any difference between the two men. According to him (xxiii. 39–43), one rebuked the other, gave expression to his own sense of sin and demerit, and at the same time asserted his belief in the innocence and Messiahship of Jesus. He also begged Jesus to remember him when He came into His Kingdom. In His reply Jesus promised more than the robber asked: "To-day shalt thou be with me in Paradise."

Some scholars find it difficult to believe that Luke's additions to the Marcan *Grundschrift* are historical. They would dismiss them as "characteristic Lucan embroideries."[1] But the story is not without psychological probability. As the malefactor's life slowly ebbed away, the weight on his conscience grew heavier and heavier. The dark deeds that had stained his past loomed blacker and blacker. He is struck with the contrast between his own merited suffering and Jesus's innocence, between his own blasphemous railings and Jesus's prayer for the forgiveness

---

[1] There is an able defence of the Lucan additions to and modifications of the Marcan *Grundschrift* in the Passion narrative in Sir John Hawkins's essay in *Studies in the Synoptic Problem*. See especially p. 92.

Conversion in Classic Christianity 33

of His murderers. It is a case of sudden conversion at the hour of death, and due, in all probability, to fear at the approach of death and the feeling that everything was slipping away from him but his need of God. It is the only case in the New Testament of a " death-bed repentance."

We have no means of telling exactly how many adherents Jesus gained during the course of His ministry, but that their number was considerable is vouched for by Paul's statement that the Risen Lord appeared to " above five hundred brethren at once " (1 Cor. xv. 6). How many of these five hundred remained loyal is difficult to say. When the third Evangelist continues his history of the infant Church in the Book of Acts, he tells us that after the Ascension there were gathered at Jerusalem some hundred and twenty disciples who were anticipating their Master's speedy return. But what most strikes the reader in passing from the Gospels to Acts is the contrast between the Gospels' picture of the quiet pastoral work of Jesus among individuals and the contagious revivalism in Acts, by means of which Christianity is spread with surprising rapidity, till in ever-widening circles it is diffused over all the world. Luke evidently intends his readers to feel that the Early Christian community entered upon a new phase of its life with the experience at Pentecost. According to Acts ii., the disciples had met for prayer when suddenly the room was filled by a rushing wind, and tongues of fire appeared on each one of them. At the same time they were filled with the Holy Spirit and found themselves able to speak in other tongues. It was the time of the Feast of Pentecost, and Jerusalem was full of " devout men " from all parts of the earth. These were amazed when they heard the disciples address each different race in its own language. But others suggested the disciples were drunk. Peter addressed the crowd, with the result that his hearers " were pricked in their hearts," and three thousand of them received his word and were baptized.

It is hard to believe that this narrative, as we find it in Acts, is strictly historical. It is incredible that at this early stage of the Church's history three thousand converts should have been made in one day—to say nothing of the impossibility of baptizing such a number. Further, the miracle was unnecessary; for the many nationalities, so carefully named as hearing their own mother-tongues, would all of them be able to follow Greek, and, after the excitement had died down, Peter delivered his sermon in Greek, and there is no hint that it needed to be translated.

That there is an historical kernel in the narrative we need not doubt. The accretions must not blind us to the fact of the remarkable change which came over the behaviour of these early believers. The narrative almost certainly points back to some memorable occasion when the little company, met for prayer in Jerusalem, first became conscious of the strange phenomena of the glossolalia. This conjecture is borne out by critical analysis. The writer of Acts seems to make use of a primitive document, to which he has added his own account of the speaking in foreign languages. In the speech of Peter, which belongs to the primitive document, there is no reference to the miracle, and the suggestion he rebuts is that he and his colleagues are drunk.[1] But we can go farther than this. The gift of the glossolalia was a clear indication of the gift and presence of the Holy Spirit, as Peter claimed. The occasion marked an epoch in the life of an infant community, for their ecstatic experience, the direct result of the Spirit's presence in their midst, conferred on them energy, illumination and power, and lifted them to a mood of elevation and confidence, in which they were able to add to their community not a few " devout persons " from among those who had come to Jerusalem at the Feast. " Pentecost was a day of power—a day on which the Spirit of God manifested Himself through the disciples as a power for the conversion of others." [2]

This power for the conversion of others is a marked feature of the Church in the Apostolic Age, but the purpose with which Luke drew up his narrative causes him " to

---

[1] Cf. E. F. Scott, *The Spirit in the New Testament*, 94 ff., who offers suggestions as to the motives which led Luke to transform the story.
[2] McGiffert, *History of Christianity in the Apostolic Age*, 50. Cf. Weizsäcker, *Apostolic Age*, E.T. ii. 50 f.

concentrate attention on critical steps," and to narrate only those conversions which have a special significance.[1]

The conversion of Simon Magus and his fellow-Samaritans is narrated in chap. viii. as marking the first step towards a more liberal policy. Though the Samaritans were akin to the Jews in blood and faith, the action of Philip was an innovation. The apostles Peter and John were sent down from Jerusalem to Samaria to investigate the matter. But when in answer to the Apostles' prayers and the laying on of their hands the Holy Spirit came upon the newly made converts, the *testimonium Spiritus Sancti* could no longer be withstood, and the action of Philip was fully ratified (Acts viii. 17 and 25). The next conversion to be narrated is that of the Ethiopian eunuch, whom Luke evidently regards as already a convert to Judaism and not strictly a heathen (Acts viii. 27).[2] The conversion is recorded here as part of the evangelist Philip's activities. Philip, at the direct prompting of the Holy Spirit, as Luke is careful to point out, takes the southern route to Jerusalem, and in the neighbourhood of Gaza falls in with the Ethiopian eunuch reading Isa. liii. To him the evangelist "preached Jesus." The eunuch had been drawn into Judaism by religious needs which the religion of his fathers could not satisfy. His religious zeal had brought him up to Jerusalem to worship, and yet he seemed to be returning to his native land in a mood of doubt and perplexity rather than of exaltation (viii. 31). But his spirit of diligent inquiry, humility and teachableness was such that he responded with joy to the fuller light which Philip was able to throw upon the sacred scriptures.

Next follows the conversion of Paul, which the author of Acts evidently intends to place in its proper chronological sequence. The story of the conversion of the Apostle to the Gentiles is so well known that it need not be repeated here. We may briefly point out that Acts contains three

[1] In ii. 47 he writes: "And the Lord added to them day by day those that were being saved." "One of those phrases," says Ramsay, "in which Luke often hits off a long, steady, uniform process" (*St. Paul the Traveller*, 364).

[2] If we do not take this view, the conversion of the eunuch is a case of irregular and unauthorized conversion of a Gentile before Peter was divinely led to accept the conversion of Cornelius.

36 *Conversion : Christian and Non-Christian*

accounts of the event—one by the historian himself (ix. 3–10), and two in the form of speeches put into the mouth of Paul (xxii. 6–21 and xxvi. 12–18). Nowhere in his extant epistles does the apostle give a detailed account of his conversion. He was writing with other purposes in mind, and, doubtless, some of his readers had already heard the story from him by word of mouth. The chief passages in which he refers to the great event are Gal. i. 12–17, 1 Cor. ix. 1, 1 Cor. xv. 5–9, in all of which passages the apostle is on his defence. But scattered throughout his letters are allusions and references which would be sufficient, apart from any other evidence, to warrant the conjecture that he was a " twice-born " soul. Phil. iii. 4–12 is a specially fine passage.

The next conversion recorded is that of the centurion Cornelius. Here again Luke has chosen a special case, not because of any psychological features attaching to it, but with a view to showing how Peter was led, not only to receive a Gentile "God-fearer" into the Church, but to have table-companionship with the uncircumcised (Acts xi. 3). Cornelius was a centurion stationed at Cæsarea, and, being a " God-fearer," was anxious to hear the preaching of Peter (x. 17 f.). The apostle had some scruples about going to preach to a Gentile, but was reassured by a vision. After hearing Peter's discourse, Cornelius and his household began to speak with tongues. As in the early community the glossolalia was always interpreted as a gift of the Spirit, Peter was forced to the conclusion that Cornelius, Gentile though he was, might be formally admitted into the Christian community by baptism, for he and his household displayed all the marks of " being filled with the Spirit."

Having told the story of the conversion of Cornelius, Luke goes back for a moment and "starts a new thread of history from the death of Stephen "[1] (vii. 60). The bold

---

[1] Ramsay, op. cit. 41. Possibly Luke's reason for putting xi. 19–21 out of its true chronological order is more or less to regularize the conversions of Gentiles at Antioch by relating their conversion after the episode of Cornelius. " In reality God's providence did not wait upon the caution of Peter and the Eleven " is B. W. Bacon's characteristic comment (*The Story of St. Paul*, 85).

line taken by Stephen had provoked a persecution, which had dispersed the Church. But the refugees were the Church's earliest missionaries and played a great part in the spread of the Gospel. Luke has already given hints of the foundation of churches in Judæa and Samaria (viii. 14, 25, 40; ix. 31, 32, 35, 42; x. 44) by these itinerant missionaries. In xi. 19–21 he returns to the events following Stephen's death, and tells of the foundation of the Church in Antioch by some "who spake the word to Jews and to none save Jews," but he adds that some of the missionaries, certain Cypriote and Cyrenaic Jews, who had been brought up in Greek lands and had consequently a wider outlook than the average Palestinian Jew, were guilty of the innovation of addressing, not merely Jews, but Greeks also.[1] Their preaching was successful, for "the hand of the Lord was with them, and a great number that believed turned unto the Lord." Barnabas was sent to inquire into this anomalous state of affairs, but again the *testimonium Spiritus Sancti*, the divine evidence of conversion, could not be gainsaid, and, as a result of Barnabas's ministry, "much people was added unto the Lord" (xi. 24). Paul was brought to assist Barnabas in building up the congregation, and Antioch now became the base for missions to the Gentile world.

We turn now to the conversions which took place during the missionary journeys of Paul. The first missionary journey began with a preaching tour through the whole island of Cyprus, and the first recorded conversion is that of Sergius Paulus, the pro-consul of Cyprus (Acts xiii. 4–12). As Ramsay points out, it was customary for high Roman officials to have in their train "provincials, men of letters or of scientific knowledge or of tastes and habits that rendered them agreeable or useful to the great man."[2] Sergius Paulus, a cultivated man, interested in science and philosophy, had among his train a Magian named Elymas. When the news reached him of the preaching of Paul and Barnabas in the island, he sent for the two teachers of

[1] Whichever reading be accepted as original in xi. 20, the narrative gains coherence only on the assumption that Gentiles were converted. See McGiffert, op. cit. 108 n 2, and Bacon, op. cit. 85.
[2] Op. cit. 77.

rhetoric and moral philosophy (as he would doubtless regard them), and listened to their message with such evident pleasure that the jealousy of Elymas was aroused, and he tried to dissuade his patron from hearing them. When Elymas was struck blind for a season the governor was greatly impressed. " Then the pro-consul, when he saw what was done, believed, being astonished at the teaching of the Lord " (xiii. 12).

Whether this is a genuine case of conversion to the Christian faith is open to doubt, for nothing is said about the governor's baptism and the subsequent course of his life. The verb πιστεύειν is used in the New Testament to describe something less than full Christian faith (see John xx. 8, Acts viii. 13). We may well believe that the educated governor, interested in science and philosophy, " did make some profession of faith which sent the apostles on their way rejoicing in the Christian victory. We are not told whether the man's heart was the good soil in which the seed bears fruit, or the shallow soil in which the shoot is scorched, or the pre-occupied soil in which the growing corn is choked. We are told only that the seed took root and sprang up." [1]

Paul and his companions crossed to the mainland and made many converts at Pisidian Antioch. The mission was so successful that the whole region soon heard the word of the Lord (xiii. 49). The converts were drawn, as usual, from the Gentiles, and from the " God-fearers " in particular (xiii. 43, 48). But Luke gives us no details about the converts made or the psychological processes through which they passed. There is just the brief note that " the disciples were filled with joy and with the Holy Ghost " (xiii. 52). With similar brevity conversions are recorded at Iconium (xiv. 1), Derbe, Lystra and Iconium (xiv. 20–22).

There is the same meagreness of psychological details in Luke's account of the second missionary journey, his real interest being to show how Christianity was carried from the continent of its birth westward to the great centres of ancient civilization. Paul and his companion, Silas,

[1] D.A.C. ii. 471.

Conversion in Classic Christianity 39

make it their first business to "confirm" the churches planted during the first journey. In this connection occurs the earliest mention of Timothy (xvi. 1). He is described as "a certain disciple" who was "well reported of by the brethren that were at Lystra and Iconium" (xvi. 1 f.). Paul seems to have seen in this highly esteemed young believer a promising helper, so in preparation for his missionary work he had him circumcised, lest the presence in his company of an uncircumcised son of a Jewish mother should prejudice his influence among the Jews. It is not Timothy's conversion that is here described, but his admission into the inner circle of Paul. Nevertheless, it seems reasonable to assume that he had been converted by Paul at Lystra or Derbe during the first missionary journey. This seems borne out by 1 Cor. iv. 17, where Paul speaks of him as "my beloved and faithful child in the Lord" (cf. verse 15 and Philem. 10). From 2 Tim. i. 5, iii. 14 f., we learn that Timothy had inherited from his grandmother Lois, and from his mother Eunice, the finest traditions of Hebrew piety. His conversion was probably one of the quiet, non-explosive type, the natural development of pious surroundings and early training, but Bartlet[1] sees in 1 Tim. iv. 14 an allusion to the time when the *charismata* were first manifested in young Timothy's life.

Strictly speaking, the first converts made during the second journey of which Luke takes any notice are those made on the soil of Europe. Landing at Neapolis, the missionaries made their way along the Egnatian Way to the Roman military colony of Philippi. The Jews were evidently few in numbers, for there was no synagogue in the town, and the apostle found such adherents to Judaism as there were gathered together for prayer outside the city gates by the side of a river. Acts xvi. 13 looks as if only women attended the Philippian place of prayer, and from among them Paul won his first European convert, the "God-fearer" Lydia (xvi. 14). The phrase which is used to describe her conversion is interesting: "whose heart the Lord opened." It would seem as if this pious woman's whole moral and religious nature responded as soon as

[1] *The Apostolic Age*, 95.

40 Conversion : Christian and Non-Christian

she heard the preaching of Paul, and that his message fitted the needs of her nature as perfectly as a key fits the wards of a lock. She at once showed the fruits of her conversion in the generous hospitality she offered the missionaries. So begins the conversion of " honourable women " to the new religion which forms such a conspicuous feature of Macedonian Christianity.

An outburst of pagan hatred, caused by the healing of the girl who was a soothsayer, led to the scourging and imprisonment of Paul and Silas. That night there was an earthquake which resulted in the conversion of their jailor. Writers like Weizsäcker, Holtzmann, Harnack, Bacon regard the story of the earthquake and the conversion of the jailor as legendary, but most of their objections have been met by Ramsay, who uses his acquaintance with Turkish prisons to remove some of the difficulties.[1]

An earthquake is, after all, a natural occurrence, and it may well have happened on that very night, and it was entirely natural for the writer of Acts to treat it as a special providential intervention. The jailor, who is designated a δεσμοφύλαξ, occupied a position of supreme authority in the prison. He is not to be confused with a keeper, φύλαξ (Acts v. 23, xii. 6). Rackham[2] suggests he was a Roman officer, occupying the rank of a centurion. Into his custody Paul and Silas had been committed by the magistrates, with the injunction that he should " keep them safely." It seems reasonable to assume that he knew something of the missionaries and their teaching, for the cure of the girl had caused a sensation in the town. Nor would the conduct of the apostles be without influence upon his mind. Lacerated with stripes and their feet fast in the stocks, they yet prayed and sang praises to God. Then he was suddenly awakened out of his sleep to find that his charges had, as he thought, escaped. Such a sudden and unexpected calamity, which might have meant the ruin of all his worldly prospects, drove him to desperation. His desperation is all the more credible when we remember that severe earthquake shocks invariably cause a panic fear, which is often greatest in the breasts of those who are

[1] Op. cit. 220–223.   [2] Cty. in loco.

conscious of guilt. He would have committed suicide. He heard the reassuring voice of Paul, and, threatened with temporal ruin, his mind turned to religion, as many another's has done, both before and since, when driven to despair by some personal or domestic trial. After further instruction he was baptized, and showed the fruits of the new life in the manner in which he washed the missionaries' stripes, set food before them, and " rejoiced greatly " (xvi. 34). Acts mentions no other converts at Philippi except Lydia and the jailor and their households. But the opening verse of the Epistle to the Philippians shows that by that time the Church must have had a considerable membership, and in the body of the letter mention is made of two women, Euodia and Syntyche, and of two men, Epaphroditus and Clement (Phil. iv. 2, ii. 25, iv. 18, iv. 3). Further, in Acts xvi. 40, " the brethren " are referred to as though they were substantial in number.

The next stopping-place seems to have been Thessalonica. According to Acts xvii. 2, Paul preached for three weeks in the synagogue there to the Jews and the " God-fearers." The result of his preaching was a few conversions among the Jews and a great many among the " God-fearers," including not a few of the " chief women," the Thessalonian Church being thus founded. The names of some of the Thessalonian converts have come down to us. Jason seems to have been the host of Paul and Silas during their stay in the city (Acts xvii. 6), and in Acts xx. 4 Aristarchus and Secundus are mentioned as two of the Thessalonians who went with Paul to Jerusalem with the collection for the poor. To these we should probably add the Gaius of Acts xix. 29, a companion of Paul, who with Aristarchus was seized at Ephesus. Both he and Aristarchus are described as Macedonians, possibly with the intention of distinguishing him from the Gaius of Derbe mentioned in Acts xx. 4.

Compelled to leave Thessalonica, Paul and Silas made their way to Berœa, where many Jews were converted " and of Greek ladies of position, and of men, not a few " (Acts xvii. 12). From Berœa Paul went on alone to Athens, where certain believed, among whom were Dionysius, a

42 Conversion : Christian and Non-Christian

member of the council of the Areopagus, a woman named Damaris, " and others with them " (Acts xvii. 34). Ramsay [1] suggests that Damaris was one of the educated *hetairai*. But conversions were evidently few. Paul's " apostolate was never so nearly a failure as in this city of wisdom and renown ; and, when he quitted it and went on to the next stage, Corinth, he was, we know, from his own words, in a state of ' weakness and fear and much trembling.' " [2] But when, after some weeks, Silas and Timothy rejoined him, the apostle "was constrained by the word " ($\sigma\upsilon\nu\epsilon\acute{\iota}\chi\epsilon\tau o\ \tau\hat{\wp}$ $\lambda\acute{o}\gamma\wp$) (xviii. 5). This probably means that all his thoughts were " compressed " in one channel, and he abandoned the method of philosophical disquisition, which had proved a failure at Athens, and determined to know nothing " save Jesus Christ and Him crucified " (1 Cor. ii. 2). The intensity of spirit with which he preached the " word of the cross" had its effect, and in a city renowned throughout the ancient world for its licentiousness moral miracles were wrought in the lives of many. He hints at the black sins which stained the former lives of his converts (1 Cor. vi. 9-11). They had been fornicators, idolaters, adulterers, effeminate, thieves, drunkards, robbers, extortioners. " Such were some of you," he avows, " but ye were washed, but ye were sanctified, but ye were justified in the name of the Lord Jesus Christ and in the Spirit of our God." It is impossible to miss here the missionary's note of exaltation in the triumph of the " word of the cross." The apostle continued for about two and a half years in the city, and his preaching met with a considerable amount of success, for many of the Corinthians believed and were baptized. Certain of the converts were men of some social standing, such as Crispus, the ruler of the synagogue (Acts xviii. 8) ; Erastus, the city treasurer ; and Gaius, who was hospitable to Paul and to " the whole of the Church " (Rom. xvi. 23 ; 1 Cor. i. 14). But other converts were poor enough, for they had nothing ($\tau o\grave{\upsilon}s\ \mu\grave{\eta}\ \acute{\epsilon}\chi o\nu\tau as$), and were put to shame by their more comfortably placed brethren when the Church met " to eat the Lord's supper " ; for the latter, instead of sharing their supplies, devoured what they had brought,

[1] Op. cit. 252.   [2] Stalker in D.A.C. ii. 148.

and the poor were left hungry (1 Cor. xi. 20-22; cf. 1 Cor. i. 26-28). Other converts we hear of are Stephanas, Fortunatus, Achaicus (1 Cor. xvi. 15-17), and, perhaps, Chloe, who may possibly have been an Ephesian (1 Cor. i. 11). To these Lucius, Jason, Sosipater, Quartus and Tertius should possibly be added (Rom. xvi. 21 ff.).

On his third missionary journey Paul settled down at Ephesus for a considerable time, with the intention, probably, of making a deliberate attempt to capture for Christianity this great centre of population, art, commerce and religion. The preaching of the missionaries seems to have met with wonderful success, for within two years " all they which dwelt in Asia heard the word of the Lord, both Jews and Greeks " (Acts xix. 10). That the new teaching proved morally revolutionary, a new way of life, is shown by the fact that the magicians burnt books to the value of 50,000 pieces of silver.[1] " So mightily grew the word of the Lord and prevailed " (xix. 20).

The runaway slave Onesimus is known to us only through the Epistle to Philemon and Col. iv. 9, but a characteristic phrase of Paul's in the former letter makes it clear he was a convert of the apostle's. Paul describes him as " my child, whom I have begotten in my bonds." Philemon 11 and 18 are usually taken to warrant the assumption that Onesimus was a thief. He had absconded and fled to Rome, where he fell in with the apostle. He may have heard Paul preach in Ephesus during his three years' stay there, for Ephesus was only about a hundred miles from Colossæ; or he may have heard something of Paul in the household of Philemon and have been drawn to the apostle by a desire to listen to one who had taken a special interest in slaves; or he may have met the apostle quite by accident. But whatever the circumstance of their meeting, he was converted by the apostle and showed the fruits of his conversion in loyal and devoted service to his father in the Lord (Philem. 13). He cannot have been a Christian when he met the

---

[1] B. W. Bacon's characteristic note runs: " The valuation must be understood as representing their worth in the eyes of those who believed in them. If inventoried at cost, the figures would hardly be accepted by fire-insurance adjusters." Op. cit. 179 n. Cf. Ramsay, op. cit. 272.

44 Conversion : Christian and Non-Christian

apostle, for in that case Paul would scarcely have used the striking phrase about the slave's "spiritual begetting."

The Book of Acts gives anything but a complete account of Paul's missionary labours, but enough has now been said to demonstrate how large a place conversion occupied in New Testament times. It was the aim and purpose of the apostolic preaching. Early Christianity began as a religious revival and spread with astonishing rapidity through the Græco-Roman world. To the names of the converts mentioned above many others could be added, but the New Testament is silent about the details of their conversion. McGiffert points out [1] that about fourscore companions and disciples of Paul are mentioned by name in his epistles and about a score more in the Book of Acts. The greater proportion of them were doubtless his own converts, though some owed their Christianity to others. Nor, in view of the accidental manner in which the names are often referred to in the Epistles, can it be doubted that the apostle had many other companions and converts. One would like to know, for instance, how persons like Silas, Mark, the mother of Rufus, Phœbe, Andronicus, Junias, Aristarchus, Euodia and Syntyche, Persis, Epaphras and Epaphroditus were brought to a living knowledge of the Christian faith. What of Priscilla and Aquila, tentmakers like Paul himself, "who for my life laid down their own necks" (Rom. xvi. 3)? And Luke? Was he called in to render medical aid to the apostle in some illness, and did he receive as his reward a knowledge of the gospel? What was it that won the hearts of the "saints in Cæsar's household?" Certain answers to these questions we may never find, but one thing is clear. There run through the New Testament writings strong tides of religious life and emotion. The Early Church was a Church of converted men and women. They speak as converts, they write as converts, and they exult as converts. Their characters adorned the Early Church and their services edified it, but beyond a casual reference in the New Testament we know nothing of them. The casual reference is, however, enough to show that these "unknown and forgotten in-

[1] Op. cit. 423 f.

habitants of the great cities of antiquity, some by their names recognizable as slaves, are striving upward from the dull, vegetating mass, upward to the light, having become personalities, saints in Christ." [1]

At this point we must close our somewhat lengthy review of the evidence for the fact of conversion in New Testament times. Sufficient has been said to make it clear where primitive Christianity placed its emphasis, and to show that it is a sound and healthy instinct that has led many Christian circles to regard conversion as the *articulus aut stantis aut cadentis ecclesiæ*.

[1] Deissmann, *St. Paul the Apostle*, E.T. 224.

CHAPTER IV
CONVERSION IN HINDUISM

VEDIC religion was much more favourable to the "once-born" than to the "twice-born" type of religious experience. The Vedic hymns are full of a passionate love of life, and their authors are more concerned with the attainment of happiness in this world and with its continuance in the next than with entering into personal relations with the gods. In this period the shadows had not yet fallen which were to darken the whole religious landscape of the Indian peoples, rendering the best minds among them consciously inferior, divided and unhappy. These shadows were due to the rise of the doctrines of transmigration and karma, which have ever since fettered the Hindu mind and created within it a poignant sense of the misery and futility of life. According to these associated doctrines, souls "exist in infinite numbers everlastingly from beginningless time, and pass from body to body in an eternal course of experience, of which every instant is determined by the merit or demerit of previous works (karma)."[1]

These two closely associated doctrines must always be kept in mind in dealing with the religious experiences of India's saints and sages, for they are the logical *prius* of all their thought, giving shape, especially, to their doctrine of redemption. "The sum and substance, it may almost be said, of Indian philosophy is from first to last the misery of metempsychosis and the mode of extrication from it."[2] Darkened as their souls were by the karma-transmigration theory, it was natural for all earnest, awakened spirits to seek a way of release (*mukti, moksa*) from the cycle of birth

[1] Barnett, *Bhagavadgita*, 10.
[2] Gough, *Philosophy of the Upanishads*, 20 f.

and death (*samsara*). Firmly convinced of the misery of mundane existence, they believed that real happiness could only be found by release from *samsara*. The prayer with which Tulsi Das concludes his version of the *Ramayana* would find a response in all Hindu hearts. "There is no one so poor as I am, and no one so gracious to the poor as you, O Raghubir; remember this ... and rid me of the grievous burden of existence." Release from *samsara*, then, was their quest, and only when they reached the goal of their strivings did they find themselves unified and at peace.

Within the bounds of Hindu orthodoxy three paths have long been recognized as leading to release. The lowest of the three paths is the Way of Works (*karma-marga*), "the faithful fulfilment by followers of Siva or Visnu of the rites of their particular creed: at birth, marriage, death, and the other great crises of life; at the great feasts; at their daily private worship; and in the temple courts."[1] This path does not lead immediately to final release, and those who follow it can never hope to be *jivanmuktas*.[2] The faithful followers of the path may attain at death a temporary heaven of bliss, but they are still held in the bonds of *samsara*, and must again be born in this troubled world. The most that they can hope for is to acquire sufficient merit to ensure their entering upon a higher stage of existence when next they come to birth. More ardent spirits naturally turned to other paths, which offered immediate release. The other paths are the Way of Devotion (*bhakti-marga*) and the Way of Knowledge (*jnana-marga*). According to the former, release from *samsara* comes by loving devotion to a personal deity, and we shall find men entering upon this way through experiences which cannot fail to remind us of Methodist conversions. According to the latter, release comes through knowledge, and here we shall find a certain amount of evidence that some found happiness and unification of soul by following it to the end.

It is in the Upanishads that the doctrine of release by knowledge first arises. By knowledge in this connection

---

[1] Mrs. Sinclair Stevenson, *The Rites of the Twice-Born*, 418.
[2] Delivered while yet on earth.

the Upanishads mean much more than mere book-learning. It is possible for a man to be acquainted with all branches of human knowledge and yet not be in possession of saving knowledge. Saving knowledge consists in the recognition of the unity of the individual soul and the World Soul. Such knowledge will deliver a man from the flux of time and from the cycle of rebirth. The doctrine of the unity of the self with Brahman had been hinted at before the time of the Upanishads,[1] but in them it is for the first time elevated into a message of redemption.

In the much later teaching of Sankara the speculations of the Upanishads receive their final formulation. He taught that " knowledge, and knowledge alone, can lead to *moksa*. For *moksa* is not something to be obtained or produced. It is only a realization of our real nature, of which we can never be really deprived, but of which we have been only forgetful; it is therefore only knowledge that can be the means of *moksa*."[2] With Sankara, as with the authors of the Upanishads, saving knowledge is the knowledge that nothing exists save Brahman. When this truth is known, the fetters that bind the soul to the wheel of rebirth are broken and *mukti* is attained.

The average Westerner is inclined to doubt whether such teaching would ever bring unification to souls divided and depressed. But it is impossible to plod through the strange mixture of religion, ritual, philosophy and poetry contained in the Upanishads without feeling that their authors are convinced that they have a gospel to proclaim the blissful effects of which they have tasted in their own lives. They testify to the unity and peace of mind that came to them when they reached the intuition that the soul of man is one with the Absolute, and that they were, therefore, free from the painful necessity of rebirth. There are passages in the Upanishads that are much more than mere pieces of argumentation for the position of absolute idealism. They are transcripts from experience. We can trace in them that happiness and that feeling of relief and elevation which are so characteristic of the converted man. We quote a few passages :

[1] *Satapatha Brahmana*, x. 6. 3.   [2] Prof. Ghate in E.R.E. xi. 189.

" From the dark (the Brahman of the heart) I come to the nebulous (the world of Brahman), from the nebulous to the dark, shaking off all evil, as a horse shakes his hairs, and as the moon frees herself from the mouth of Rahu. Having shaken off the body, I obtain, self-made, and satisfied, the uncreated world of Brahman—yea, I obtain it." [1]

" He therefore that knows it, after having become quiet, subdued, satisfied, patient and collected, sees self in Self, sees all as Self. Evil does not overcome him : he overcomes all evil. Evil does not burn him : he burns all evil. Free from evil, free from spots, free from doubt, he becomes a (true) Brahmana ; this is the Brahma-world, O King—thus spoke Yajnavalkya." [2]

" There is one ruler, the Self within all things, who makes the one form manifold. The wise who perceive him within their Self, to them belongs eternal happiness, not to others."

" There is one eternal thinker, thinking non-eternal thoughts, who, though one, fulfils the desires of many. The wise who perceive him within their Self, to them belongs eternal peace, not to others." [3]

The feeling of elation was, evidently, known to show itself in the face.

"Friend, your face shines like that of one who knows Brahman. Who has taught you ? " [4]

Though the Upanishadic philosophy of release came as a gospel to many, it failed in other cases to bring peace to troubled spirits. This, doubtless, was largely due to the fact that it offered men nothing more than the intuitive realization of what already is, and effected no great change in their lives. How could the follower of the path ever be certain that release had actually taken place ? Hence the tendency to abandon purely intellectual methods in favour of psychophysical methods, in order to produce the union of " I " and " It." These psychophysical practices have always been a feature of India's religious life. They may be traced far back beyond Buddhism, and connect themselves with the austerities of the earliest days. In this way the system of Yoga was brought in as an auxiliary to the *jnana-marga*. The aspirant retired to the forest, and, seating himself, sought to control every wandering thought

---

[1] *Chhand. Up.* viii. 13 (S.B.E. i. 143). Rahu is the monster who swallows the moon in times of eclipse.
[2] *Brihad. Up.* iv. 4. 23 (S.B.E. xv. 180).
[3] *Katha Up.* ii. 5. 12 f. (S.B.E. xv. 19 f.)
[4] *Chhand. Up.* iv. 14. 2 (S.B.E. i. 67). See also iv. 9. 2.

by long suppressions of the breath, by peculiar methods of inspiration and respiration through the right and left nostrils alternately, by the frequent repetition of the syllable *Om*, by the prolonged concentration of the visual attention on such near objects as the tip of the nose and the navel. Such practices were carried on in solitude until a state of autohypnosis was reached, in which the aspirant became insensible to all external stimuli. This state signified the attainment of Yoga (Union), and was attended by the beatific vision and unutterable bliss. In the later Upanishads these new ideas are already jostling the older ones long before they were fully expounded in the *Yoga-sutras* of Patanjali. That they were an effective means of unifying the self is shown by the following quotations:

"That happiness which belongs to a mind which by deep meditation has been washed clean from all impurity and has entered within the Self cannot be described here by words; it can be felt by the inward power only."[1]
"He who has known that cause which is to be apprehended by Sankhya and Yoga, he is freed from all fetters."[2]
"If a man practises Yoga for six months and is thoroughly free (from the outer world), then the perfect Yoga (Union), which is endless, high, and hidden, is accomplished."[3]

To pass from *Jnana-marga* to *Bhakti-marga* is to enter another world of thought and feeling. The one is cold and logical; the other mystical and passionate. The god of one is a meaningless cipher; the god of the other a personal being, who becomes incarnate among men for their salvation, and confers redemption from *samsara* on all who come to him with loving devotion (*bhakti*). This is the theme of the *Gita*, which Professor Garbe has described as a poem in praise of *bhakti*. "The entire poem is full of this thought. . . . To everyone, without distinction of birth or regard to his former conduct, *bhakti* assures deliverance, even to evil-doers, women, Vaisyas and Sudras."[4]

In spite of its undeniable attractions, Bhagavatism did

[1] *Mait. Up.* vi. 34 (S.B.E. xv. 334).
[2] *Svet. Up.* vi. 13 (S.B.E. xv. 264).
[3] *Mait. Up.* vi. 28 (S.B.E. xv. 326). [4] E.R.E. ii. 538.

Conversion in Hinduism

not win general acceptance till the Middle Ages.[1] It had little chance so long as India lay under the spell of the genius of Sankara. But the day was bound to come when the craving of the human heart for a personal deity and a God of Grace, who would respond to the faith of his worshippers, would again assert itself. Hence the time came when the heart of India received with passionate welcome the apostles of the Bhakti movement, who declared that, not by austerity or penance, nor by the outward forms of ritual and ceremony, nor yet in the chilling atmosphere of pure thought, was God to be found, but by the way of loving, passionate devotion. "No other Yoga we recognize than conversation relating to Krishna. If there are other ways of Yoga, abandon them, and offer your service to Krishna alone. Visiting shrines and sacred places is only a superstition and unnecessary toil. The highest bliss we can aspire to may be found in self-dedication to Krishna."[2] So wrote an enthusiastic Bengali Vaishnava *bhakta* in the sixteenth century.

The revival of Bhagavatism began in the south through the teaching of the four great leaders, Ramanuja, Madhva, Visnuswamin, and Nimbarka; but it was Ramananda who made it the leading religion of India. Fourth or fifth in descent from Ramanuja, he quarrelled with the head of the monastery in Seringapatam, of which he was a member, and migrated to Northern India, where he founded a sect of his own. He gained his large influence largely because he abandoned Sanscrit and preached and taught in the vernacular, so bringing his doctrine within the reach of all classes. The following brilliant summary by Grierson will show that India experienced the refreshing of a mighty religious revival:

"No one who reads the Indian religious literature of the fifteenth and following centuries can fail to notice the gulf that lies between the old and the new. We find ourselves in the face of the greatest

---

[1] We are not here concerned with the early history of Bhagavatism, but with the religious experiences of its saints. For the early history see Grierson's elaborate art. "Bhakti-marga" in E.R.E.; Bhandarkar's *Vaisnavism, Saivism, and Minor Religious Systems* in the *Grundriss;* and Carpenter, *Theism in Mediæval India*, 244 ff.

[2] *Prema Bhakti Chandrika* of Narottama Das. Cited by Sen, V.L. 229 f.

religious revolution that India has ever seen—greater even than that of Buddhism, for its effects have persisted to the present day. Religion is no longer a question of knowledge; it is one of emotion. We visit a land of mysticism and rapture, and meet spirits akin, not to the giant schoolman of Benares, but to the poets and mystics of mediæval Europe, in sympathy with Bernard of Clairvaux, with Thomas à Kempis, with Eckhart and with St. Theresa. In the early years of the Reformation the converts lived and moved in an atmosphere of the highest spiritual exaltation, while over all there hovered with healing in its wings a Divine Gospel of love, smoothing down inevitable asperities, restoring breaches, and reconciling conflicting modes of thought. Northern India was filled with wandering devotees vowed to poverty and purity. Visions, trances, raptures, and even reputed miracles, were of everyday occurrence. Rich noblemen abandoned all their possessions and gave them to the poor, and even the poorest would lay aside a bundle of sticks to light a fire for some chance wandering saint. Nor were the converts confined to the male sex. Of devout and honourable women there were not a few—Mira Bai, the queen-poet of Udaipur, who gave up her throne rather than join in the bloody worship of Siva; Barika, the poor woodcutter's wife, who could not be tempted by a purse of gold; the chaste Surasuri, with her tiger guardian; Ganesa Derani, the queen of Madhukara Sahi of Orchha, who hid the wound inflicted by a mad ascetic, lest her husband should take indiscriminate vengeance; the penitent Magdalen of Delhi, who gave her life and the only art she possessed, her dancing, to the service of the deity in whom she had taken refuge; and many others. Of men there were Hari-Dasa, the sweet singer, to hear whom Akbar disguised himself as a menial servant and travelled far; Nanda-Dasa, the hymn-writer, whose last words were a prayer that his soul might stand ' very close and near ' the Adored; Chaturbhuja, the apostle to the savage Gonds, who taught that right initiation meant ' being born again '; Gopala, who, when smitten on one cheek, turned the other to the smiter; Vilvamangla, who looked after a woman to lust after her, and, because his eye offended him, made himself blind; the unnamed king, who for the same reason cut off his right hand and cast it from him; Sura-Dasa, the blind bard of Agra; and, most famous of all, perhaps the greatest poet that India has produced, Tulasi-dasa, the teller of the deeds of Rama."[1]

All the above examples are taken by Grierson from the *Bhakta-mala* of Nabha Dasa, which, with its commentary by Priya Dasa, is all-important for an understanding of the reformed Bhagavatism. The *Bhakta-mala* is an *acta sanctorum* of the Bhakti movement. Originally written in

[1] E.R.E. ii. 548.

Middle Hindi, it has been frequently translated into the Indian vernaculars, but never into English. Its many difficulties have hitherto deterred most students from the task of studying it.[1] An English version would, in all probability, make available some valuable psychological material. It is greatly to be regretted that materials are not forthcoming in the existing biographies of men like Ramanuja, Madhvacharya, and Ramananda, which would enable us to see the inner motives which led them to make the great renunciation and become *sannyasis*, living hard lives as strenuous peripatetic religious teachers. But in the case of other apostles and prophets of the *Bhakti-marga* we are much more fortunately placed.

A thirteenth-century *Life* of Ramanuja records a number of conversions which took place under the saint's teaching and influence. Considerations of space forbid our citing more than the case of the archer-athlete, Dhanurdasa, who lived near Trichinopoly:

" To his caste-men he looked as terrible as death. He loved a girl by name Kanakamba, who was very beautiful. So much was he enamoured of her that he never left her side for a moment and never took his eyes off her moon-like face. One day Ramanuja's eyes fell on the loving pair, and he said to his disciples: ' Sons, look at this curious spectacle. Here is a despicable specimen of humanity who is the slave of a woman ! Shameless, in the public streets, he pays such attentions to a courtesan. Let me try to turn this man's love from the girl to the Lord Ranga.' He then gently chided the athlete for his open violation of public morality. Dhanurdasa replied: ' Holy sire, how can I help it ? Her eyes are more beautiful than the lotus. My heart and those eyes are one.' Ramanuja said: ' But, son, if I could show you better eyes than those ? ' So saying, he led him to the temple and showed him the figure of Ranga, recumbent on his couch. ' Look at those witching eyes,' said he; ' they are the eyes of Lord Ranga, the Father of the Universe; look steadily and study their beauty.' Dhanurdasa did so, and found that he could neither stir from the spot nor move his eyes from the figure before him. He was completely hypnotized, as it were. ' God's grace has descended on this person,' murmured Ramanuja to himself. The athlete gave up food and sleep, and was daily found in the temple gazing with straining eyes on the figure of Ranga. Ramanuja now sent

[1] Articles by Grierson on the *Bhakta-mala* may be found in the J.R.A.S for 1909 and 1910.

for him and asked him how he felt. He replied: 'Master, how can I be grateful enough to you for the bliss in which you have deigned to steep a wretch like myself? Make me thy slave, and complete the work of salvation you have, unasked, taken into your hands.' Ramanuja smiled and admitted him into his flock. When Kanakamba came to know of all this, she, too, repented and implored Ramanuja to take her into his Vaishnava fold. The saint, overcome by her solicitations, did so, and allowed both of them (now husband and wife) to work as servants in his monastery."[1]

Namdev, the fourteenth-century exponent of Krishna-bhakti in the Maratha land, who preceded Ramananda and prepared the way for him, is said to have been a converted dacoit.

" On one occasion, when Namdev went to behold his god in the temple, he was not allowed to enter because a Brahman, who had brought cooked food to offer to the god, would not suffer persons of Namdev's degraded caste to stand under the same roof with him. Namdev, while detained outside the temple, saw approach a very needy low-caste woman with a child on her hip. The child was crying piteously for a morsel of the food brought by wealthy persons as offerings to the god. The woman then began to beat the child. Namdev's heart melted at the sight, and he remonstrated with the mother for her behaviour. She replied: 'The child is hungry and wishes me to give her the god's food, which is impossible. . . . My husband was one of the eighty-four horsemen recently cut down by the inhuman dacoits. . . . I only possess the bones in my body. Dost thou . . . desire me to feed her with them ? '

" Her words pierced Namdev's heart, and he began to reflect how many families had been ruined by his reckless and lawless career. On leaving the temple precincts, he bestowed his mare and whatever clothes he could dispense with on the Brahmans, and, to use his own words, made a friend of repentance."[2]

The best-known and most influential of the Maratha *bhakti* poets was Tukaram (1608–1649). He was a petty shopkeeper, and the story of his conversion is a typical story of the poignant sorrows of Indian life. A succession of disasters fell on his business and home. First, death took both his parents and his eldest brother's wife. Then his brother left home for ever to become a *sannyasi*. After

[1] I have used and abridged A. Govindacharya's translation of the *Life* of Ramanuja (Madras, 1906), 158-160. For other cases of conversion, see 92, 150.
[2] Macauliffe, *The Religion of the Sikhs*, vi. 21 f.

Conversion in Hinduism

that his business failed and he became bankrupt. The climax came in the famine of 1630, when he lost his eldest son and his favourite wife died, crying for bread. Stunned with grief, he sat for seven days with his eyelids closed. He called to memory the god Vithoba of Pandurang, who appeared to him in a vision. Then, after throwing into the river the account-books which showed who owed him money, he committed his business to his younger brother, and left the world and all attachments to it to spend the remainder of his life in the service of Vithoba and in the composition of those songs, which have sustained the spiritual life of thousands in the Maratha country to this day.[1]

Who, after reading the following hymns of Kabir, the founder of the Kabirpanth, can doubt that he was a twice-born soul? Kabir was a disciple of Ramananda, and the groundwork of his teaching is Hindu, though Islamic and Sufi elements enter into it. His date is disputed, but, according to Farquhar, he died in 1518.

"This day is dear to me above all other days, for to-day the Beloved Lord is a guest in my house.
My chamber and my courtyard are beautiful with His presence.
My longings sing His name, and they are become lost in His great beauty.
I wash His feet and I look upon His face; and I lay before Him as an offering my body, my mind, and all that I have.
What a day of gladness is that day in which my Beloved, who is my treasure, comes to my house!
All evils fly from my heart when I see my Lord.
'My love has touched Him; my heart is longing for the Name which is Truth.'
Thus sings Kabir, the servant of all servants." [2]

"Thou hast drawn my love, O Fakir!
I was sleeping in my own chamber, and Thou didst awaken me, striking me with Thy voice, O Fakir!
I was drowning in the deeps of the ocean of this world, and Thou didst save me; upholding me with Thine arm, O Fakir!
Only one word and no second—and Thou hast made me tear off all my bonds, O Fakir!
Kabir says, 'Thou hast united Thy heart to my heart, O Fakir.'" [3]

[1] I have taken this account from Frazer and Edward's *Life and Teachings of Tukaram* (Madras, 1922), 83 f.
[2] Tagore, *One Hundred Poems of Kabir*, Poem 88
[3] Ibid., Poem 10. The Fakir is, of course, God.

56 Conversion : Christian and Non-Christian

Chaitanya was probably about twenty-four when, in the first decade of the sixteenth century, he passed through that experience which made him an apostle of Krishna-bhakti, and set in motion a religious revival which changed the face of Bengal. About this time the death of his father seems to have made a deep impression upon him. He was restless, and could not settle down in his home in Navadipa. His whole desire was to go to Gaya to offer there the *pindas* for the repose of his father's soul. Arrived at Gaya, he entered the temple and heard the *pandas* singing the virtues and praises of Vishnu's footprint, at the sight of which he fell into a swoon.

"And when he heard from the mouth of the Brahmans the glory of the footprint, the Master became possessed with love and bliss. Floods of tears flowed from his two lotus eyes. His hair stood on an end and he trembled at the sight of the footprint. The Master, Gaurchandra,[1] for the good fortune of the whole universe, began his manifestations of *prem* and *bhakti*. Incessant floods flowed from the Master's eyes. The Brahmans present there saw this most extraordinary sight."[2]

While at Gaya he met with Iswar Puri, a famous Vaishnava Sannyasi of the Madhvacharya sect, whom he took as his spiritual guide.[3] He came back from Gaya to his native town a changed man. He was now "god intoxicated." He sang and chanted Krishna's name for hours together till he became delirious with *bhakti*. He found it impossible to resume his old habits and pursuits. His calling as the head of a *tol* had to be given up, for, instead of teaching his pupils, he for ever indulged in reveries about Krishna. The revival which Chaitanya set on foot inspired countless lives of devotion and won converts from every class of society. Many of the conversions will be referred to in the course of this work, and in Chapter XV the Chaitanyite revival is dealt with in some detail.

The story of the conversion of Tulsi Das, the author of the *Ramacharit-manasa*, which popularized *bhakti* in Northern India, is worth telling. Born in 1532, he was

[1] Another name for Chaitanya.
[2] *Chait. Bhagabat*, Adi Khanda, chap. xii.   [3] Ibid.

Conversion in Hinduism

abandoned by his parents at birth, but was picked up by a wandering *sadhu*, with whom he roamed all over Northern India. When he grew up he married and lived as a householder.

"He was devoted to his wife and could not bear to be separated from her. She was a firm Vaishnava, and on one occasion, when she had gone on a visit to her people, she reproached him for following her and not showing equal affection for Rama. Struck with remorse, Tulasi at once left her and took to an ascetic life. He is said to have seen her only once again in after years, and then not to have recognized her. With his headquarters, first in Ayodhya and subsequently in Benares, he made long journeys over Northern India preaching the gospel of Rama."[1]

We have up to now confined our attention to the Vaishnava *bhaktas;* we may now turn to a South Indian system, in which *bhakti* is directed to Siva. At first it comes with something of a shock to find loving devotion directed toward the dread and terrible Siva. Well has Dr. Macnicol said: "Of all the deities in the Hindu pantheon, Siva seems the one least likely to attract a theistic devotion. ... The fact that even about this ghoulish god, more devil than deity, who battens on corpses and smears himself with ashes from the burning ground, has gathered a gracious devotion that has been able to remould an object so repulsive nearer to its heart's desire, is in itself a remarkable testimony to the strength in the Indian peoples of the theistic instinct.... The human spirit has surely seldom found material harder to subdue to its purpose of devotion than was Siva."[2]

For roughly four or five centuries (*circa* 700–1200 A.D.), Saivism in South India was engaged in a life and death struggle with Buddhism and Jainism. The victory was with Saivism, largely because the struggle gave birth to a great spiritual revival and a remarkable intellectual awakening among the Saivites. To this victory not only

[1] Grierson in E.R.E. xii. 470; cf. Farquhar, O.R.L.I., 328 f.
[2] *Indian Theism*, 160. The literature on Siva-bhakti is meagre. Bhandarkar, in his volume in the *Grundriss*, is disappointing. He has only two pages on the subject. Grierson says: "Very little is known, and the subject deserves more study than it has hitherto received" (E.R.E. ii. 551). The difficulty is that the literature, being in Tamil, is not accessible to the average orientalist.

scholars contributed, but also saints and devotees, who were remarkable for their unceasing activities, poetic fervour and spiritual power. These poets produced a devotional literature which is unsurpassed among the literatures of the Indian people. Dr. Barnett, who combines with his Sanscrit learning a knowledge of the Dravidian languages, says: "No cult in the world has produced a richer devotional literature or one more instinct with brilliance of imagination, fervour of feeling and grace of expression." [1]

Foremost among these poet-saints was Manikka Vachakar, whose collection of songs, the *Tiru-Vachakam*, is beloved by all the Tamil people. In his songs Manikka lays bare his heart to our gaze with pretty much the same frankness as Augustine in his *Confessions*. The experimental note in religion is sounded throughout, and, as one reads his songs, one is reminded now of Jeremiah and now of Augustine. In many respects Manikka represents Sivabhakti at its highest and best. Regarding the outward events of his life, little is certainly known. Even his date is uncertain.[2] Round him, as so often in India, there soon sprang up a thick jungle of legend. He is said to have been born in a Brahman family in the neighbourhood of Madura. He early attracted the attention of the King of Madura, who made him his Prime Minister. Amid the pomp and splendour of the Court his soul found no lasting satisfaction. He was filled with pity for the thronging multitudes, who were condemned to the ceaseless round of rebirth, and his mind ever sought a way of release. One day news came to the Court that a large shipment of horses had arrived at a harbour on the coast. The King at once commissioned his Minister to buy the horses, and furnished him with the necessary money and a splendid escort. "The curtain here falls at the end of the first act in the drama of the sage's history. His secular life is really ended. Like Paul journeying to Damascus, he is on the eve of an unexpected and decisive experience."[3] The god

[1] *Heart of India*, 82.   [2] See Farquhar, O.R.L.I., 197.
[3] Pope, *Tiruvasagam*, xx. f. I have followed Pope's account of the conversion.

Siva appeared to him, on his way to the port, in order that he might convert and initiate him.

> "And now how changed is the youthful Minister of State! He has become a Jivan-muttar, who lives in a body still for a little while, but is one in feeling, soul, power and faculty with the Infinite Eternal. He has to put off his rich garments and adornments, is besmeared with white ashes, and wears the peculiar habiliment of the ascetic. From his head depends the braided lock of the Caiva devotee; one hand grasps the staff and the other the mendicant's bowl: he has for ever renounced the world. . . . Whatever deductions we are compelled to make for the exaggerations that have grown up . . . there stands out a real historical character which seems to be a mixture of St. Paul and St. Francis of Assisi. . . . This is his conversion, as South India believes it, and in almost every poem he alludes to it, pouring forth his gratitude in ecstasies of thanksgiving."[1]

We quote from Dr. Pope's translation of the *Tiru-Vachakam* a few stanzas, which go far to show that the validity of his experience would have been recognized at a Methodist class meeting.

> "By lust bewilder'd; in this earthly sphere
>   caught in the circling sea of joyous life—
> [By whirling tide of woman's charms engulf'd;
>   lest I should sink with mind perturb'd,
> He gave His sacred grace, that falseness all
>   my soul might flee, and showed His golden feet!
> The TRUTH Himself—He stood in presence there:
>   This matchless miracle I tell not, I!
>
> "I gave no fitting gift with lavish hand
>   of full-blown flowers; nor bowed with rev'rence meet.
> He grace conferr'd, lest I should tread the paths
>   of grief, with mind bewildered by soft dames
> With fragrant bosoms fair. He came to save
>   and showed to me His golden jewell'd feet!
> As King in presence manifest He stood.
>   This matchless miracle I tell not, I!
>
> "Busied in earth I acted many a lie;
>   I spake of 'I' and 'mine'—illusions old;
> Nor shunned what caused me pain; while sins increased.
>   I wandered raving. Me, that Being Rare—

---

[1] Pope, *Tiruvasagam*, xxii. f.

60 Conversion : Christian and Non-Christian

By the great mystic Vedas sought in vain—
  held fast in presence there ; to lowly me
Essential sweetness was the food He gave:
  This miracle of grace I know not, I !

" To ' birth ' and ' death ' that cling to man, I gave no thought,
  and uttering merest lies went on my way.
By eyes of maids with flowing jet-black locks
  disturbed, with passion filled, I helpless lay.
He came ! the anklets on His roseate feet—
  I heard their tinkling sound ; nor parts the bliss !
In grace my precious Helper made me His :
  This miracle of Love I know not, I !

" I wealth and kindred and all other bliss
  enjoy'd ; by tender maidens' charms was stirr'd ;
I wandered free in joyous intercourse ;
  such goodly qualities it seemed were there.
He set me free ; to stay the course of ' deeds,'
  my foes, He showed His foot-flowers' tender grace,
My spirit stirred, entered within, and made me His !
  This matchless miracle I know not, I !

" I gave no thought to ' birth ' and ' death ' that yield
  their place successive ; but with maidens joined
I sank engulfed as by a mighty flood :
  their rosy lips my death ! I madly roamed.
The Sea of Excellence, Whom neither quality
  nor name of excellence defines—
He came, and tenderly embracing made me His :
  This miracle of grace I know not, I !

" Though born a man, unfailing gifts
  I laid not at the golden feet ; nor did I cull
The cluster'd flowers, by rule and wont prescrib'd,
  nor chaunted the ' Five Letters ' due. O'ercome
By the full-bosomed damsels' jet-black eyes
  I prostrate lay. Showing His flow'ry feet,
To me the Father came, and made me His :
  This miracle of grace I know not, I !

" He caused the ' twofold deeds ' to cease, that cause
  this swing of soul with body joined. He, Whom
'Tis hard to learn by uttered sound to know,
  gave me to know Himself : thus made me light !
He cut asunder bonds that clung ; fulfilled
  with His own mercy's gift sublime my soul's
Desire ; and joined me to His servant's feet :
  This miracle of grace I know not, I !

Conversion in Hinduism

" In tangled wilderness of ' birth ' supine
   I lay ; like wretched cur diseased I roamed ;
Did as I lusted ; dwelt with creatures vile,
   with them complying, satisfied in soul !
He showed me there His flowery fragrant feet,
   by Hari and by Ayan unattained.
Th' Imperishable made ev'n me His own.
   This miracle of grace I know not, I !

" I gave no thought to thronging ' births ' and ' deaths,'
   but dwelt on tricks, and wiles, and glancing eyes
Of maids with wealth of braided tresses fair ;
   and thus I lay, The King, Our Lord Supreme,
His jewell'd feet, that traverse all the worlds,
   to me made manifest like clustering blooms ;
He wisdom gave, and made me all His own :
   This miracle of grace I know not, I ! " [1]

" Lest I should go astray, He laid His hand on me !
As wax before the unwearied fire,
With melting soul I worshipt, wept, and bent myself,
Danced, cried aloud, and sang, and prayed.
They say : ' The tooth of elephant and woman's grasp relax not.'
So I with love, real, intermitting never,
Was pierced, as wedge driven into soft young tree.
All tears, I like the refluent sea was tossed ;
Soul was subdued, and body quivered with delight.
While the world called me demon, mocking me,
False shame I threw aside ; the folk's abusive word
I took as ornament ; nor did I swerve.
My mind was rapt—a fool, but in my folly wise—
The goal I sought to reach infinity ! All wondering desire,
As cow yearns for its calf, I moaning, hurried to and fro.
Not ev'n in dreams thought I of other gods.
The One most precious Infinite to earth came down :
Nor did I greatness of the Sage superne contemn,
Who came in grace. Thus from the pair of sacred feet,
Like shadow from its substance parting not,
Before, behind, at every point, to it I clung.
My inmost self in strong desire dissolved, I yearned ;
Love's river overflowed its banks :
My senses all in Him were centred ; ' Lord ! ' I cried.
With stammering speech, and quivering frame
I clasped adoring hands ; my heart expanding like a flower.
Eyes gleamed with joy and tears distilled.
His love that fails not day by day still burgeons forth ! " [2]

    [1] Hymn xli.   [2] Hymn iv.

62 Conversion : Christian and Non-Christian

That Manikka's experience was by no means solitary may be seen from the testimony of three other saints of the same school. Tirunavukkarasu Swami, who flourished about the seventh century A.D., writes :

" The moving water He made stand unmoving in His hair ;
And He my thoughtless heart hath fixed in thought of Him alone ;
He taught me that which none can learn, which none can see laid bare ;
What tongues tell not He told ; me He pursued and made His own.
The spotless pure, the Holy One, my fell disease He healed,
And in Punturutti to me, e'en me, Himself revealed." [1]

Sundaramurti Swami, who flourished in the first quarter of the ninth century A.D., thus hymns what was evidently a very definite experience of the divine grace :

" O madman with the moon-crowned hair,
    Thou Lord of men, Thou fount of grace,
    How to forget Thee could I bear ?
    My soul hath aye for Thee a place.
Venney-nallur, in ' Grace's Shrine,'
    South of the stream of Pennai, there,
My father, I became all thine ;
    How could I now myself forswear ?

" I roamed a cur, for many days
    Without a single thought of Thee,
Roamed and grew weary, then such grace
    As none could win Thou gavest me.
Venney-nallur, in ' Grace's Shrine,'
    Where bamboos fringe the Pennai, there,
My Shepherd, I became all Thine ;
    How could I now myself forswear ? " [2]

It is impossible not to see in the following hymn the warm after-glow of a conversion experience. Its writer, Tayumanavar, was a Tamil Saivite belonging to the early eighteenth century A.D.

" I was like copper-alloy in the midst of my body, which answers to the copper-mine. But thou, O God, didst start the fire of wisdom in me, and didst melt me into a liquid, and, knowing the right

[1] Trans. from Kingsbury and Phillip's *Hymns of the Tamil Saivite Saints*, 47.
[2] Ibid. 75 ff.

Conversion in Hinduism 63

moment, didst touch me with thy medicinal pill of grace, and, as in the process of the alchemist, didst change me from copper into the finest gold. Oh, how can I praise this great love of thine?" [1]

When through contact with Western thought in general, and Christian Missions in particular, Hinduism began to throw off a number of reformed societies, we find that the leaders were often men who had gone through a conversion crisis. I have not been able to discover any evidence for a spiritual crisis in the life of Raja Ram Mohan Ray, the founder of the Brahma Samaj, but it is significant that at the age of fifteen or sixteen he braved his father's anger by renouncing polytheism and idolatry.[2] The Raja's successor, Debendranath Tagore, and the latter's brilliant disciple, Keshab Chandra Sen, both underwent a profound spiritual change in their adolescent years. The same is true of Dayananda Saraswati, the founder of the Arya Samaj. These three cases will be dealt with more fully in a later chapter.[3] In all these modern cases, with the exception of Dayananda Saraswati, we are safe in assuming some Christian influence. In educated Indian circles the main ideas of Christianity were known and appreciated, and in many cases there was a profound reverence for the life and teaching of Christ. It is true that Debendranath Tagore never took the name of Christ upon his lips in his public teaching, and disclaimed any Christian influence upon his thought, but the influence was real, nevertheless. In the conversion of P. C. Mozoomdar, the faithful disciple and friend of Keshab through many vicissitudes, we see this Christian influence at its height. His conversion is typically Christian in all its essentials. Mozoomdar remained a Brahma all his life, but his glowing admiration and reverence for the person of Christ prevented him being elected Keshab's successor by his fellow-members of the New Dispensation Samaj. We give here an account of his conversion from his own pen:

[1] I owe this reference and its translation to my former pupil, the Rev. J. S. Masillamony, B.D., now lecturer in Tamil Literature in the Pasumalai Theological Seminary.
[2] Farquhar, M.R.M., 30. See also *Calcutta Review*, vol. iv. (1845), 360.
[3] See below, Chapter X.

64 Conversion : Christian and Non-Christian

"About the year 1867 a very painful period of spiritual isolation overtook me. . . . I was almost alone in Calcutta. My inward trials and travails had really reached a crisis. It was a weekday evening—I forget the date now. The gloomy and haunted shades of the summer evening had suddenly thickened into darkness, and all things, both far and near, had assumed an unearthly mysteriousness. . . . I sat near the large lake in the Hindu College Compound. Above me rose in a sombre mass the giant, grim old seesum-tree. . . . A sobbing, gusty wind swam over the water's surface. . . . My eyes, nearly closed, were yet dreamily conscious of the gloomy calmness of the scenery. I was meditating on the state of my soul, on the cure of all spiritual wretchedness, the brightness and peace unknown to me, which was the lot of God's children. I prayed and besought heaven. I cried, and shed hot tears. It might be said I was almost in a state of trance. Suddenly, it seemed to me, let me own it was revealed to me, that close to me there was a holier, more blessed, most loving personality upon whom I might repose my troubled head. Jesus lay discovered in my heart as a strong, human, kindred love, as a repose, a sympathetic consolation, an unpurchased treasure to which I was freely invited. The response of my nature was unhesitating and immediate. Jesus from that day became to me a reality whereon I might lean. It was an impulse then, a flood of light, love and consolation. It is no longer an impulse now. It is a faith and principle; it is an experience verified by a thousand trials. . . . Christ has been the meat and drink of my soul." [1]

The early critics of the Brahma Samaj often asserted that its influence was confined to the intellectuals, who wished to break away from the restraints of orthodox Hinduism. But this was by no means the case. In its best days the Samaj drew its converts from all classes of society. There was Hazarilal, who had been carried away by the temptations which abound in a large city like Calcutta. He fell into bad company and led a dissolute and depraved life. "In this evil plight he obtained by the grace of God a refuge in Brahmaism. The strength of the Brahma Dharma entered into his heart, and with its help he overcame his sinful tendencies and was restored to the path of a virtuous life." [2]

[1] From the Preface of his *The Oriental Christ* (Boston, 1883).
[2] Debendranath Tagore's *Autobiography*, 115. Debendranath speaks very gratefully of Hazarilal, who had been a menial servant in the family establishment, as the only one who stood by him when he refused to countenance idolatry in performing his father's *shradda* ceremony. This

Conversion in Hinduism 65

No one can read the files of the *Indian Mirror* for the sixties without feeling the note of proud confidence that throbs in its pages. The Samaj, whose organ it was, was winning spiritual victories in many places. The issue for August 1, 1864, gives an account of the conversion of forty-two poor, illiterate families in the village of Bagachia. It was in 1868 that a great religious revival took place at Monghyr, where there was a large colony of Bengali clerks.

" The ordinary services, and occasional Brahma Utsabs, in the form of festivals, took place in the little bungalow which Keshab had rented in the Fort. They were most numerously attended, and the emotions awakened on such occasions were uncontrollable—in fact, the devotional excitement through which Keshab and his friends had passed during the last eighteen months broke out with increased violence at Monghyr, and a great religious revival seemed to be at hand. The whole congregation, which multiplied every week, would often be moved to tears and sobs and ejaculations that were well-nigh hysterical. The women vied with the men in expressing their devotedness and enthusiasm; even the ignorant people from the bazaar were sometimes attracted. Processions perambulated through the streets at any hour of the day and night, sang at the *ghâts* on the river-side, and sometimes kept watches and vigils on the hills in the neighbourhood. The whole town was in a ferment. Some danced, one or two fell into fits of unconsciousness, not a few saw visions. Some left worldly avocations and joined Keshab's missionary body." [1]

One other remarkable conversion belonging to the period of conflict between Hinduism and Christianity may be noted—that of Ramakrishna Paramahamsa. Born in 1834,

---

was one of the crises in Debendranath's life, when even his brothers deserted him. Hazarilal's story is also told by Pundit Sivanath Sastri in his *History of the Brahmo Samaj* (Calcutta, 1911 and 1912), i. 93-95.

[1] P. C. Mozoomdar, *The Life and Teachings of Keshub Chunder Sen* (2nd ed., Calcutta, 1891), 111. See also Sivanath Sastri, op. cit., vol. i. 226 f. I have been unable to consult the files of the *Indian Mirror* for 1868. They would doubtless contain some valuable psychological material for the further study of the revival at Monghyr. The *Mirror* is no longer in the hands of the Samaj. The present proprietor very kindly allowed me to search the room where the back numbers are kept, but I could not find those for 1868; nor are they available at the libraries of any of the existing Samajes in Calcutta or at the Imperial Library. The state of the late Pundit Sivanath Sastri's health did not permit of my troubling him for his reminiscences. After completing his two volumes on the history of the Samaj, he intended to give some account of its converts in a third volume. This he was never able to do.

in a poor but orthodox Brahman family, he early showed a religious bent of mind. In his early twenties he was appointed an assistant priest in a temple dedicated to the goddess Kali, to whose image he manifested a passionate devotion. He frequently fell into a state of *Samadhi*, and would remain unconscious for hours. This caused him to neglect his duties, and he was therefore deprived of his position in the temple. He then spent twelve years in a wood near by in a ceaseless endeavour to obtain union with the divine by means of the *jnana-marga* and the Yoga praxis. Peace and unification did not come to his divided soul till 1871, when he adopted the way of *bhakti* and became a devotee of Krishna.[1]

[1] I have summarized Farquhar, M.R.M., 188 ff., and Macdonell in E.R.E. x. 568 f. Pratt (op. cit. 129 ff.) has a study of this conversion, but he does not seem aware of the part played by *bhakti* in the process of unification.

CHAPTER V

CONVERSION IN EARLY BUDDHISM

To some minds it may come as a surprise to find that an avowedly agnostic system like Early Buddhism was capable of bringing to large numbers of men and women that victorious sense of self-realization which we describe as conversion, and that it developed for itself a technical terminology relating thereto. It is not open to doubt that Buddha himself was a " twice-born " soul. During a public ministry of more than forty years he gathered around him a great many followers, many of whom underwent a definite conversion experience at the time they accepted his teaching.

The problem of the historicity of the early Buddhist writings is a difficult one, but happily it need not here be discussed in any detail. Attention will be confined to those cases of conversion which bear the marks of historicity. But it has to be borne in mind that, even if certain stories are unreliable as history, they are good evidence for the fact of conversion at the time they were drawn up.

The first book of the *Maha-Vagga* (the principal part of the *Vinaya Pitaka*) gives an account of the events which took place after Gotama's attainment of Buddhahood down to the conversion of his two chief disciples, Sariputta and Mogallana. Of this section of the *Maha-Vagga* Oldenberg and Rhys Davids write: " It contains the oldest version accessible to us now, and, most probably, for ever, of what the Buddhist fraternity deemed to be the history of their master's life in its most important period."[1]

Gotama Buddha was born in affluent circumstances about the middle of the sixth century B.C. in the little kingdom

---
[1] S.B.E. xiii. 73 n. See also Oldenberg, *Buddha*, E.T. 113, and Poussin, *The Way to Nirvana*, 144 n.

of Kapilavastu, on the borders of Nepal. At that time the doctrine of transmigration and karma hung like a nightmare over the sensitive Indian mind, and many were the systems put forward which propounded some way of release from the incessant round of birth and rebirth. From the crucible of his own experience Gotama was to give to the world another way of release. As far as we can judge, the first stage in his conversion experience dates from his twenty-ninth year. At that time he took the step which was afterwards called the Great Renunciation. He did what thousands of Indians have done both before him and since —he abandoned his wife, his infant son and his home, and went out to live the homeless life of a wandering ascetic. How long he had been debating the question before he took the decisive step, which must have shaken to its foundation his particularly sensitive nature, we cannot say. This much, however, seems clear. He had tasted the joys of life in comfortable circumstances, but had found them unsatisfying. Like so many other earnest souls of his age, he was oppressed and saddened with the doctrine of karma, and had early begun to reflect on the hard and bitter facts of life, nowhere more patent than in a land like India. Pain seemed to be the great, ever-present reality.[1] The desire arose within him to find a way of escape, a path of salvation, and he left everything in fulfilment of that quest.

The Great Renunciation, however, did not bring him peace. Seven more weary years were to pass before unification came to his divided soul. He first became the pupil of two wise teachers, but they had no solution of his doubts and questionings. Next he joined five ascetics, and soon outstripped them in fervour and zeal. For six years he continued his austerities with such severity that he was brought to the point of death. Finding that asceticism was nothing more than a *cul-de-sac*, he gave it up. His five companions were very indignant at his apostasy, and he himself was sorely tempted to return to the home which his departure had left desolate. He overcame the tempta-

[1] For the embellishments of a later age see the *Buddha-Karita* of Asvaghosa, iii. 28 (S.B.E. xlix. 30 ff.).

tion and made his way to Budh-Gaya, fully determined on winning for himself a solution of the problem that had darkened his life. Sitting one cool night under a peepul-tree, the weary conflict came to an end in a moment of insight. The way of deliverance had become clear. The knot of existence could be untied, for he had obtained perfect insight into the nature of sorrow, its cause and the means of its destruction. One *sutta* thus describes what must have been an upheaval of his whole mental and moral nature:

"When this knowledge, this insight, had arisen within me, my heart was set free from the intoxication of lusts, set free from the intoxication of becomings, set free from the intoxication of ignorance. In me, thus emancipated, there arose the certainty of that emancipation. And I came to know: 'Rebirth is at an end. The higher life has been fulfilled. What had to be done has been accomplished. After this present life there will be no beyond.' This last insight did I attain in the last watch of the night. Ignorance was beaten down, insight arose, darkness was destroyed, the light came, inasmuch as I was there strenuous, aglow, master of myself." [1]

Modern psychology would give much for a more complete account of the mental states here described.

After Buddha had overcome the temptation to keep to himself the insight he had won, he decided to preach this doctrine first of all to the five ascetics who had been his companions in self-mortification. Accordingly, with the light and joy of conquest shining in his face, he went to Benares and there found them in the Deer Park. They saw him coming, and agreed to receive him rudely on account of his apostasy, but something about him made them unable to keep their compact. He told them that he had won immortal insight, and said:

"I will teach you; to you I preach the doctrine. If you walk in the way I show you, you will, ere long, have penetrated to the truth, having yourselves known it and seen it face to face; and you will live in possession of that highest goal of the holy life." [2]

They expressed their doubt as to his having attained the supreme enlightenment, since he had abandoned the life

[1] *Maha-saccaka.* Quoted by Rhys Davids in his *Early Buddhism*, 36.
[2] This and the following quotations from the *Maha-Vagga* are taken from S.B.E. xiii.

of austerity and was "living in abundance." He then expounded to them his doctrine, as a mean between a life devoted to pleasure and a life devoted to mortification, both of which are ignoble and profitless. This middle path is the Noble Eightfold Path. The five were delighted with his teaching. One of them immediately " obtained the pure and spotless Eye of Truth (that is to say, the following knowledge) : whatsoever is subject to the condition of origination is subject also to the condition of cessation." In turn the other mendicants obtained the pure and spotless Eye of Truth, and so the mission of conversion was begun and the Sangha duly founded. After an exposition of the unreality of the "self," the minds of the five became free from all attachment to the world, and were released from Asavas. So the five became *arahats*, of whom there were now six in the world. At this point the first section or recitation portion of the *Maha-Vagga* comes to an end. Copleston [1] thinks that the succeeding portions are not so historically trustworthy as the preceding section, and must therefore be used with care.

The next converts are drawn from the *jeunesse dorée*, and include the noble youth Yasa, fifty other noblemen, and thirty rich young men whom Buddha found sporting in a grove when he was on his way to Uruvela.[2]

Arrived at Uruvela, the Buddha fell in with three fire-worshipping ascetics. After a number of extravagant miracles they were converted, together with their followers, to the number of a thousand.[3]

By this time the fame of the Master had reached the ears of Bimbisara, King of Magadha. Accompanied by a vast number of Brahmans and householders, he went to visit the saint, who preached to them in the same words that he had used to convince the noble youth Yasa. They all obtained "the pure and spotless Eye of Truth," and became lay disciples.[4]

The next recorded conversion is that of Sariputta and

---

[1] *Buddhism*, 27.
[2] The conversions of Yasa and the thirty rich young men are more fully dealt with in Chapter X of this work.
[3] *Maha-Vagga*, i. xv. ff.   [4] Ibid. i. xxii.

Mogallana, who afterwards became Buddha's chief disciples. At this time they were numbered among the followers of an ascetic named Sanjaya. They had given their word to each other that "he who first attains to the immortal (*amata*, i.e. Nirvana) shall tell the other one." One day, at Rajagaha, Sariputta saw a member of the Sangha going on his begging rounds. Greatly struck by his decorous and dignified deportment, he sought a convenient time, and said to him: "Your countenance, friend, is serene; your complexion is pure and bright. In whose name, friend, have you retired from the world? Who is your teacher? Whose doctrine do you profess?"[1] The *bhikshu* replied that he had retired from the world in the name of the Blessed One. When asked for an exposition of the doctrine, the *bhikshu* hesitated to give it, on the ground that he was but newly ordained, and was unable to expound the doctrine in detail. But he offered to tell his questioner in short what it meant. Sariputta replied: "Well, friend, tell me as much or as little as you like, but be sure to tell me the spirit (of the doctrine); I want but the spirit. Why do you make so much of the letter?" The *bhikshu* then quoted the following text: "Of all objects which proceed from a cause, the Tathagata has explained the cause, and He has explained their cessation also; this is the doctrine of the great Samana." On hearing these words Sariputta "obtained the pure and spotless Eye of the Truth." He at once sought out his friend, Mogallana, who on seeing him said: "Your countenance, friend, is serene; your complexion pure and bright. Have you, then, really reached the immortal, friend?" On hearing his friend's story, Mogallana at once became a convert. Together they went to the Buddha, and were admitted into full membership in the Order.

The conversions, which were now occurring in great numbers, caused a great stir and no little resentment.

"At that time many distinguished Magadha noblemen led a religious life under the direction of the Blessed One. The people were annoyed, murmured, and became angry, (saying): 'The Samana Gotama causes fathers to beget no sons; the Samana

[1] *Maha-Vagga*, i, xxiii. 3.

72 Conversion : Christian and Non-Christian

Gotama causes wives to become widows; the Samana Gotama causes families to become extinct." [1]

At this point the continuous history of the Foundation of the Kingdom of Righteousness comes to an end, and from this point onward we have nothing like a continuous narrative of the life of Buddha until we come to the *Sutta of the Great Decease*. But the *Maha-Vagga* contains records of other conversions. There is the touching story of the conversion of Rahula, Buddha's own son,[2] and of the courtesan Ambapali, with whom the Master dined.[3] There are others, too, but their historicity is doubtful. The story of the conversion forms a preface to some new piece of legislation laid down by the Blessed One for the *bhikshus*. The story of Siha leads up to the permission to eat meat; [4] that of Sona, the delicately nurtured youth, to permission for *bhikshus* to wear shoes with one lining and no more.[5]

When we come to the *Sutta of the Great Decease* we seem to be treading on much firmer ground.[6] In this book we have the record of the conversion of the last disciple made by the Buddha before his death. He was a mendicant named Subhadda, who dwelt in the little town of Kusinara, where the Master died. The news came to him that in the third watch of the night the Samana Gotama would pass away.

" Then thought the mendicant, Subhadda : this have I heard from fellow-mendicants of mine, old and well-stricken in years, teachers and disciples, when they said : ' Sometimes and full seldom do Tathagatas appear in the world, the Arahat Buddhas.' Yet this day, in the last watch of the night, the final passing away of the Samana Gotama will take place. Now a certain feeling of uncertainty has sprung up in my mind ; and this faith have I in the Samana Gotama, that he, methinks, is able so to present the truth that I may get rid of this feeling of uncertainty." [7]

He went to the grove where the Buddha was lying, tended by the faithful Ananda, and told the latter of his

[1] *Maha-Vagga*, i. xxiv. 5.   [2] Ibid. i. liv.
[3] Ibid. vi. xxx. The story is also told, with slight discrepancies, in the *Maha-Parinibbana Sutta*, ii. 16 ff.
[4] Ibid. vi. xxxi.   [5] Ibid. v. i.
[6] Cf. Rhys Davids's judgment in S.B.E., xi. p. xxxiii.
[7] *Maha-Parinibbana Sutta*, v. 52 ff. (S.B.E. xi. 103 ff.).

doubts and fears, asking three times that he might be allowed to see Gotama. Three times the good Ananda refused his request. But the Blessed One, overhearing the conversation, called out to Ananda to allow Subhadda to come near to him. Subhadda told the dying sage of his doubts and fears. The different teachers and founders of schools of doctrine are greatly esteemed by the multitude, and, according to their own assertions, they thoroughly understand things. Is this really the case with them or not? he asks Gotama. The Blessed One characteristically replied: "Enough, Subhadda! Let this matter rest, whether they, according to their own assertion, have thoroughly understood things, or whether some have understood and some have not! The truth, Ananda, will I teach you." He then proceeded to expound to the doubting mendicant the Eightfold Noble Path, and affirmed that it led to true saintliness, whereas the systems of other teachers are void of true saints. Subhadda accepted the teaching, and Ananda was instructed to admit him to the Order.

Copleston remarks[1] that Subhadda "was converted with curious ease." But it is extremely probable that we have here a genuine fragment of tradition. Subhadda was, apparently, an earnest seeker after truth, and must have heard previously of the Buddha and his teaching, but he was unable to make up his mind definitely to accept it. When, however, he heard that the aged saint was dying, some impulse drove him to seek an interview with the man whose teaching had had some fascination for him. All that we know of the Buddha makes it probable that as he lay dying he consented to receive the inquirer and to instruct him, while nothing is more natural than to assume that the sight of the dying saint hushed into calm all Subhadda's doubts. He had an object lesson before his own eyes. Even the Buddha himself was no exception to the universal law of death and decay. The pathos of the situation and the calm demeanour of the dying man may well have urged his will to the choice before which he had hesitated so long.

But only when we turn from the historical books to the

[1] Op. cit. 49.

collection of poems called the *Thera-theri-gatha* are we able to form any adequate idea of the power of early Buddhism to bring peace and joy to the anguished and divided spirit. This collection of poems, found in the *Sutta Pitaka*, is of supreme interest, because they all claim to be written by men and women who belonged to the Order during the lifetime of its founder, and who attained Nirvana in their own lifetime. The poems are of the greatest importance to the student of the psychology of religion, because they show us Buddhism at work, so to speak. They do not expound doctrine so much as give lyrical expression to a religious experience. Two hundred and sixty-four of the poems were written by men and seventy-three by women. Mrs. Rhys Davids has translated the former under the title *Psalms of the Brethren*, and the latter under the title *Psalms of the Sisters*. It is to be regretted that her translations are not more widely known, for many who would take fright at her *Buddhist Psychological Ethics* would find it a pure delight to share the religious experience of these ancient brothers and sisters. There is also extant a commentary by Dhammapala, belonging to the fifth or sixth century A.D., which gives a short account of the life-history of each author, and purports to tell the circumstances under which the poems were composed. Mrs. Rhys Davids discusses the value of this commentary, and adduces good reasons for accepting many of the data it affords for the interpretation of these songs. But, apart altogether from the commentary, the psalms themselves bear unmistakable testimony to the fundamental change wrought by Gotama's gospel in the lives of their authors. To a much greater extent than the historical and doctrinal books they make it clear that Early Buddhism was a gospel which brought healing on its wings to the people of India, and was able to bring men into a state of mind wherein they were confident that all the fetters that bound them to the wheel of birth and rebirth were broken for ever, and they were no longer under the dire necessity of being born again in this weary world. In the present work considerable use will be made of the material these psalms afford. At present, however, it will be sufficient to quote a few

Conversion in Early Buddhism 75

passages as evidence of the fact of conversion in Early Buddhism.

Here is the testimony of a man who had for years tried to find release from karmic bonds by the way of austerity :

> " Borne on the flood of false austerity,
> Full three-score years lived I in misery !
> Clothed me with dirt, and plucked out beard and hair,
> Fed me with dung, and sitting did forswear ;
> Refusing proffered hospitality,
> I practised penances which lead to hell,
> Until I came beneath the Buddha's spell.
> Behold the Dharma's glorious work in me !
> Behold the Threefold Lore hath set me free ! " [1]

One of the women thus describes her experience :

> " The path of insight I neglected, turned
> From highest good to follow baser ends.
> I lay enthralled to worldly vice, and naught
> To win the goal of my high calling wrought.
> But anguish crept upon me, even me,
> Whenas I pondered in my little cell :
> Ah me ! how have I come into this evil road !
> Into the power of Craving have I strayed !
> Brief is the span of life yet left to me ;
> Old age, disease, hang imminent to crush.
> Now, ere this body perish and dissolve,
> Swift let me be : no time have I for sloth.
> And contemplating as they really are,
> The Aggregates of life that come and go,
> I rose and stood with mind emancipate !
> For me the Buddha's word had come to pass." [2]

Infinitely touching is the testimony of another sister, though the cause of her unhappiness was very different :

> " Now here, now there, light-headed, crazed with grief,
> Mourning my child, I wandered up and down,
> Naked, unheeding, streaming hair unkempt,
> Lodging in scourings of the streets, and where
> The dead lay still, and by the chariot roads—
> So three years long I fared, starving, athirst,

---

[1] *Theragatha*, 283. Translation, in this case, from Saunders, *Heart of Buddhism*, 52.
[2] *Therigatha*, 93–96. Mrs. Rhys Davids's translation, which is used in all subsequent citations from the *Thera-theri-gatha*.

76 Conversion : Christian and Non-Christian

> And then at last I saw Him, as he went,
> Within that blessed city Mithila ;
> Great tamer of untamed hearts—yea, Him,
> The Very Buddha, Banisher of fear.
> Came back my heart to me, my errant mind,
> Forthwith to Him I went low worshipping,
> And there, e'en at His feet, I heard the Norm,
> For of His great compassion on us all,
> 'Twas He who taught me, even Gotama." [1]

Pride and insolence were the besetting sins of one brother, but both were overcome when he was " born again."

> " Infatuated with my birth, my wealth,
> And influence, with the beauty of my form
> Intoxicated, thus I led my life.
> O'ermuch I fancied none was like to me,
> A poor young fool by overweening spoilt,
> Stubborn with pride, posing and insolent.
> Mother and father—aye, and others too
> Claiming respect and honour—never one
> Did I salute, discourteous, stiff with pride.
> Then saw I Him the Guide, Leader Supreme,
> The peerless Chief 'mong drivers of mankind,
> In glory shining like the sun, with all
> The company of brethren in His train.
> Casting away deceit and wanton pride,
> A pious gladness filling all my heart,
> Lowly I rendered homage with the head
> To Him among all creatures Best and Chief.
> Well extirpated now and put away
> Is both o'erweening and hypocrisy ;
> The *what* and *that* ' I am ' is snapt in twain,
> Yea, every form of self-conceit is slain." [2]

For twenty-five years the woman who wrote the following poem strove for self-mastery :

> " Full five-and-twenty years since I came forth !
> But in my troubled heart in no way yet
> Could I discern the calm of victory.
> The peace of mind, the governance of thoughts
> Long sought, I found not ; and with anguish thrilled
> I dwelt in memory on the Conqueror's word.
> To free my path from all that breedeth ill,

[1] *Therigatha*, 133-136. [2] *Theragatha*, 423-428.

Conversion in Early Buddhism

> I strove with passionate ardour, and I won !
> Craving is dead, and the Lord's will is done.
> To-day is now the seventh day since first
> Was withered up within that ancient Thirst." [1]

The brother who wrote the following poem had no difficulty in dating his conversion :

> " O welcome was to me that day of spring,
> When at Gaya, at Gaya's river-feast,
> I saw the Buddha teach the Norm supreme,
> Saw the great Light, Teacher of multitudes,
> Him who hath won the highest, Guide of all,
> The Conqueror of men and gods, unrivalled Seer.
> Mighty magician, hero glorious,
> Far-shining splendour, pure, immune of mind,
> The master who hath slain all *asavas*,
> And hath attained that where no fear can come.
> Long lay I bound and harassed by the ties
> Of sect and dogma—ah ! but now 'tis He,
> The Blessed Lord, hath rescued Senaka
> From every bond and set at liberty." [2]

To those who know India the following utterance has all the marks of verisimilitude :

> " On Ganga's shore three palm-tree leaves I took
> And made my hut ; my bowl like funeral pot
> Wherewith men sprinkle milk upon a corpse ;
> My cloak from refuse of the dust-heap culled.
> Two years, from one rain-season till the next,
> I (there abode) nor spake a word save once.
> So till the third year passed—then the long night
> Of gloom asunder burst (and broke in light)." [3]

Before we leave the testimony of the *Thera-theri-gatha* to the fact of conversion in Early Buddhism, it may be well to point out that these poems help us to correct the view once held that the gospel of Gotama appealed only to the higher and educated classes of society, and had little power to draw the lowly, the wretched, or the young. " I am not aware," wrote Oldenberg, " of any instance in which a Candala—the pariah of that age—is mentioned in the sacred

---

[1] *Therigatha*, 39–41.   [2] *Theragatha*, 287–290.
[3] Ibid. 127.

78 Conversion : Christian and Non-Christian

writings as a member of the Order. For the lower order of the people, for those born to toil in manual labour, hardened by the struggle for existence, the announcement of the connection of misery with all forms of existence was not made, nor was the dialectic of the law of the painful concatenation of causes and effects calculated to satisfy 'the poor in spirit!' 'To the wise belongeth the law,' it is said, 'not unto the foolish.' Very unlike the word of that Man, Who suffered 'little children to come unto Him, for of such is the Kingdom of God.' For children and those who are like children the arms of Buddha are not opened."[1]

If regard be had only to the *Maha-Vagga*, Oldenberg's conclusion would be sound enough; but Mrs. Rhys Davids has taken a census of the various classes from which the 259 poets of the *Theragatha* are said, by the Commentary, to have sprung. The Brahmans and Khattriyas naturally preponderate. The former were the custodians of the religious lore, the latter were of the same caste as Gotama. But 10 out of the 259 belong to the despised of the earth, being pariahs, labourers, slaves, fishermen. Another group of 10 includes craftsmen, elephant-trainers, caravan guides, and an actor. Further, according to the Commentary, a number of the authors left the world as youths, and became *arahats* on the threshold of manhood.[2]

As far as I know, Mrs. Rhys Davids has taken no such census of the women who wrote the *Therigatha*, but I have noted four who had been courtesans before their conversions: Addhakasi, Vimala, Abhaya's mother, and Ambapali.[3] This is further evidence that Early Buddhism was able to attract those who were sadly in need of moral renewal, and was able to save not only proud Brahmans and kings, but also the outcasts of the streets. Thus does Vimala hymn her moral renewal. The first part of the poem describes her beauty and the manifold wiles she had used to devour the virtue of many:

[1] *Buddha*, E.T. 155-158. See also 205. So also Copleston, op. cit. 37. Contrast Poussin, op. cit. 8 f., and Rhys Davids, *Dialogues of the Buddha*, 102.
[2] *Psalms of the Brethren*, p. xxxi. We return to the point in Chapter X.
[3] See Psalms xxii., xxvi., xxxix., lxvi.

"To-day with shaven head, wrapt in my robe,
I go forth on my daily round for food ;
And 'neath the spreading boughs of forest tree
I sit, and Second-Jhana's rapture win,
Where reas'nings cease, and joy and ease remain.
Now all the evil bonds that fetter gods
And men are wholly rent and cut away.
Purg'd are the *asavas* that drugg'd my heart.
Calm and content I know Nibbana's Peace." [1]

[1] *Therigatha*, 75.

CHAPTER VI

CONVERSION IN ISLAM

ANY account of Islamic conversions might well be expected to begin with an examination of Muhammad's own religious experiences. As is well known, it was only after long internal conflict that he became convinced of his mission as a prophet of God. Are there any grounds for thinking that this consciousness of the prophetic call was associated with a conversion experience ? Unfortunately, the question as to the precise nature of Muhammad's pathological states is still an open one, and modern scholarship has not taken kindly to Sprenger's suggestion that Muhammad's was a case of epileptic mendacity. Nor can we believe that the Prophet was a conscious impostor, at any rate during the Meccan period of his career. His sincerity is vouched for by the fact that his preaching against idolatry, licentiousness, infanticide, drunkenness and gambling aroused the bitter hostility of the Quraysh, who held out many inducements to him to be silent. From what we know of the Old Testament prophets and the close connection between their call to the prophetic office and their conversion, the conjecture seems plausible that Muhammad may have passed through a somewhat similar experience, though specific evidence in support of the conjecture is wanting.

Islamic tradition has preserved pretty elaborate accounts of the Prophet's earliest adherents, but it is difficult to detect in these records the vibration of the subtler strings of religious emotion. Not even Professor T. W. Arnold can produce evidence of a spiritual revolution in the lives of the earliest converts.[1] Perhaps, if we knew more of

[1] Chap. ii. of his *Preaching of Islam* is !devoted to a study of the converts made during the Prophet's own lifetime ; and Arnold is anxious to show that Islam from the beginning was " a missionary religion that seeks to win the hearts of men."

Conversion in Islam 81

the gentle-hearted Abu Bakr, we might find in him an exceptional case. After his conversion he spent the greater part of his fortune in the purchase of Moslem slaves, who were being persecuted by their owners because they had adopted the new faith.[1]

Another interesting case is that of Mus'ab b. 'Umayr, whom Muhammad sent to Medinah as a missionary before the Hijrah.

> "In early life he had been a fop, who rejoiced in fine raiment and dainty perfumes. He had concealed his conversion till the secret was betrayed to his parents by one who saw him. Then he openly espoused the cause, losing his all. He fled to Abyssinia, and returned with the others. Poverty and privation had changed his dainty complexion, so that the Prophet wept to see it; rags scarcely sufficient to cover him were the substitute for his smart apparel. Presently a martyr's death awaited him. If other Moslems reaped some of their reward in this world, the first Refugee reaped none. Fops and dandies were thought good material by Epictetus, who perhaps knew men well." [2]

The conversion of the famous Omar is of interest as an example of a complete and sudden *volte face*, but the religious element is difficult to trace. So bitter was his opposition to Muhammad that he set out one day, sword in hand, to slay him. On the way he was reminded that his sister, Fatimah, and her husband, Sa'id, had become Moslems. He rushed into their house and found them being taught to recite the Koran. Whereupon he rushed at Sa'id and struck him. Fatimah, in order to protect her husband, flung herself between the two men, and in the struggle was wounded. When Omar saw the blood on her face, he relented, and asked to see the roll from which they had been reading. As he read, conviction suddenly overcame him, and he asked to be taken to Muhammad as a convert.[3]

After the flight to Medinah and the turn in the tide of the Prophet's fortunes, conversions multiplied rapidly,

---

[1] Arnold, op. cit. 12.   [2] Margoliouth, *Mohammed*, 199.
[3] Arnold, op. cit. 17. Cf. Margoliouth, op. cit. 164. Not unsimilar was the case of Muhammad's uncle, Hamzah. His Arab blood changed him from a bitter foe to a stanch adherent when he heard of an insult inflicted upon and patiently borne by his kinsman. See Arnold, op. cit. 14.

82 Conversion : Christian and Non-Christian

but naturally their religious value decreased as their numbers increased.[1] In spite of Professor Arnold's *apologia*, we may acquiesce in Margoliouth's judgment. " The men whose accession to Islam after the migration led to its great military successes, especially Khalid b. al-Walid and 'Amr b. al-'As, appear to have had little or no religious conviction, but to have been moved by admiration for the Prophet's military and diplomatic skill, and anxious to serve under so able a chief. So far as religion entered into their considerations, they probably thought of the god of the community as leading it in war, and found the deity of the Muslim society able to defeat others. More devout members of the society regarded the Prophet as able to call in the divine aid whenever he was in need of it." [2]

How superficial the conversion of the Arab tribes had been is seen by the widespread apostasy that followed the Prophet's death ; [3] while the subsequent conversion of millions of non-Arabs was the work, not of apostles, but of generals. With the rise of Sufiism, however, we get a return to greater inwardness in religion.

The Sufis, not content with the five canonical prayers of Islam, nor with the obligatory fast of Ramadan, invented extra devotions and fasts ; and their ascetic morality led them to favour celibacy in spite of the Prophet's saying, " There is no monkery in Islam." They also replaced Muhammad's entirely legalistic conception of salvation with one of greater inwardness. The aim of the Sufi system was nothing less than mystical union with God by the cultivation of spiritual feelings and the purification of the inner man. The movement was marked by intense religious exaltation, and, without question, Sufiism furnished Islam with its saints. Cases of genuine spiritual awakening abound, as might be expected, in a system which made repentance or conversion the first of the Seven Stages on the Unitive Way.

[1] Cf. Hurgronje, *Mohammedanism*, 40.
[2] E.R.E. viii. 876. Similarly Hurgronje, op. cit. 97. The curious may find an account of the conversion of Khalid and 'Amr in Margoliouth, op. cit. 374 f. For other conversions see 96–102, 110, 162–164, 199 f.
[3] This is noted by Arnold, op. cit. 41.

Conversion in Islam 83

Fortunately the *Kashf al-Mahjub* of al-Hujwiri,[1] the oldest extant Persian treatise on Sufiism, contains a long section which gives a considerable amount of biographical detail about eminent Sufis, many of whom abandoned their evil ways at their conversion. Hujwiri tells us that Habib al-'Ajami, before his spiritual awakening, had been a usurer and had committed all sorts of wickedness.[2] The celebrated Fudayl was a brigand before his conversion. One day, as he was lying in ambush, he heard the rider of one of the camels in the caravan he was about to waylay reciting the Koran aloud. The verse that came to his ears was: " Is not the time yet come unto those who believe, that their hearts should humbly submit to the admonition of God ? " " Fudayl's heart was softened. He repented of the business in which he was engaged, and, having written a list of those whom he had robbed, satisfied all their claims upon him. Then he went to Mecca and resided there for some time, and became acquainted with certain saints of God."[3]

Bishr b. al-Harith al-Hafi is said to have been converted in the following manner:

"One day, when drunk, he found a piece of paper on which was written: 'In the name of God, the Compassionate, the Merciful.' He picked it up with reverence, perfumed it, and laid it in a clean place. The same night he dreamed that God said to him: 'O Bishr, as thou hast made My name sweet, I swear by My Glory that I will make thy name sweet both in this world and in the next.' Thereupon he repented and took to asceticism."[4]

Other eminent Sufis were of royal descent, but they turned their backs on this world, God having bestowed upon them a true repentance.[5] Shibli, once a chief chamberlain to the Caliph, was converted by a sermon of Khayr al-Nassaj.[6] When Abu Yazid was asked how old he was, he replied, " Four years." His questioner asked, " How can that be ? " The saint replied: " I have been

---

[1] Hujwiri, who died about 1076 A.D., represents a moderate type of Sufiism, which set its face against the extreme pantheism and antinomianism of the radicals. All the citations that follow are from the translation by R. A. Nicholson (London, 1911).
[2] Hujwiri, 88.   [3] Ibid. 97 f.   [4] Ibid. 105.
[5] Ibid. 103, 158.   [6] Ibid. 155; cf. 144.

veiled (from God) for seventy years, but I have seen Him during the last four years: the period during which one is veiled does not belong to one's life."[1] Husri, who defined Sufiism as " the heart's being free from the pollution of discord,"[2] had almost certainly had experience of the unification of the divided self.

The following four stories of conversion will present no difficulties to those who have any knowledge of the psychology of the Eastern soul:

'Abdallah b. Mubarak al-Marwazi "was in love with a girl, and one night in winter he stationed himself at the foot of the wall of her house, while she came on to the roof, and they both stayed gazing at each other till daybreak. When 'Abdallah heard the call to morning prayers he thought it was time for evening prayers; and only when the sun began to shine did he discover that he had spent the whole night in rapturous contemplation of his beloved. He took warning by this, and said to himself: ' Shame on thee, O son of Mubarak! Dost thou stand on foot all night for thine own pleasure, and yet become furious when the Imam reads a long chapter in the Koran?' He repented and devoted himself to study, and entered a life of asceticism."[3]

Abu 'l-Hasan Sari b. Mughallis al-Saqati "used to carry on the business of a huckster in the bazaar at Baghdad. When the bazaar caught fire, he was told that his shop was burnt. He replied: ' Then I am freed from the care of it.' Afterwards it was discovered that his shop had not been burnt, although all the shops surrounding it were destroyed. On seeing this, Sari gave all that he possessed to the poor and took to the path of Sufiism. He was asked how the change in him began. He answered: ' One day Habib Ra'i passed my shop, and I gave him a crust of bread, telling him to give it to the poor. He said to me, "May God reward thee!" From the day when I heard this prayer my worldly affairs never prospered again.' "[4]

The conversion of Abu 'Ali Shaqiq b. Ibrahim al-Azdi took place in the following manner:

" One year there was a famine in Balkh and the people were eating one another's flesh. While all the Moslems were bitterly distressed, Shaqiq saw a youth laughing and making merry in the bazaar. The people said: ' Why do you laugh? Are you not ashamed to rejoice when everyone else is mourning?' The youth said:

[1] Hujwiri, 331.   [2] Ibid. 38; cf. 160.   [3] Ibid. 95 f.
[4] Ibid. 110. For a slightly different account see Margoliouth, *Early Development of Mohammedanism*, 173.

'I have no sorrow; I am the servant of a man who owns a village as his private property, and he has relieved me of all care for my livelihood.' Shaqiq exclaimed: 'O Lord God, this youth rejoices so much in having a master who owns a single village, but Thou art the King of Kings, and Thou hast promised to give us our daily bread; and nevertheless we have filled our hearts with all this sorrow because we are engrossed with worldly things.' He turned to God and began to walk in the way of Truth, and never troubled himself again about his daily bread."[1]

Ahmad Hammadi gave the following account of his conversion to Hujwiri:

"Once I set out from Sarakhs and took my camels into the desert and stayed there for a considerable time. I was always wishing to be hungry, and was giving my portion of food to others, and the words of God—'They prefer them to themselves, although they are indigent' (Kor. lix. 9)—were ever fresh in my mind; and I had a firm belief in the Sufis. One day a hungry lion came from the desert and killed one of my camels and retired to some rising ground and roared. All the wild beasts in the neighbourhood, hearing him roar, gathered round him. He tore the camel to pieces and went back to the higher ground without having eaten anything. The other beasts—foxes, jackals, wolves, etc.—began to eat, and the lion waited till they had gone away. Then he approached in order to eat a morsel, but seeing a lame fox in the distance, he withdrew once more until the new-comer had eaten his fill. After that he came and ate a morsel. As he departed, he spoke to me, who had been watching from afar, and said: 'O Ahmad, to prefer others to one's self in the matter of food is an act only worthy of dogs: a *man* sacrifices his life and his soul.' When I saw this evidence I renounced all worldly occupations, and that was the beginning of my conversion."[2]

As far as I know, there is no extant record of the conversion of the famous female Sufi, Rabi'a, who died in A.D. 752, but echoes of it appear to ring in the following striking lines:

"I love thee with two loves, a love that is a passion
  And one which besides thou hast earned as thy due.
The passionate love is the thought which forgetting
  All else is of you—aye, for ever of you.
Thou earnedst the other by rending asunder
  All veils and disclosing thyself to my view.
Not mine be the praise for the one or the other;
  The praise and the thanks are all thine for the two."[3]

[1] Hujwiri, 112. [2] Ibid. 193. [3] Margoliouth, op. cit. 175.

86 Conversion : Christian and Non-Christian

Nasir ibn Khusraw was turned from the world by a dream. I quote D. B. Macdonald's account of his conversion:

"He was a secretary in the service of the State at Merv, and devoted to wealth and the pleasures it brings. In October, A.D. 1045, he confesses that he took the opportunity of a favourable astrological situation to address to Allah a special prayer for wealth. Under such circumstances he believed it would be heard. Then he went to a neighbouring town, and gave himself up for a month to wine. He was plainly in a completely unregenerate condition, and jumbled together religion, astrology, his worldly ambitions, and his pleasures. But one night he saw in a dream a figure which addressed him thus : ' How long wilt thou drink wine that deprives men of reason ? It were better that thou shouldest return to thyself.' He answered : ' The wise have found nothing better than wine to dissipate the cares of this world.' ' The loss of reason and of the possession of thyself,' the figure replied, ' do not give peace to the spirit. The wise cannot commend to anyone to give himself to be guided by madness ; there is rather need to seek that which will increase wisdom and inheritance.' ' How,' he replied, ' can I get it for myself ? ' ' He who seeks, finds,' added the form, and indicated with a gesture the direction of Mecca.

" This dream changed his life. However his own psychological condition may have been prepared, there was no question to his mind of the suddenness with which his conversion came. With the morning he determined to give up everything for which he had lived for forty years. His secretaryship he resigned ; his wealth he abandoned, except what was needed for the journey ; on March 6, 1046, he set out on a pilgrimage to Mecca. Thereafter his life was that of a wandering religious, and he died as a hermit in the mountains of Badakhshan in 1088. His is in many respects a perplexing personality . . . but the great fact of this sudden conversion is firm." [1]

From R. A. Nicholson's erudite study of Abu Sa'id ibn Abi 'l-Khayr I take the following account of that famous Persian Sufi's conversion. Abu Sa'id was a great preacher and teacher of the pantheistic, antinomian school. He also did much for the organization of Sufiism as a monastic system. For some time before his conversion he had been seeking spiritual peace, but all his efforts to win it by the method of intellectual proof had ended in failure, though he spent ten years under well-known teachers in the study of Koranic exegesis and Islamic theology.

[1] *The Religious Attitude and Life in Islam*, 87 f. See 88-91 for the sudden conversion of al-Ashari, the founder of the Asharite system.

Conversion in Islam

"Abu Sa'id said as follows: 'At the time when I was a student I lived at Sarakhs and read with Abu 'Ali, the doctor of divinity. One day ... I saw Luqman of Sarakhs seated on an ash-heap near the gate sewing a patch on his gaberdine. I went up to him and stood looking at him, while he continued to sew. As soon as he had sewn the patch on, he said: "O Abu Sa'id! I have sewn thee on this gaberdine along with the patch." Then he rose and took my hand, leading me to the convent of the Sufis in Sarakhs, and shouted for Shaykh Abu 'l-Fadl Hasan, who was within. When Abu 'l-Fadl appeared, Luqman placed my hand in his, saying: "O Abu 'l-Fadl, watch over this young man, for he is one of you." The Shaykh took my hand and led me into the convent. I sat down in the portico, and the Shaykh picked up a volume and began to peruse it. As is the way of scholars, I could not help wondering what the book was. The Shaykh perceived my thought. "Abu Sa'id," he said, "all the hundred and twenty-four thousand prophets were sent to preach one word. They bade the people say 'Allah' and devote themselves to Him. Those who heard this word with the ear alone, let it go out by the other ear; but those who heard it with their souls ... their whole being became this word. ..." This saying took hold of me and did not allow me to sleep that night. In the morning, when I had finished my prayers and devotions, I went to the Shaykh before sunrise and asked permission to attend Abu 'Ali's lectures on Koranic exegesis. He began his lecture with the verse, "Say Allah! then leave them to amuse themselves in their folly." At the moment of hearing this word a door in my breast was opened, and I was rapt from myself.'"[1]

The following record of a conversion made under the influence of the preaching of Abu Sa'id is of interest, because the convert resisted successfully for some time the pressure of crowd conditions upon him, but yielded in the end:

"One day I went to the hall where he preached, with the intention of putting him to the proof,[2] and sat down in front of his chair. I was handsomely dressed and had a turban of fine Tabari stuff wound on my head. While the Shaykh was speaking, I regarded him with feelings of hostility and disbelief. Having finished his sermon, he asked for clothes on behalf of a dervish. Everyone offered something. Then he asked for a turban. I thought of giving mine, but again I reflected that it had been brought to me from Amul as a present and that it was worth ten Nishapuri dinars, so I resolved not to give it. The Shaykh made a second appeal,

---

[1] *Studies in Islamic Mysticism*, 6–8.
[2] The reference is to Abu Sa'id's telepathic gifts, which he knew how to exhibit impressively, and to which his age ascribed a miraculous character.

88 *Conversion : Christian and Non-Christian*

and the same thought occurred to me, but I rejected it once more. An old man who was seated beside me asked : ' O Shaykh ! does God plead with his creatures ? ' He answered : ' Yes, but He does not plead more than twice for the sake of a Tabari turban. He has already spoken twice to the man sitting beside you and has told him to give to this dervish the turban which he is wearing, but he refuses to do so, because it is worth ten pieces of gold and was brought to him from Amul as a present.' On hearing these words, I rose, trembling, and went forward to the Shaykh and kissed his foot and offered my turban and my whole suit of clothes to the dervish. Every feeling of dislike and incredulity was gone. I became a Moslem anew, bestowed on the Shaykh all the money and wealth I possessed, and devoted myself to his service." [1]

Some of the better-known Sufi poets appear to have undergone a real spiritual awakening. Very little is known of Saadi and Hafiz, but the latter is said to have led a riotous life before he became a Sufi. Fariduddin 'Attar (A.D. 1119–1229) was a druggist, as his cognomen implies. His conversion reminds one of the call of the evangelist Matthew from the seat of custom.

" One day, while he was seated in his shop surrounded by his servants busily attending to his orders, a wandering dervish paused at the door and regarded him silently, while his eyes slowly filled with tears. Attar sharply told him to be off about his business. ' That is easily done,' replied the dervish ; ' I have only a light bundle to carry—nothing, in fact, but my clothes. But you, with your sacks full of valuable drugs, when the time comes to go, what will you do ? Had you not better consider a little ? ' The appeal went home ; he promptly abandoned his business in order to devote himself to a religious life." [2]

Jalaluddin Rumi (A.D. 1207–1273) also was led into the mystic way by a wandering dervish.

" After several years of study at Aleppo and Damascus, Jalal returned to Qoniya, where he was appointed professor and gained a great reputation for learning. About this time he seems to have devoted himself to theosophy under the guidance of . . . one of his father's pupils ; but the crisis of his spiritual life was his meeting with Shams al-din of Tabriz, a wandering dervish who came to Qoniya in A.D. 1244. . . . The illiterate, God-intoxicated man

[1] *Studies in Islamic Mysticism*, 28.
[2] Field, *Mystics and Saints of Islam*, 123.

exerted upon Jalal an extraordinary influence, almost amounting to possession." [1]

It is surely not altogether fanciful to hear the echoes of this conversion experience in the following lines by Jalal:

> " When first the Giver of the grape my lonely heart befriended,
> Wine fired my bosom and my veins filled up.
> But when His image all mine eye possessed, a voice descended,
> ' Well done, O Sovereign Wine and peerless Cup!'" [2]

Jami (1414-1492) is said to have been converted to Sufiism by a vision in which S'ad al-din appeared to him and said: " Go, O Child, and wait on one who is indispensable to you." Jami obeyed the command and went to S'ad al-din for spiritual instruction.[3]

The story of the conversion of al-Ghazali, the greatest constructive theologian in Islam, has often been told,[4] and need not be repeated here in detail. Born in 1058, he went through a well-marked conversion about 1095, and spent the remaining years of his life as a wandering Sufi, teaching the Sufi doctrines. His autobiography reveals the inner movements of his soul with a keenness of spiritual and psychological insight that cannot fail to remind one of the *Confessions* of Augustine, whom in many respects he closely resembles. For about six months he was " torn asunder," he tells us, " by the opposite forces of earthly passions and religious aspirations."

Finally, we notice that within modern times the rise of the Babi movement in Persia was followed by a number of surprising conversions, the reality of which is placed beyond doubt by the pitiless persecution to which the Babis were subjected.[5]

[1] R. A. Nicholson in E.R.E. vii. 474. Details of the meeting between Jalal and Shams may be found in Redhouse's translation of *The Acts of the Adepts*, prefixed to his translation of the *Mesnevi* of Jalal (London, 1871), 24 f. Many conversions are recorded in *The Acts of the Adepts*, but the psychological details given are extremely meagre.
[2] Nicholson, *Mystics of Islam*, 107.
[3] F. Hadland Davis, *The Persian Mystics: Jami*, 17.
[4] James, 402 ff.; Macdonald, op. cit. 174 ff.; Moore, *History of Religions*, ii. 457 ff.; Field, op. cit. 106 ff. A convenient English trans. of the *Confessions* was published by Field in the Wisdom of the East Series in 1909.
[5] The curious may find some details of these conversions in Nicolas, *Seyyed Ali Mohammed dit Le Bab* (Paris, 1905), 233 ff., 248-254, 262, 273 ff., 293, 301, 328 f., 344, 389-393.

CHAPTER VII

CONVERSION IN THE RELIGIONS OF GREECE AND ROME

FOR the highest flights of the religious spirit in Greece and Rome we must look in the writings of their poets and philosophers. The priests of the different temples were content to preserve the old traditions and rites, but the great poets and thinkers set out to ethicize the traditional religion so that it might commend itself to thinking men. The scandalous stories of the gods had been for some time an offence to many, when Æschylus and Sophocles took their own line in dealing with the moral problem thus created and sought to show the unity of the moral order of the world. Euripides, however, adopted another and a different attitude toward the gods—an attitude of philosophic agnosticism. How, then, are we to explain the deeper religious note that breathes through his last play, the *Bacchæ*? Some scholars think that it indicates that at the end of his life he abandoned his scepticism for an attitude of genuine religious enthusiasm. " The poet writes throughout as if he felt profoundly what he so rapturously says. The greater part of the play is pervaded by a kind of joyous exaltation which accompanies a new discovery or illumination."[1] Have we here a genuine religious conversion ? It is doubtful if the evidence will take us farther than the conclusion that " the poet threw his soul more unreservedly into his subject than was his wont."[2]

Socrates shared to the full the view of the great poets

[1] Adam, *The Religious Teachers of Greece*, 317. See also 306. Cf. Gilbert Murray, *Euripides and His Age*, 141. Prof. Murray speaks of his impression " of some profound change that has worked into the writer's soul."

[2] Moore, *History of Religions*, i. 489.

that the gods must be wise and good and incapable of any action repugnant to the moral sense of men. In him, however, we see an intense practical interest in the problems of the inner, ethical life. While his teaching gave the greatest impetus to speculative inquiry, his peculiar method of question and answer was designed to bring inquirers to a clear knowledge of the state of their own souls, and its end was to produce a regeneration of character by means of education. "He made me feel," says Alcibiades in the *Symposium*,[1] "as though I could hardly endure the life which I am living."

The strain of moral earnestness in Socrates was inherited by the Cynics and transmitted by them to the Stoics, whose precursors they were. Epictetus well calls the Cynics "athletes of righteousness." In an age when there was no deep and earnest religion to satisfy the cravings of the religious temper, both Cynics and Stoics almost equated philosophy with ethics and made it take the place of religion and do its work. They preached virtue as the only good, and called men to the way of virtue and happiness. Philosophy, they held, was the only cure for the maladies of the soul.

Many well-known Cynics and Stoics were converted men. Of Antisthenes, Gomperz writes: "His history was probably that of a worldling, who had recklessly broken with his own past, and henceforth judged himself with the same inexorable severity which he meted out to others."[2] Diogenes of Sinope, after his frauds had been discovered in his native town, fled to Athens, where he was arrested by the character of Antisthenes, who at first drove him away, as he did all other would-be pupils. Diogenes, however, could not be kept away by blows, and in the end Antisthenes accepted him as his pupil.[3] Diogenes Laërtius[4] recounts two stories that had come down as to the manner in which Crates entered the philosophic life. According to one story he

---

[1] The passage may be found in Jowett's trans. of the *Dialogues of Plato*, i. 523. The whole section is worthy of attention. I owe the reference to Adam, op. cit. 335 f. In very similar terms Epictetus speaks of his teacher, Musonius Rufus. See Davidson, *The Stoic Creed*, 54.
[2] *Greek Thinkers*, ii. 143.
[3] Diog. Laërt., vi. ii. 2.   [4] Ibid. vi. v. 4 f.

was the possessor of a large estate and flocks. These he discarded and his money he threw into the sea. According to another account he placed it in the hands of a banker with the charge to deliver it to his sons if they turned out ordinary ignorant people, and to the poor if they became philosophers. Whichever story be the true one, it is clear that on entering the philosophic life he attained complete equanimity of temper and was full of missionary zeal.

The conversion of Zeno, the Stoic, who began as a pupil of Crates, but afterwards founded a school of his own, is thus told by Diogenes Laërtius :

" Having purchased a quantity of purple from Phœnicia, he was shipwrecked close to the Piræus ; and when he had made his way along the coast as far as Athens, he sat down by a bookseller's stall, being now about thirty years of age. And as he took up the second book of Xenophon's *Memorabilia* and began to read it, he was delighted with it, and asked where such men as were described in that book lived ; and as Crates happened very seasonably to pass at that moment, the bookseller pointed him out, and said, ' Follow that man.' From that time forth he became a pupil of Crates." [1]

Some of the early Cynics were full of missionary zeal, and sought the conversion of the ignorant multitude by their direct appeals to conscience. Later, in the Antonine Age, philosophic missionaries of almost every school sought to win the multitude to the way of righteousness. Their preaching bore fruit. " An edifying discourse under a Stoic portico or in an academic school has been as effective in its practical results," says Oakesmith, [2] " as a religious oration by Bossuet or a village preaching by Whitfield." We notice later two cases of conversion under such preaching.[3]

How familiar the Stoics were with the fact of conver-

[1] Diog. Laërt., vii.i. 3 (Bohn's trans.) In vii. i. 5 Diog. Laërt. says: "As some relate the affair, he was not shipwrecked at all, but sold all his cargo at Athens and then turned to philosophy." For a good description of the new world that opened on Zeno at Athens see Bevan, *Stoics and Sceptics*, 15 f.
[2] *The Religion of Plutarch*, 15. Martha, in his *Les Moralistes sous l'Empire Romain*, writes : " On entrait dans la philosophie par une sorte de conversion édifiante ; on ne pouvait en sortir que par une apostasie scandaleuse," 297 (ed. 1865).
[3] See below, Chapter X.

sion may be seen by the way in which they worked out a systematic doctrine of it. Professor E. V. Arnold gives the following able summary of their teaching:

"The stages of progress are variously expounded by Stoic writers, but on one principle all are agreed. Progress is not a half-way stage between vice and virtue, as the Peripatetics teach; it is a long preparation, to be followed by a change, sudden and complete (μεταβολή, *conversio*). The final step by which a foolish man becomes in an instant wise is different in kind from all that has gone before. This position is a necessary consequence of the doctrine that 'the good is not constituted by addition,' and it is enforced by various illustrations. The probationer is like a man who has long been under water; little by little he rises to the surface, but all in a moment he finds himself able to breathe. He is like a puppy in whom the organ of sight has been for days past developing; all at once he gains the power of vision. Just so, when progress reaches the end, there dawns upon the eyes of the soul the complete and dazzling vision of the good, of which till now only shadows and reflections have been perceived. For a moment he is wise, but does not even yet realize his own wisdom; then again in a moment he passes on to the complete fruition of happiness." [1]

Very striking, too, is the language used by Apollonius in his advice to the young man who wasted his time training birds to talk. "What you want is some splendid diversion which will instantly make some alteration in your character" [2] (Δεῖ δέ σοι ἐκτροπῆς λαμπρᾶς καὶ μεταβολῆς ἤδη τινὸς τῶν τρόπων).

In spite of its magnificent missionary effort, the philosophic gospel failed to touch the lives of the masses of people on any considerable scale. Philosophy might furnish a religion for the cultured few, but the many turned for the satisfaction of their spiritual needs to the rites and mysteries that were coming in from the East. In these warmer worships they found something which neither philosophy nor the ceremonial of ancient Roman religion could give. They found sacraments designed to meet the soul's sense of guilt and to prepare it for its reception at the confines

---

[1] *Roman Stoicism*, 327 f. Cf. Zeller, *Stoics, Epicureans and Sceptics*, 275.
[2] *Life*, by Philostratus, vi. 36. Trans. by Conybeare in the Loeb Classical Library.

of the next world. The story of the invasion of the West by the cults of the Magna Mater, Isis and Mithras has been graphically told by Cumont in his *Les religions orientals dans le paganisme romain*, and need not be repeated here. As Cumont points out,[1] a great religious conquest can be explained only on moral grounds. The instinct of imitation and the contagion of example may account in large part for the rapid spread of these faiths, but in the last analysis much must be set down to individual conversions. A discussion of the evidence for such conversions may be reserved for Chapter IX, in which the dramatic representation of the idea of rebirth, which is so conspicuous in these cults, is dealt with.

In closing, we notice that even Epicureanism served as a religious force. With a zeal and enthusiasm that must surely be counted religious, Lucretius in his *De Natura Rerum* sets forth the materialism of his master as a gospel which brings deliverance from the fear of death and hell. But, as Warde Fowler points out, the real force of Epicureanism was its " profound and touching belief in the founder himself as a saviour, which is so familiar to all readers of Lucretius."[2] " At the beginning of almost every book of his poems Lucretius repeats," says Masson,[3] " the same acknowledgment of his debt to his master. It is now his spiritual bravery, now his marvellous insight into nature, now his power to cleanse the heart and save mankind from the miseries of ambition, from lust, care and fear." This feeling of indebtedness is expressed with such passionate fervour in the exordium to Book III that a modern scholar[4] has argued that we have there clear indications of a psychological conversion of Lucretius.

[1] Op. cit. (E.T., Chicago, 1911) 27 ff.
[2] *Religious Experience of the Roman People*, 361.
[3] *Lucretius: Epicurean and Poet*, 355. Cf. 318 f. and the quotations there given.
[4] W. A. Heidel in a paper, " Die Bekehrung im klassischen Alterthum mit besonderer Berücksichtigung des Lucretius," in the *Zeitschrift für Religionspsychologie* for 1910. This paper is now out of print, and I have not been able to consult it. I owe the reference to Warde Fowler, op. cit. 376.

CHAPTER VIII

CONVERSION IN VARIOUS NON-CHRISTIAN RELIGIONS

IN seeking evidence for the fact of conversion in the religions of Babylonia and Assyria, we naturally turn to the so-called Penitential Psalms, in which the religious spirit of these countries reached its highest expression. The finest specimen is the hymn addressed to Ishtar,[1] but even here, as Jastrow reminds us,[2] the footsteps of spiritual religion are dogged by incantation and magic.[3] Yet the inference is not altogether precarious that the royal person who here pours out his soul before the goddess had undergone a spiritual awakening. What oppresses him is the feeling that his many afflictions are due to the anger of the goddess, whom he has provoked by unintentional disobedience and insufficient reverence. His spiritual experience, however, is on a much lower level than that of the writer of Psalm li. in the Hebrew Psalter.

When we turn to the religion of Egypt, we are confronted with an absence of documents relating to personal religion. The practical and materialistic tendencies of the Egyptians, and their disposition to concentrate attention on the future life, were unfavourable to the emergence of the "twice-born" type of religious experience. The Egyptians of the Old and Middle Kingdoms and of the Early New Empire never admitted to the gods that they were other than models of excellence. They had no sense of sin. "The Egyptian mind is rather akin to the Greek mind, which sought out

[1] Text and trans. in Rogers, *Cuneiform Parallels to the Old Testament*, 153 ff.
[2] H.D.B. v. 567.
[3] The psalm concludes with what is an anti-climax: directions for a magical rite of expiation. See Rogers, op. cit. 160 f.

96 Conversion : Christian and Non-Christian

a fair and noble life without introspection or self-reproach." [1] But in the later period of the New Empire we can see the dawn of an age of personal piety and inner aspiration to God—an age in which man can now pray, "Chastise me not according to my many sins." [2]

A little earlier arose the splendid figure of Akhnaton, the reality and inwardness of whose religious experiences none can doubt. Ascending the throne of the Pharaohs as Amenhopis IV, at the age of twelve or thirteen, he reigned from 1375–1358 B.C. He was not more than nineteen when he broke away from orthodoxy and changed his name to Akhnaton (The Disk is pleased), and launched his magnificent but unsuccessful attempt to make an exclusive solar monotheism the religion of Egypt. When he was about twenty-two or twenty-three he composed the remarkable hymn to Aton, which stands out among the greatest utterances of the religious spirit of man. In it he says :

> "Thou art in my heart,
> There is no other that knoweth thee
> Save thy son Ikhnaton.
> Thou hast made him wise
> In thy designs and in thy might." [3]

Professor H. W. V. Jackson has collected in his *Zoroaster* an immense amount of material relating to the career of the prophet of Iran, but he has made no attempt to sift this material, the unhistoricity of much of which is immediately apparent. It is safer, therefore, to follow Moulton, who confines himself to the Gathas in attempting to sketch the career of the prophet. Moulton says that the following passage "may be regarded as a record of later reflection on the prophet's conversion." [4]

"As the Holy One I knew thee, Mazdah Ahura, when Good Thought came to me, when first by your words I was instructed.

---

[1] Flinders Petrie, *Religion and Conscience in Ancient Egypt*, 122.
[2] Erman, *A Handbook of Egyptian Religion*, 83. For the earlier protestations of innocence see Breasted, *Development of Religion and Thought in Ancient Egypt*, 168 f., 253 f., 299 ff.
[3] Breasted, op. cit. 328.
[4] *Treasure of the Magi*, 17.

Conversion in Non-Christian Religions 97

Shall it bring me sorrow among men, my devotion, in doing that which ye tell me is the best?

"And when thou saidst unto me, 'To Right shalt thou go for teaching,' then thou didst not command what I did not obey."[1]

This passage, however, is extremely vague, and to attempt to fill in the picture with non-Gathic material is to use matter of doubtful authenticity.

Zoroaster's first convert was his cousin, Maidhyoi-maonha, and his most important convert King Vishtaspa, but a thick incrustation of legendary matter now conceals the historical kernel of these conversions.[2]

I have not been able to discover any authenticated cases of conversion in the religions of China. While it would be unsafe to say that the phenomenon was unknown, it cannot be doubted that the whole religious atmosphere of China was inimical to its appearance. Confucianism is not a religion in the sense in which a European would use the term. Its sanctions are political and practical in character. The emphasis is everywhere on filial obedience, propriety, courtesy, and orderly conduct. With transcendental matters Confucius felt no concern. Moreover, the fundamental Confucian dogma that man is born good tended to blind men's eyes to the need and possibility of spiritual rebirth. Nor is the case radically different with Lao-tse, in spite of his mystic flights. Both he and Confucius left the religion of China where they found it—on that animistic level where it remains to this day. There is no hint in the records of the life of either sage of a spiritual awakening that filled life with a deeper meaning. And the same may be said of their respective disciples, Mencius and Chuang Tzse.

When we turn to the history of religion in Japan, we find the records of which we are in search. Kobo, one of the reformers of Buddhist monasticism in Japan, was born in a noble family in A.D. 774. He enjoyed a university education and made a careful study of the ethics of Confucius, in preparation for an official career. Dissatisfied with the

[1] Ys, 43. Trans. from Moulton, loc. cit.
[2] The curious may find all the stories in Jackson, op. cit. 54 ff. For other conversions see 77 f., 81-88.

secular tone of Confucian ethics, he turned to Taoism, but found no lasting satisfaction in it.

"The mystical tendencies of his spirit, combined with the spiritual upheaval of his conversion, urged him to leave the capital to dwell in the midst of nature. In the midst of the mountains and in the seclusion of the forests and in the shadows of the ravines little by little his troubled soul found peace.

"It was after several years of travel and self-discipline that he attained spiritual illumination by a revelation of Buddha, on a day when he was on a high cliff jutting out like a spur in the midst of the waves. At the time of this definitive conversion he was twenty-four years of age, and shortly afterwards he was ordained in the Buddhist Church." [1]

The twelfth and thirteenth centuries in Japan witnessed a marked religious revival, of which the leaders were Honen and Nichiren, both of whom were converted men. Honen (1133–1212) was placed at an early age in a Tendai monastery on Mount Hiei, where he carried on his studies for more than thirty years.

"He acquired a great reputation for talent and virtue, and he might have aimed at the highest honours of the hierarchy, had he not preferred to honours the satisfactions which the soul draws from a well-founded faith.

"Starving for spiritual ambrosia, he cut himself off from his companions to dwell in a hermitage at Kurodani, a dark glade completely isolated from the world. . . . When he was about thirty his conversion, which had matured little by little, was completed, and he was forty-two years of age when he declared it publicly in his book, *The Choice*. . . .

"In spite of inward agitation, his life at Mount Hiei was not marked by any incident even before his conversion; later, his life continued to float on the calm sea of piety, bathed in the sunlight of the grace of Buddha. It was a peaceful existence, firmly established on his belief and wholly consecrated to repeating the name of Buddha and to inspiring the same faith in his admirers.

"Finally, he left Mount Hiei to live in greater isolation than ever at Yoshimizu, 'The Fountain of Joy.' Although he did not give himself at all to propaganda, his saintly character drew to the hermitage men and women of all classes. The Fountain of Joy became, indeed, a source of peace and inspiration for many thirsty souls . . . nobles and ladies of the Court, whom the sudden decline of imperial splendour had unsettled and who were seeking happiness

[1] Prof. Anesaki, *Quelques pages de l'histoire religieuse du Japon*, 40.

in the beyond ; warriors tired of drawing the sword and who were longing for eternal peace ; poor folk whom the aristocratic Church had kept at a distance and who were hoping at length to quench their spiritual thirst."[1]

Of the conversion of Nichiren, Professor Anesaki has given us a detailed account, which I here summarize. In the work just quoted he describes him, with a pardonable touch of extravagance, as an Isaiah and a Savonarola and at the same time an Augustine and a Dominic.[2] Born in 1222, he was placed by his father, a fisherman, at the age of eleven in a monastery. As he pursued his studies, doubt assailed him, and he became dissatisfied with the incongruous mixture of beliefs and practices included in the Buddhism of his day. His religious distress was so great that he fell into a swoon and had an attack of blood-spitting. In his quest for truth he left the monastery and visited the great centres of Buddhist learning, and extended his studies to Shintoism and Confucianism. His distress came to an end when he rose to the conviction that " the scripture, ' the Lotus of Truth,' was the deposit of the unique truth, the book in which the Lord Buddha had revealed his real entity. . . . Nichiren's firm belief was that the Lotus of Truth was not only the perfect culmination of Buddhist truth, but the sole key to the salvation of all beings in the latter days of degeneration. Thus, all other branches of Buddhism, which deviated from the principle of the exclusive adoration of this scripture, were denounced as untrue. . . . But all these doctrines and arguments were fused into the white-heat of his faith and zeal ; that is, he simplified the whole practice of religion to an easy method, that of uttering the ' Sacred Title ' of the Scripture."[3] Inflamed by this conviction, he spent the rest of his life in propagating his doctrines with somewhat turbulent zeal. He died in 1282.

[1] Prof. Anesaki, *Quelques pages de l'histoire religieuse du Japon*, 69–71.
[2] Op. cit. 89.
[3] *Nichiren, the Buddhist Prophet* (Harvard, 1916), 15.

CHAPTER IX

THE DRAMATIC REPRESENTATION OF REGENERATION

AT all stages of their religious development men have displayed a tendency to give dramatic representation to their religious beliefs and feelings. Particularly is this true of the earliest stages of human development. "On the lower cultural levels everything is more concrete—the man does what he feels; he acts rather than proclaims his feelings."[1] In this chapter we are concerned with dramatic rites of initiation in which the idea of rebirth is central.

We may begin with those initiatory ceremonies, taking place at puberty, which take the form of a pretended death and resurrection. On the lowest cultural levels this rebirth is often dramatized in a very realistic fashion. Among the Kikuyu of East Africa "the mother stands up with the boy crouching at her feet; she pretends to go through all the labour pains, and the boy, on being reborn, cries like a babe and is washed."[2] Among some tribes a pretence is made of killing the lad and bringing him to life again. Thus in the west of Ceram the youths who are to be initiated into the Kakian association are taken blindfolded into a darkened wooden shed in the depths of the forest. Each novice is led by the hand by two men, who act as his sponsors. When all are assembled before the shed, the high priest calls on the devils, and immediately a hideous uproar is heard to proceed from the shed. It is made by men secreted within, but the women and children think it is made by

[1] S. A. Cook, *The Study of Religions*, 351.
[2] Frazer, *Totemism and Exogamy*, i. 228.

Dramatic Representation of Regeneration 101

the devils, and are greatly terrified. The priests then enter the shed with the boys, one at a time. As each boy disappears within the precincts, a sound of chopping is heard. Dreadful cries ring out, and a sword or spear dripping with blood is thrust through the roof. This is a token that the boy's head has been cut off, and that the devil has taken him away to the other world to regenerate him. The mothers of the lads bewail the murder of their sons, who are kept in the shed for five or nine days, during which time they are taught the secrets and traditions of their tribe. The men who acted as sponsors return to the village and inform the mourning mothers and sisters that the devil, at the intercession of the priests, has restored the lads to life again. The men who bring this glad news come in fainting and daubed with mud, like messengers newly arrived from another world. When at last the boys leave the shed and return home, they totter in their walk and enter the house backward, as though they had forgotten how to walk. If a plate of food is given to them, they hold it upside down. They pretend they cannot speak, and indicate their wants by signs. Their sponsors have to teach them all the common arts of life, as though they were new-born children.[1]

Sometimes the pantomimic representation of death and rebirth is performed, not on the initiates themselves, but on other persons in their presence. Thus in one of the Fijian Islands the novices were led within the sacred enclosure and there shown a row of seemingly dead men with their bodies cut open and their entrails protruding. But at a yell from the priest the men started to their feet and ran to the river and cleansed themselves from the blood and entrails of pigs, with which they had been besmeared. Afterwards they marched back to the sacred enclosure, as if they had come to life again, clean, fresh and garlanded.[2]

Besides these graphic methods of simulating death and rebirth, other means are used to suggest that the initiate has been born again. A new name is given, on the principle that with the change of name the individual becomes another person, so indissolubly are a man's name and his personality

[1] I have summarized Frazer in *The Golden Bough*, iii. 442 ff.
[2] Ibid. iii. 425.

connected.[1] Just as a man's name is part of his soul, or life, so also is his dress. Hence the change of dress at initiation ceremonies betokens the changed identity of the novice. "Wanika boys are smeared all over with white earth, so that they cannot be recognized. At the end of the initiation they wash."[2] The Lokele people of the Upper Congo likewise use chalk or yellow clay.[3] On the Lower Congo those who have been initiated into the Ndembo mysteries show how utterly they have forgotten their old life by pretending not to know their parents and relatives. They also pretend to be like new-born babes, for when food is offered to them they affect not to know how to eat it; someone has to masticate it for them.[4] The new life of the initiates is sometimes emphasized by the giving of new food, the food of adults having been tabued till maturity is reached.[5]

On higher cultural levels the ritual takes a more refined form. The most important moment in the life of the three upper castes of India is their investiture with the sacred thread (Upanayana). Until that has taken place, the boy's spiritual life has not begun, and he is only a Sudra, with no place among the "Twice-born." Mrs. Sinclair Stevenson has given a careful and elaborate account of the ceremony as practised to-day by the Saivite Brahmans of the Maratha country.[6] The boy spends the night before the day of the actual ceremony in absolute silence, having been previously smeared all over with a yellow substance. In the morning the father and mother take the lad to a booth, where the sacrificial fire is burning on an altar, and his head is then shaved. Next the yellow powder is rubbed off and his body is bathed in warm water. After that he partakes of a little sweet food with his mother, and for the last time mother and son eat together. Henceforth the boy will eat with the men and sleep in the men's part of the house.

[1] Many cases are cited by Crawley in his *Mystic Rose*, 299 f., and by Webster in his *Primitive Secret Societies*, 40 f.
[2] Crawley, op. cit. 299.
[3] Sutton Smith, *Yakusu, the Very Heart of Africa*, 63.
[4] Sir Harry Johnston, *George Grenfell and the Congo*, ii. 668.
[5] Crawley, op. cit. 302 f.
[6] *The Rites of the Twice-Born*, 27–46, to which I am here much indebted.

Dramatic Representation of Regeneration 103

Then follows the solemn investiture with the sacred thread. This is succeeded by the giving of a new name, though, curiously enough, the new name is used only at this ceremony and is then immediately forgotten. Finally the boy is taught the famous *Gayatri* mantra, whose life-giving syllables no woman or low-caste person is permitted to hear. To prevent it being overheard, the heads of the boy and the *guru* are covered with a silk shawl, and it is whispered into the boy's right ear. Another feature of the ceremony is of interest. The boy is given a deer-skin, or, if in these days a whole skin cannot be managed, a small piece of deer-skin is threaded on a string and hung round the boy's neck. It is noteworthy that the *Satapatha Brahmana*[1] says that the antelope-skin represents the womb, and, when the young Brahman in the course of his initiation sits upon it, he is to assume the attitude of an embryo by closing his hands, " since embryos have their hands closed."

A kindred rite of initiation, to mark the beginning of the religious life, is found among the Parsis, but by them it is administered to both boys and girls. It is called the Naojote. After a purificatory bath, the child is solemnly invested with the sacred girdle (*kusti*) and shirt (*sudrah*), which every follower of Zoroaster must wear for the remainder of his life, whatever be the other costume he adopts. The ceremony takes place after the child has attained the age of seven, and is never postponed till later than the fifteenth year.[2]

As is well known, the dramatization of the death and rebirth of the initiated played a great part in the rites of the Mystery-Religions of the Græco-Roman world. The most impressive rite in the worship of the Magna Mater was the *taurobolium*. Various descriptions describe the baptized as *renatus in æternum*.[3] There is a famous description by Prudentius[4] of this bath in bull's blood. Some scholars hold that the *taurobolium* was also practised

---

[1] III. ii. 6 (S.B.E. xxvi. 27). Mrs. Sinclair Stevenson appears to have missed this small but interesting point.
[2] Further details may be found in Dr. Jivanji Modi's elaborate art. in E.R.E. vii. 325 f., and in Moulton, op. cit. 160 ff.
[3] Dill, *Roman Society from Nero to Marcus Aurelius*, 547, n. 4.
[4] Cited by Cumont, *Oriental Religions in Roman Paganism*, 66.

by pious Mithraists. In a syncretistic age the close connection between the two cults would pave the way to this, as would also the fact that the favourite symbol of Mithra depicted him slaying a bull. In the Cybele-Attis rites the idea of spiritual infancy was still further emphasized, for Sallustius tells us that, after the cutting of the tree and a fast, comes "the feeding on milk, as though we were being born again." [1]

Writing of the Isis cult, Cumont says: "Through initiation the mystic was born again, but to a superhuman life, and became the equal of the immortals." [2] Thus at the initiation of Lucius the high priest is made to say: "The goddess is wont to choose such as, having fulfilled a course of life, stand at the very threshold of departing light, to whom nevertheless the great mysteries of religion can be safely entrusted; and after they have been made, by her providence, in a sense born again (*quodam modo renatus*), she places them again on the course of a new life in salvation." [3]

Baptism in water often found a place in the ritual of the Mystery-Religions,[4] and we have the explicit testimony of Tertullian [5] that such baptisms were regarded as regenerating those who submitted to them.

Before we turn to the dramatic representation of Christian conversion in Christian baptism, it may be well to pause at this point to ask two questions: What was the psychological effect of these rites of initiation upon those who underwent them? How were they thought to bring about the desired rebirth? The second question is more easily answered than the first. In the initiation ceremonies of savage peoples the novice passes, as we have seen, from a purely profane world, in which he passed his infancy,

---

[1] *De Diis et Mundo*, 4. There is an English trans. by Gilbert Murray in his *Four Stages of Greek Religion*, 187 ff. In some parts of the Christian Church at the eucharist, which followed baptism, the neophyte partook of a cup of milk and honey mixed. The new-born in Christ partook of the food of babes, as though to emphasize their spiritual infancy. The *Canones Hippolyti* expressly say this. See Duchesne, *Christian Worship*, 3rd ed., 534. The custom is still observed among the Coptic and Ethiopic communities. Duchesne, op. cit. 330, n. 6.
[2] Op. cit. 100.
[3] *Metam.* xi. 21. Trans. from Kennedy, *St. Paul and the Mystery-Religions*, 101.
[4] Details in E.R.E. ii. 373 f. [5] *De Baptismo*, 5.

Dramatic Representation of Regeneration

into a world of sacred things. Durkheim is on sound lines when he says: "This change of state is thought of, not as a simple and regular development of pre-existent germs, but as a transformation (*totius substantiæ*) of the whole being. It is said that at this moment the young man dies, that the person that he was ceases to exist, and that another is instantly substituted for it. He is reborn under a new form. Appropriate ceremonies are felt to bring about this death and rebirth, which are not understood in a merely symbolic sense, but are taken literally."[1]

The Mystery-Religions of the Græco-Roman world stand on a much higher plane than the rites of initiation among savage peoples, for they demanded personal allegiance based on belief, and were not imposed on all members of the clan, and refused to all who stood outside it. At the same time we may take it as practically certain that their rites were thought of as possessing a similar *ex opere operato* character. The *taurobolium* and the water-baptisms were held to have an objective efficacy which, independent of the conscious faith of the recipient, was able to change his nature and raise him to a sphere of existence beyond the reach of Fate. Those who described themselves as *renatus in æternum* were using no empty phrase. They ascribed to the sacramental act the power actually to effect what happened to them in symbolism.

When we seek to investigate the religious and psychological effect these ceremonies of initiation had upon the novices, we are left, in the main, to sympathetic conjecture. There is also the further difficulty of translating into terms of our own consciousness a type of religious experience remote from our own. It cannot, however, be doubted that these ceremonies left an indelible impression on the mind of the initiates. The painful nature of some features of the rites (knocking out a tooth, biting the scalp till the blood flows, circumcision, sub-incision, and the ordeal by fire) would ensure this, and would at the same time teach hardihood and self-restraint. Among the Kurnai the youths who have been initiated remain in the bush with their sponsors,

[1] *Elementary Forms of the Religious Life*, 39. See also Marett, *The Threshold of Religion*, 191.

106 *Conversion : Christian and Non-Christian*

and their probation does not end till the old men are satisfied as to their conduct and obedience to tribal laws.[1] Writing of the rites among the Murring community, Howitt says they " are intended to impress and terrify the boy in such a manner that the lesson may be indelible, and may govern the whole of his future life."[2] The extraordinarily powerful effect produced by the teaching received at the ceremonies is seen in those cases where novices have broken food tabus and have thereafter died of fright.[3]

We are, therefore, driven to conclude that even among savage peoples the initiation rites are powers that work for righteousness by making the adolescents of the tribe more worthy members of it according to their lights; and in all probability a profound religious agitation[4] is a frequent concomitant. This may be crude, but there is no more need to doubt its occurrence than to doubt that it accompanies the rite of confirmation in Christian Churches.

Turning now to the Mystery-Religions, we notice first that they all, by their ritual, sought to produce a profound emotional effect. The aim of the Eleusinian Mysteries was not so much to communicate esoteric doctrine as to create an overpowering impression by the stimulus of collective excitement and the pageantry of dramatic ceremonial. The preliminary purifications were also intended to put the initiates in a state of mind which fitted them to receive the consummate experience. Synesius[5] quotes Aristotle as saying, with reference to the Eleusinian rites, that the aim of those who submitted to them was " not to learn anything, but to feel a certain emotion, and to get into a certain state of mind, after first becoming fit to experience it." The final rites must have been enacted in an atmosphere of intense feeling.[6]

The later mysteries were not less impressive, though their methods were more bizarre. Cumont warns us against

[1] Howitt, *Native Tribes of South-East Australia*, 637.
[2] Op. cit. 532.   [3] Ibid. 769 for such a case.
[4] For evidence of hallucination attending the initiation of adolescents see Marett, *Anthropology*, 247 ff., and Durkheim, op. cit. 162.
[5] *De Dione*, 10.
[6] See, e.g., Sir William Ramsay in *Enc. Brit.* (9th ed.) xvii. 126, and Farnell in E.R.E. vi. 409.

supposing that Mithraism "exhibited nothing more than a benignant phantasmagoria of a species of freemasonry."[1] "The gradual initiations," he says, "kept alive in the heart of the neophyte the hopes of a truth still more sublime, and the strange rites which accompanied them left in his ingenuous soul an ineffaceable impression. The converts believed they found, and, the suggestion being transformed into reality, actually did find, in the mystic ceremonies a stimulant and a consolation. They believed themselves purified of their guilt by the ritual ablutions, and this baptism lightened their conscience of the weight of their heavy responsibility."[2] In a kindred manner the rites of the Cybele cult were designed in a most skilful manner to raise the feelings of the onlookers into a state of rapturous ecstasy.[3] The profound impression which the rites of the Isis cult were capable of producing is vouched for by the famous description in Apuleius of the initiation of Lucius at Cenchreæ, "The prayer of thanksgiving offered by Lucius might," says Dill,[4] "*mutatis mutandis*, be uttered by a new convert at a camp-meeting or a Breton peasant after her first communion. It is the devout expression of the deep, elementary religious feelings of awe and gratitude, humility and joy, boundless hope and trust."

If further evidence be required of the emotional effect of the rites, we may quote Plutarch. "Nothing gives us more joy," he says, "than what we see and do ourselves in divine service when we carry the emblems, or join in the sacred dance, or stand by at the sacrifice or initiation. . . . It is when the soul most believes and perceives that the god is present, that she most puts from her pain and fear and anxiety, and gives herself up to joy—yes, even as far as intoxication and laughter and merriment. . . . In sacred processions and sacrifices, not only the old man and the old woman, nor the poor and lowly, but the thick-legged drudge that sways her at the mill and household slaves and hirelings are uplifted by joy and triumph. Rich men and kings

---

[1] *The Mysteries of Mithra*, E.T. 162.   [2] Ibid. 172 f.
[3] See a fine passage in Cumont, *Oriental Religions in Roman Paganism*, 58 f.
[4] Op. cit. 574.

have always their own banquets and feasts . . . but the feasts in the temples and at initiations, when men seem to touch the divine most nearly in their thought, with honour and worship, have a pleasure and a charm far more exceeding."[1]

It is impossible to believe that great crowds of initiates went through these emotional experiences without some of them undergoing a genuine religious change. Many of the rites must have brought before the mystics the need of moral as well as of ceremonial purity, while the need of purification and of regeneration were central to the whole cultus. Such is the power of suggestion that, when symbolic acts are performed with every accompaniment of solemnity, there is always a tendency for the outward and visible sign of the rite to produce the reality in the minds of the worshippers, and often in an abiding form.[2] That this was actually the case in connection with the Mystery-Religions no psychologist would doubt. It is, however, greatly to be regretted that none of the initiates has left behind a record of his spiritual states at the time of his initiation. The injunction to keep silence on their most sacred experiences prevented this. The extant evidence for a higher standard of moral life among the initiated is also very scanty. That the Eleusinian rites produced moral fruit is witnessed to by Aristophanes,[3] while Andocides " assumed that those who had been initiated would take a juster and sterner view of moral innocence and guilt, and that foul conduct was a greater sin when committed by a man who was in the official service of the mother and daughter."[4]

With reference to the Samothracian Mysteries, Diodorus Siculus says : " Those who had partaken in these mysteries became more pious and more just, in every respect better than their past selves."[5] In the rites of the Phrygian

[1] *Non suaviter*, 21. I owe the reference and the trans. to T. R. Glover, *Conflict of Religions in the Early Roman Empire*, 76 f.
[2] As it did in the case of Cyprian, whose conversion coincided with his baptism. See his *ad Don*. 4.
[3] *Frogs*, 455 f.
[4] Farnell in *Enc. Brit.* xix. 121 ; cf. also his *Cults of the Greek States*, iii. 191 f.
[5] Farnell in E.R.E. vii. 632.

Dramatic Representation of Regeneration

Mysteries of Dionysos-Sabazios, the initiate, after being purified with water, stood upright and said: "I have fled from evil; I have found a better thing."[1] This utterance must have stood for a genuine experience in the lives of some, at least.

The evidence for the moral effects of initiation in the later Oriental mystery cults which swarmed into the Roman world is very slight. Apuleius evidently intends us to think of Lucius as a reformed character after his initiation. Henceforth he "lives in an odour of sanctity. He never sleeps without a vision of the goddess. He passes from initiation to initiation, though the service of religion is difficult, chastity arduous, and life now a matter of circumspection—it had not been before."[2]

We may now turn from these non-Christian rites, whose aim was to effect a momentous change in the life of the novice, to the ideas regarding regeneration and baptism found in the New Testament. There we find that baptism was administered, not in order to effect a new birth, but to all who professed to have already undergone the experience of conversion, and to no others. It is a dramatic representation of something that has already taken place, as its ritual implies. John the Baptist, at the beginning of the Christian movement, borrowed an existing and familiar religious practice and adapted it, at the same time importing into it new meaning. The Pharisaic baptism of proselytes was, in the main, a ceremonial cleansing from the taint of heathenism,[3] but John made it the pledge of a moral conversion and the utterance of a purpose to live a new life. He treats it as "a bodily purification corresponding to an inward change, not as a means of remitting sins."[4]

It is generally assumed that Jesus took over John's practice of baptizing his converts, and in that way the rite passed into Christian usage. But the Synoptic data are

[1] We learn this from Demosthenes, *de Corona*, 259.
[2] Glover, op. cit. 236.
[3] The idea of rebirth is not wanting in Pharisaic baptism, for the Rabbis held that "a newly made proselyte is like a new-born child" (E.R.E. ii. 379 and 409).
[4] I. Abrahams, *Studies in Pharisaism and the Gospels*, 34.

too meagre to make possible any discussion of the relation between baptism and our Lord's teaching on conversion. The general probabilities are that He shared the views of the Baptist.

Turning to the epistles of Paul, we find that he does not view baptism simply as an outward sign of an inward repentance, but connects closely with it the gift of the Spirit and union with Christ (Rom. vi. 3 ff., Gal. iii. 27, 1 Cor. xii. 13). Hence a number of scholars, under the influence of researches into the mystery cults, have come to hold that a candid exegesis of these passages compels us to take the view that Paul shared the view-point of these cults and regarded baptism as an *ex opere operato* rite.

To go fully into the reasons for rejecting this position would, in our opinion, be slaying the slain after the work of scholars like Rendtorff, Deissmann, Clemen, Lambert and H. A. A. Kennedy. It is now generally conceded that Paul had some knowledge of the mystery cults and that he made use of his knowledge to put himself *en rapport* with those whom he sought to win for Christ. Nor need we doubt that some of his converts would bring over with them from heathenism the crude sacramental ideas that had gathered round the mysteries, but it does not follow that the apostle shared their views. A modern parallel from the mission-field may not be out of place here. The present writer has met a few converts from Hinduism who find the doctrine of transmigration in John ix. 2, but he would not venture to assume that the Christian missionaries to whom they owed their conversion favoured a similar view of the passage.

Assuming, then, that Paul does not hold a magical view of baptism, are we at liberty to conclude that he looked upon it merely as an impressive picture of the believer's experience? In Rom. vi. he works out in detail the idea that a man's baptism is a kind of dramatization of his conversion experience. But a candid exegesis of Rom. vi. and other passages must concede that the merely symbolic view of baptism does not do justice to the apostle's phrases about " putting on Christ," " dying to sin " and " being raised to newness of life " in baptism. For Paul baptism

Dramatic Representation of Regeneration 111

means an experiential union with Christ in His redeeming acts (see especially Rom. vi. 4, Col. ii. 12, Eph. iv. 4–6). It is important to bear in mind that the only baptism which Paul knew was that of adult converts. As in the mission-field to-day, "baptism must have meant a decision of momentous importance for the convert. Now for the first time he deliberately affirmed his allegiance to Christ before the world, and solemnly identified himself with the Christian brotherhood. This was the actual spiritual crisis in which he turned his back upon his old associations, faced all manner of costly sacrifices, and committed himself, in utter dependence upon the divine grace and power, to a new mode of life. Rendtorff is fully justified in saying that an act which thus liberated the most powerful ethical motives 'became a religious experience of the first rank.' In baptism (of course, adult) something happened. Faith had been there before, receptiveness toward the good news of Christ. The Divine Spirit had been already present, taking of the things of Christ and showing them to the believer. But now, once for all, the convert makes his own the movings of the divine love in his heart. And thus there would come to him in his baptism a wonderful spiritual quickening, a new enhancing of the power and grasp of faith, a fresh realization of communion with the once crucified and now risen Lord."[1] These words of Kennedy are, we believe, full of true psychological insight.

If the question be asked what the outer act of baptism contributed to these inner experiences of forgiveness, regeneration, faith and fellowship with Christ, the only possible answer is that Paul and the other New Testament writers never consider them apart in this detached manner. The baptism of which they speak is no formal act, no mere symbol, and at the same time it is never administered to any but believers. And it is, therefore, for Paul never a passive experience. The outer act and the inner experience are always found together. "The faith which welcomes the divine message of forgiveness and new life in Christ crucified and risen is invariably presupposed as the background of the solemn ritual. It is in virtue of their faith

[1] H. A. A. Kennedy, *St. Paul and the Mystery-Religions*, 248 f.

that converts proceed to baptism."[1] Hence baptism works in no magical way. It is not so much the cause of regeneration as the occasion for the bestowal of spiritual gifts. What it becomes to each individual depends upon the recipient—upon his faith.

Apart from this faith it does not effect anything. " It is not a bare symbol as of something already complete, but a sacrament, i.e. a symbol conditioning a present deeper and decisive experience of divine grace, already embraced by faith. But all is psychologically conditioned, being thereby raised above the level of the magical or quasi-physical conception of sacramental grace."[2]

It is generally thought that the author of the Fourth Gospel took up a somewhat more advanced sacramentarian position than did Paul. E. F. Scott goes so far as to say that according to him man by baptism " is ' born again,' in the sense that he has been magically changed into a new creature and possesses affinities, lacking in him before, with the supersensible world."[3] Scott, however, concedes that alongside this view we find conversion regarded as a moral change, answering to the *metanoia* of the Synoptics. The former view of conversion as a quasi-physical change is John's attempt to state his experience in terms of an alien philosophy, while the latter view is the ultimate teaching of the Gospel, and arises out of the writer's Christian experience.[4]

Many, however, would deny that the Fourth Gospel anywhere countenances a magical view of baptism. In i. 12 (cf. I John v. 1) faith is presented as a vital condition of the new birth, and no mention is made of baptism as a means by which we become children of God. Above all, the only baptism known to John was that of confessing, penitent believers, who had already been born again in conversion. They were not baptized in order to be regenerated, for their conversion was their regeneration. They were baptized in order to be admitted into the rights and privileges of the Divine Society, and with the expectation that the religious experience already theirs would be deepened and

[1] Kennedy, op. cit. 254. [2] J. Vernon Bartlet, E.R.E. ii. 377.
[3] *The Fourth Gospel*, 282. [4] Ibid. 366 f.

Dramatic Representation of Regeneration 113

heightened if they underwent the rite in the proper frame of heart and mind.

These conclusions are borne out by a study of the concept of regeneration as it occurs in the different writings of the New Testament. In the Synoptic Gospels the term is found once only—in Matt. xix. 28, where it bears an eschatological sense. But the substance of the idea is found in the logion, " Whosoever shall not receive the Kingdom of God as a little child, he shall in nowise enter therein " (Mark x. 15), and is even more emphasized in its Matthean form (Matt. xviii. 3). When Jesus exhorted His disciples to turn and become as little children, He had in mind precisely that change which in later theology the figure of rebirth was intended to convey. To become as a little child is to be born again, and is for the Synoptic teaching of Jesus a moral requirement. It is " identical with what is elsewhere in the Synoptics called *metanoia*, or repentance. It is through this moral change, the responsibility for which is laid upon man, that he becomes as a little child, that is, is born again."[1] The thought of Jesus here moves entirely within ethical limits, the metaphysical receiving no mention. In brief, the only regeneration which the Synoptic teaching of Jesus knows is a moral and ethical change.

The term " regeneration " and its cognates are not found in the genuine epistles of Paul. The absence of the figure is strange when we remember that he uses the figure of begetting with reference to his converts, and speaks of the new life as being entered upon through a death. The idea, however, comes out clearly enough in such passages as 2 Cor. v. 17 and Gal. vi. 15 ; and it is explicit in all those passages in which he insists that the Christian life is divine in its inception as well as in its continuance. His writings contain all the materials for a doctrine of regeneration, but his ideas are fluid and are not worked out with any dogmatic finality. He is much more concerned with entreaties to his converts to live worthy of the new life that has been divinely bestowed upon them than with exact definitions of regeneration. Nowhere, moreover, does he regard regeneration and conversion as separate experiences. Indeed, for

[1] Denney in D.C.G. ii. 485.

Paul the moment of conversion is the moment of regeneration, as it is also the moment of justification by faith.

In the Johannine literature the figure of the new-birth is frequent and explicit. Twice in the Gospel and nine times in his First Epistle John speaks of being born of God; and four times in his Epistle he speaks of the children of God. The necessity of regeneration is fundamental to his theological scheme, but what he has in mind is the radical change in moral values which Jesus insisted upon when He called men to repent and bade them become as little children. John iii. 3 is " a theological interpretation from the side of God of the experience which the Synoptic Gospels present as a moral change on the part of man to God's call."[1] John's supreme concern is to insist that conversion is a divine creative act—the work of the Spirit. This is the essence of his thought, which is here entirely at one with that of Paul. For both regeneration, conversion, the new-birth are one and the same experience; and that experience is always an ethico-religious one. It is called regeneration when it is regarded from the side of God, and conversion when looked at from the side of man.[2]

Thus we find in the classic Christianity of the New Testament a perfectly moralized doctrine of regeneration, which we may regard as the goal towards which the human race had been striving through long ages. Widespread rites of initiation testify to an almost universal conviction that man needs to be born again before he is fit for the spiritual kingdom. They appear to point to some permanent need of the human spirit, which Christianity alone can adequately meet. In it alone we find the idea of rebirth conceived in moral and spiritual terms, untainted by magic

---

[1] Moffatt, *Theology of the Gospels*, 196. For an elaborate discussion of the exegetical problems of John iii. 3, see Gennrich, *Die Lehre von der Wiedergeburt*, 52–59.

[2] Under the influence of the realistic tendencies of the age, Christianity later moved from this high doctrine. When conscious faith on the part of the person baptized was no longer regarded as essential, and the objective efficacy of baptism was strongly held, the necessity arose to distinguish between conversion and regeneration as separable experiences. The regenerating powers of baptism were held to be in abeyance till conversion took place; but of such a distinction the New Testament knows nothing. The development of this distinction is well sketched by Gennrich, op. cit. 98–104.

Dramatic Representation of Regeneration

and unhampered by restrictions of tribe, caste, or sex; while its initiatory rite is raised to lofty significance in that it is not compulsory, but is open only to those who have undergone the experience to which it is intended to give dramatic expression, and which it is intended to enhance.

PART II.—PSYCHOLOGICAL

CHAPTER X

CONVERSION AND ADOLESCENCE

THE cases examined by Starbuck led him to conclude that " conversion does not occur with the same frequency at all periods in life. It belongs almost exclusively to the years between ten and twenty-five. The number of instances outside that range appear few and scattered. That is, *conversion is a distinctively adolescent phenomenon.*"[1] Starbuck then goes on to note that within the period of adolescence conversion is much more likely to take place at certain years than at others. " The event comes earlier in general among the females than among the males, most frequently at thirteen and sixteen. Among the males it occurs most often at seventeen, and immediately before and after that year." These conclusions have been generally accepted,[2] and are borne out by the data we have gathered from non-Christian religions. The nature of the data, however, prevents our going into the finer distinctions drawn by Starbuck, and we must content ourselves with a corroboration of the general proposition that conversion is normally an adolescent phenomenon. But before we deal with the non-Christian cases, it will help to broaden the bases of induction if we cite a few cases of Christian conversion during adolescence drawn from other than the American Evangelical circles, from which Starbuck gathered his data, and if we choose, where possible, cases that are separated both by time as well as nationality.

[1] Starbuck, 28. See also 36. The italics are his.
[2] See, e.g., James, 199; Coe, *Psychology of Religion*, 163; Pratt, *Psychology of Religious Belief*, 218.

Keim gives reasons for thinking that many of the disciples of Jesus were adolescents when He chose them. He writes: "Though some of the disciples, as well as of the women, may have been married, yet an age of not much more than twenty years is plainly indicated in the case of the four first called, notably of the sons of Zebedee, and also of James the younger, of the youth in Judea and Gethsemane—nay, indeed, of most of them, for they are represented as coming directly from the houses of their parents, and Jesus cautions them against preferring their parents to their Teacher." [1]

Timothy may rightly be counted among the adolescent converts of New Testament times. It is true that we have no account of his conversion, but it seems reasonable to assume that he was converted as a youth by Paul at Lystra or Derbe during his first missionary journey. Acts xvi. 1 f. is not an account of Timothy's conversion, but of his admission into the inner Pauline circle.

The annals of Christian monasticism speak of many converted in their adolescent years. St. Benedict (*circa* 480–540) was eighteen or twenty when he withdrew from the world to a cave at Subiaco.[2] The brothers of St. Bernard (1090–1153) had hoped to make him a knight or, failing that, a man of letters. He wavered for a time, but, after the day on which he poured out his soul with a torrent of tears in a wayside church, he never looked back. He at once set about winning others, and, when at the age of twenty-two he entered the monastery of Citeaux, he took with him about thirty others, whom his zeal had won for the monastic life.[3]

St. Francis of Assisi (1182–1226) was in his early twenties when the day of days came to him. For nearly two years his soul had been in distress. He had been out riding and on returning to the city met a leper. The sight of the loathsome disease made him shrink back, but a wave of pity swept over him. He sprang from his horse, embraced the astounded man, and gave him all the money he had.

---

[1] *Jesus of Nazara*, E.T. iii. 279.
[2] Dom Butler, *Benedictine Monasticism*, 3.
[3] Cotter Morison, *St. Bernard*, 13 ff.

118 *Conversion : Christian and Non-Christian*

" From that moment Francis never looked back again upon the old ways : in the leper's embrace he plighted his troth to the new life in which poverty and suffering were lords demanding his liege service. He had not yet found the Lady Poverty, but he had entered her domain and had become a servant of her people, and for the present he was at peace." [1]

St. Clara was but a young girl when she first heard the preaching of St. Francis, and was only eighteen when she left her father's castle to devote herself to the life of religious poverty and to become the first member of the second Franciscan order.[2]

The spiritual life of St. Teresa began with her entry into religion at the age of eighteen, in the year 1533. She at once found great delight in the things of God, but was still held captive by the chains of the world. The happiness of the truly unified soul did not come till 1555, when in an oratory she saw an image of the wounded Christ. In a moment of extreme grief she felt God to be present in her and gave herself completely to Him. From that hour the divisive tendencies were completely suppressed.[3]

Richard Rolle, who has justly been called the Father of English Mysticism, was in his nineteenth year when, at the beginning of the fourteenth century, he forsook his studies at Oxford to give himself wholly to the anchorite life.[4]

Henry Suso, one of the Friends of God, began to be converted in his eighteenth year, but in his case final unification of the divided self came only after more than twenty years of unexampled austerity. Thereafter he lived in a state of habitual joy.[5]

Brother Lawrence, a lay brother in the Carmelite Order, was eighteen when there came the great change which made him, till his death in 1691, the great exponent of the practice of the presence of God.

[1] Father Cuthbert, O.S.F.C., *Life of St. Francis of Assisi*, 25. Cf. Sabatier, *Life of St. Francis of Assisi*, 26.
[2] Sabatier, op. cit. 152.
[3] Delacroix, *Études d'histoire et de psychologie du Mysticisme*, 11.
[4] Horstmann, *Richard Rolle of Hampole*, i. xiii.
Delacroix, op. cit. 309-315.

" He told me," says the anonymous reporter of his conversion, " that God had done him a singular favour in his conversion at the age of eighteen. That in winter, seeing a tree stripped of its leaves, and considering that within a little time the leaves would be renewed, and after that the flowers and fruit would appear, he received a high view of the Providence and Power of God, which has never since been effaced from his soul. That his view had set him perfectly loose from the world and kindled in him such a love of God that he could not tell whether it had increased in above forty years that he had lived since."

Catherine of Genoa was just over the border-line drawn by Starbuck, at twenty-five, when she was converted as she knelt before her father-confessor in her sister's nunnery at Annunciation-tide in 1474.[1] Madame Guyon was nineteen and, like Catherine of Genoa, unhappily married, when she met a Franciscan friar, who spoke the word that brought her interior struggles to an end with dramatic suddenness.[2]

Many of the converts made during the early days of the Quaker revival were adolescents, but we can cite only four cases : all of them of men who became prominent in the movement. Fox himself had been brought up in the pious household of his parents, and had never wandered into the far country.

" The hour of decision came through a simple incident, momentous in its issues. When about nineteen and on business at a fair, two Puritans, one of them a relative, asked his company over a jug of beer. After satisfying their thirst, they began drinking healths, calling for more and agreeing that whosoever refused his turn should pay all. . . . Fox had never before been asked to do such a thing, least of all by high religious professors, and the inconsistency of their profession and their conduct grieved him to the heart. In his straightforward fashion he laid a groat on the table to pay his share of the reckoning and went away ; but that night he could get no sleep, and walked up and down his chamber, praying and crying to the Lord. Then a voice spoke in his heart, saying to him: ' Thou seest how young people go together into vanity, and old people into the earth ; and thou must forsake all . . . and be as a stranger unto all.' ' Then,' says Fox, ' at the command of God, on the ninth day of the seventh

[1] Von Hugel, *The Mystical Element of Religion*, ii. 29.
[2] Delacroix, op. cit. 122 f.

month, 1643, I left my relations, and broke off all familiarity or fellowship with young or old.' There was a holy compulsion on his soul, driving it to leave the low levels of religious life around it and to fulfil itself in the society of the divine." [1]

This experience drove the young seeker after truth into a quest extending over three years, for it was not until he was twenty-two that there came to him that experience which gave birth to the message, to whose proclamation he henceforth dedicated his life. [2]

That great Quaker leader and champion of religious liberty, William Penn, was a lad of twelve when his soul was first awakened by a Quaker preacher, though his full " convincement " as a Friend was gradual and not complete till 1667, when he was twenty-three.

"When a lad of twelve, he had first heard Thomas Loe, the Oxford Quaker, at his father's house in County Cork. . . . On this occasion a black servant of the family could not contain himself from weeping aloud, and even the Admiral was in tears. Young Penn was persuaded in his heart, and thought to himself, ' What if they would all be Quakers ? ' From this time the knowledge of God, inwardly witnessed, was dear to him." [3]

The impression then created was deep enough to save him from the many temptations that must have surrounded him in Paris and in the brilliant Court of the Duke of Ormonde in Ireland. In 1671 he could write :

" I make the bold challenge to all men . . . justly to accuse me with ever having seen me drunk, heard me swear, utter a curse, or speak one obscene word. . . . I speak this to God's glory, that has ever preserved me from the power of those pollutions, and that from a child begot in me a hatred towards them." [4]

A year before William Penn's " convincement " Robert Barclay had turned Quaker at the age of eighteen, and

[1] Braithwaite, *Beginnings of Quakerism*, 30 f.
[2] The passage from his journal is too long for transcription here. Of it Braithwaite rightly remarks : " A passage like this takes us to the primitive Christian experience of Union with Christ," op. cit. 35.
[3] Braithwaite, *The Second Period of Quakerism*, 55 f.
[4] Quoted by Braithwaite, op. cit. 57, n. 3. The reference to his conversion is obvious and the challenge remarkable in view of the manners of the times.

ten years later published his famous *Apology* for the faith that was in him.[1]

Thomas Ellwood, who was afterwards Latin reader to Milton in his blindness and the editor of Fox's *Journal*, was converted at the age of twenty. Brought up as a country gentleman, he first heard the Quaker message from the lips of two of the Publishers of Truth. Of one of them Ellwood says:

> "I drank in his words with desire, for they not only answered my understanding, but warmed my heart with a certain heat, which I had not till then felt from the ministry of any man." [2]

Soon after he attended another Quaker meeting at High Wycombe.

> "This second meeting was like the clinching of a nail, confirming and fastening what he had previously heard. Light began to break forth in him, discovering the evil growths of his heart . . . so that he could no longer go on in his former ways and course of life. The vanity of superfluity in apparel was shown to him, and he took off his lace, ribbons, and useless buttons, and ceased to wear rings. He saw the evil of giving flattering titles to men —a custom in which he had been a ready master—and he also felt himself required to put away the practice of baring the head and bowing the knee in salutations, and of saying 'you' to a single person, 'contrary to the pure, plain and simple language of truth.'" [3]

Sir Harry Vane (1613-1662), "the statesman, the maker of covenants with Scottish armies, the creator of sinews of war for the battles of Marston Moor and Naseby, the organizer of a conquering navy, the man who dared withstand his old friend Cromwell," the man whom Milton called "religion's eldest son," spoke this as his dying speech:

> "About the fourteenth or fifteenth year of my age God was pleased to lay the foundation or groundwork of repentance in me, for the bringing me home to Himself, by His wonderful rich and

---

[1] Braithwaite, op. cit. 335.
[2] Quoted from Ellwood's *Autobiography* by Braithwaite in his *Beginnings of Quakerism*, 489.
[3] Braithwaite, op. cit. 490. Braithwaite gives a good account of the daily cross-bearing which Ellwood's conversion involved. His father was very embittered, and once thrashed his son before the servants for 'theeing" him.

free grace, revealing His Son in me. . . . Since that foundation of repentance was laid in me, through grace I have been kept steadfast, desiring to walk in all good conscience towards God and toward men, according to the best light and understanding God gave me."[1]

As might be expected, during the Wesleyan revival the young of both sexes were frequently converted, as the following typical extract from Wesley's *Journal* will show:

Wednesday, June 3, 1772. (Wesley is in Teesdale.) " I desired to speak with those who believed God had saved them from inward sin. I closely examined them, twenty in all, ten men, eight women, and two children. Of one man, and one or two women, I stood in doubt. The experience of the rest was clear, particularly that of the children, Margaret Spenser, aged fourteen, and Sally Blackburn, a year younger. But what a contrast was there between them! Sally Blackburn was all calmness; her look, her speech, her whole carriage was as sedate as if she had lived three-score years. On the contrary, Peggy was all fire; her eyes sparkled; her very features spoke; her whole face was all alive; and she looked as if she was just ready to take wing for heaven! Lord, let neither of these live to dishonour Thee! Rather take them unspotted to Thyself!"[2]

The well-known journalist, the late W. T. Stead, was converted during his schooldays during a revival. Writing forty-three years later, he says: " The whole of my life during all these forty-three years has been influenced by the change which men call conversion, which occurred with me when I was twelve."[3]

James Martineau was sixteen when his religious awakening took place. The death of a young Unitarian minister of Nottingham, with whom he had been very friendly, made a great impression upon him and awoke him to the realities

[1] Quoted in Rufus Jones's *Spiritual Reformers of the* 16*th and* 17*th Centuries*, 272.
[2] The next day the tireless evangelist is in Weardale, where he finds many children among those who have been newly awakened. He notes: " Phebe Teatherstone, nine years and a half old, a child of uncommon understanding; Hannah Watson, ten years old, full of faith and love; Aaron Ridson, not eleven years old, but wise and staid as a man; Sarah Smith, eight years and a half old, but serious as a woman of fifty; Sarah Morris, fourteen years of age, is as a mother among them, always serious, always watching over the rest, and building them up in love."
[3] Quoted by Jackson (*The Fact of Conversion*, 35) from a pamphlet written by Stead at the time of the Welsh Revival in 1904–5.

and solemnities of life. He afterwards said that at that time his religious life really began. The experience drove him from the profession of engineer, to which he had just been apprenticed, to that of evangelist. It started him on that ministry and life-work which was to draw Unitarian theology into deeper and more spiritual channels.[1]

In the Græco-Roman world the best-known case of conversion during adolescence is that of Polemon. The son of a rich Athenian, his youth had been extremely profligate and intemperate. One day, at the head of a band of revellers, he burst into the school of Xenocrates, who was discoursing on temperance. The master calmly continued in spite of the interruption. The youth was so arrested that he flung away his garland, and from that day changed his manner of life and continued to frequent the school, of which, on the death of Xenocrates, he became the head.[2]

Apollonius of Tyana was sixteen when he became an enthusiastic disciple of Pythagoras and set himself to observe the almost monastic rule ascribed to Pythagoras.[3] In later years Apollonius was once discoursing in Athens, and there was present " a young dandy who bore so evil a reputation for licentiousness that his conduct had once been the subject of coarse street-corner songs." During the discourse, which was directed against intemperance, the youth laughed so loudly and coarsely as to drown the lecturer's voice. Apollonius regarded it as a case of demon possession, and he exorcised the demon.

"The young man rubbed his eyes as if he had just woke up . . . and won the consideration of all who had now turned their attention to him; for he no longer showed himself licentious, nor did he stare madly about, but he returned to his own self, as thoroughly as if he had been treated with drugs; and he gave up his dainty dress and summery garments and the rest of his

[1] Drummond and Upton, *Life and Letters of James Martineau*, i. 24 f.
[2] Diogenes Laërtius, iv. iii. 1, where Polemon is described as a " young man " at the time. See also Horace, *Sat.* ii. iii. 253 f.
[3] *Life*, by Philostratus, bk. i., chaps. vii. and xiii. Cf. Seneca's picture of his early life in Rome. As an adolescent he was greatly influenced by the Stoic, Attalus, and the Pythagorean, Sotion. See his epistle 108. I owe the reference to Glover's *Conflict of Religions*, 41 f.

sybarite way of life, and he fell in love with the austerity of philosophers and donned their cloak, and, stripping off his old self, modelled his life in future upon that of Apollonius."[1]

Such an intellectualistic system as Early Buddhism might scarcely be expected to have appealed to any save those of mature intelligence. Indeed, as we have seen, Oldenberg plainly says it was not for children nor for the childlike.[2] It is true that most of the conversions recorded in the *Maha-Vagga* are not those of adolescents, but there are striking exceptions. We have the case of the noble youth Yasa, whose senses appear to have been glutted, and who appears to have grown weary of life before he had really begun it. He had been delicately brought up and possessed three palaces. During the rainy season he stayed in one of the palaces, surrounded by female musicians. One night, awaking from his sleep sooner than usual, he " saw his attendants sleeping : one had her lute leaning against her arm-pit ; one had her tabor leaning against her neck ; one had her drum leaning against her arm-pit ; one had dishevelled hair ; one had saliva flowing from her mouth ; and they were muttering in their sleep. One would think it was a cemetery one had fallen into. When he saw that, the evils (of the life he led) manifested themselves to him ; his mind became weary (of worldly pleasures). And Yasa, the noble youth, gave utterance to this solemn exclamation : ' Alas ! what distress—alas ! what danger ! ' "[3] He flung himself outside of the house and the city walls, and went to the Deer Park, where he found the Buddha walking up and down in the open air at dawn. The Master taught the truth to the youth, expounding to him the doctrine of the impermanency of all things and the blessings of the abandonment of desire. Then, " just as a clean cloth free from black specks properly takes the dye," so the noble

[1] *Life*, by Philostratus, bk. iv., chap. xx. F. C. Conybeare's trans. I ought to add that, as far as I can judge, Conybeare and other scholars have established their claim that the *Life* is not a romance, but in the main historical.
[2] *Buddha*, E.T. 155 ff. 205.
[3] *Maha-Vagga*, i. vii. 2. Attention should be called to Copleston's warning as to the trustworthiness of the incident. *Buddhism*, 2nd ed., 27.

youth, while sitting there, "obtained the pure and spotless Eye of the Truth."

Shortly after this incident, when on his way to preach the doctrine at Uruvela, the Buddha happened to rest under a tree in a grove, in which thirty rich young men were sporting with their wives. For one of their number, who had no wife, a harlot had been procured. While their attention was diverted, she stole some articles belonging to them and ran away. Roaming about the grove in their search for her they came upon the Buddha, and asked if he had seen a woman passing by. They explained the reason of their search, and he asked: "Now what think you, young men? Which would be better for you: that you should go in search of a woman, or that you should go in search of yourselves?" They replied that it would be better for them to go in search of themselves. Thereupon Buddha expounded to them the truth, and they were converted.[1]

In the *Maha-Vagga*, i. iv., we have the touching story of Buddha's visit to his father's house, where he went to beg for alms. His wife said to her son, the young Rahula: "This is your father, Rahula; go and ask him for your inheritance." The lad approached him, and said: "Your shadow, Samana, is a place of bliss." Then the Blessed One rose from his seat and went away, and the young Rahula followed the Blessed One from behind, and said: "Give me my inheritance, Samana." Then the Buddha told Sariputta to ordain the lad as a novice, admitting him into the community.

According to the Commentary on the *Thera-theri-gatha*, composed by Dhammapala in the fifth or sixth century A.D., quite a number of the authors of these psalms left the world as youths and became *arahats* on the threshold of manhood. Mrs. Rhys Davids accepts these statements in the Commentary, and points out that they are confirmed by internal evidence, for some of the authors betray their youth in their childlike diction and ideas. She remarks, in direct opposition to Oldenberg, that "these may possibly give us a truer picture of the movement sometimes held to be

[1] *Maha-Vagga*, i. xi. 1.

126 *Conversion : Christian and Non-Christian*

reserved for the middle-aged well-to-do, and even may dispose us to adapt to it a later divine saying : ' Suffer *me to come to* the little children, for of such, too, is my Kingdom that is within you.' "[1] To this we may add that the inborn instinct of hero-worship in boys of thirteen or fourteen would draw them instinctively to the gracious personality of the Buddha.

According to Dhammapala's Commentary, the following authors of the psalms, among others, were adolescents when they became "stream-entrants." Atuma, the author of Psalm 72, was the son of a councillor. When he was at the adolescent stage his mother proposed to find him a wife, and consulted with their kinsfolk. But he said: "What have I to do with house-ways? Now will I leave the world." Though his mother sought to corrupt his pious wish, he went out into the houseless life.

Of Ajjuna, the author of Psalm 88, it is said that when grown up he came into contact with the Jains, and entered their Order very young, thinking among them to win salvation. But he failed in his purpose till he met the Buddha.

Jenta, the author of Psalm 111, was the son of the raja of a district. While still young his mind inclined to leave the world, and he turned the matter over and pondered what he should do. So doubting, he heard the Master preach, and from that day became devoted to the religious life and entered the Order.

Dhammapala, the author of Psalm 162, was a Brahman's son. As he was returning home, his schooldays being finished, he saw on his way a certain Thera in a single cell, and, hearing from him the Norm, he believed.[2]

According to a widely accepted story, Kabir was a boy when he hid himself on the steps of the Ganges, where Ramananda usually came to bathe. The master, coming down to the water, trod on his body unexpectedly, and in astonishment exclaimed, "Ram! Ram!" The lad then declared that he had received the *mantra* of initiation from

---
[1] *Psalms of the Brethren*, p. xxxi.
[2] For other cases see the Commentary on *Theragatha*, Pss. 5, 33, 73, 123, 240, 261, and on *Therigatha*, Ps. 56.

Ramananda's own lips, and in spite of the protests of orthodox Brahmans and Moslems (for the lad had been brought up a Moslem), he was received into discipleship.[1]

Mira Bai, Queen of Udaipur, born in 1504, was but a child when she fell in love with Krishna and steadfastly refused to be another's bride, though married in 1516 to the son of the Rajah of Mewar. She is said to have given up her throne rather than join in the bloody worship of Siva, traditional in her husband's house.[2]

The revival which Chaitanya's teaching set on foot inspired countless lives of devotion and won converts from every class of society. Two adolescents are specially noteworthy. Young Ragunath Das, the only son of a wealthy landowner, fell at Chaitanya's feet in "a rapture of love," and repeatedly tried to run away from his father's house to become a disciple. "But his father seized him on the way and kept him tied up, with five watchmen to guard him day and night and four servants and two cooks—in all eleven guards."[3] But he frustrated all his father's efforts and left home and fortune for ever to become Chaitanya's disciple, finally becoming one of the six fathers of the Chaitanyite Church. Narottoma Datta was also the only son of a Raja. When as a lad he heard from his tutor the pathetic story of the passing away of Chaitanya, he determined to turn ascetic. He was twelve years old when one day, as he stood on the bank of the mighty Padma River, he saw the vision splendid which called him to the higher life.[4]

The story of the religious development of the Mogul Emperor, Akbar the Great (1542–1605), is full of interest.

---

[1] G. H. Westcott, in his *Kabir and the Kabirpanth* (Cawnpore, 1907), denies that Kabir was a disciple of Ramananda, and quotes from the *Bhakta-mala* in support of his position. Grierson, however, adduces further passages from the *Bhakta-mala* in support of the generally accepted view. See the J.R.A.S. for 1908, 247 f., and note the hymn translated as Poem 29 in Rabindranath Tagore's translation:

"I became suddenly revealed in Benares, and
Ramananda illumined me."

[2] Macauliffe (op. cit. vi. 342 ff.) has collected what is known of the Queen and has translated a number of her poems that are found in the *Granth*, but his material still needs careful sifting.

[3] Sarkar, 196.   [4] Sen, V.L. 95.

Beginning as an orthodox Sunni, he became a rationalizing Moslem, and finally evolved an eclectic religion of his own, which he hoped would reconcile the opposing religious factions in his vast domains. However much he may have failed in practice, it is not open to doubt that he was a sincerely religious man. His son, Jahangir, declared that his father "never for one moment forgot God."[1] Akbar's devout life, doubtless, went back to the remarkable religious awakening he underwent during his later adolescence. "On the completion of my twentieth year," he wrote, "I experienced an internal bitterness, and from lack of spiritual provision for my last journey my soul was seized with exceeding sorrow."[2]

Before passing from India we pause to notice the evidence afforded by the religious experience of some of the great leaders of modern societies like the Brahma and the Arya Samajes. The saintly Debendranath Tagore had been brought up, like Francis of Assisi, to a life of luxury, but at eighteen came the experience which changed for him all life's values. As a lad he had been very fond of his grandmother. In expectation of her death, she was taken to the bank of the Ganges to die by the sacred river.

> "She was kept in a tiled shed on the banks of the Ganges, where she remained living for three nights. On the night before Didima's death I was sitting at Nimtola Ghat on a coarse mat near the shed. It was the night of the full moon; the moon had risen; the burning ground was near. They were singing the Holy Name to Didima. . . . The sounds reached my ears faintly borne on the night wind; at this opportune moment a strange sense of the unreality of all things suddenly entered my mind. I was as if no longer the same man. A strong aversion to wealth arose within me. The coarse bamboo mat on which I sat seemed to be my fitting seat, carpets and costly spreadings seemed hateful; in my mind was awakened a joy unfelt before. I was then eighteen years old."[3]

Keshab Chandra Sen, who was destined to figure so largely in the life and work of the Samaj, likewise went through a similar conversion during adolescence. He was eighteen

---

[1] Vincent A. Smith, *Akbar, the Great Mogul*, 349.
[2] Ibid. 62. The celebrated Sufi, Hallaj, was sixteen when he entered upon the ascetic and mystical life (Nicolson in E.R.E. vi. 481).
[3] *Autobiography of Maharshi Debendranath Tagore*, 37 f.

when he found peace through prayer. Here, again, we have the advantage of possessing his own first-hand account. In a lecture delivered in England he thus describes his experience:

"English education unsettled my mind, and left a void. I had given up idolatry, but had received no positive system of faith to replace it. And how could one live on earth without a system of positive religion? ... I was passing from idolatry to utter worldliness. Through divine grace, however, I felt a longing for something higher; the consciousness of sin was awakened within me; sin was realized in the depth of my heart in all its enormity and blackness. And was there no remedy? Could I continue to bear life as a burden? Heaven said: 'No! Sinner, thou hast hope;' and I looked upward, and there was a clear revelation to me. I felt that I was not groping in the dark as a helpless child, cast away by his parents in some dreary wilderness. God spoke to me in unmistakable language, and gave me the secret of spiritual life, and that was prayer, to which I owed my conversion. I at once composed forms of prayer for every morning and evening, and used them daily, although I was still a member of no Church on earth and had no clear apprehension of God's character and attributes." [1]

Not less interesting is the following record of his own experience from the pen of the poet Rabindranath Tagore, son of the Maharshi. He was in his early twenties when the experience took place.

"The end of Sudder Street and the trees on the Free School grounds opposite were visible from our Sudder Street house. One morning I happened to be standing on the verandah looking that way. The sun was just rising through the leafy tops of the trees. As I continued to gaze, all of a sudden a covering seemed to fall away from my eyes, and I found the world bathed in a wonderful radiance, with waves of beauty and joy swelling on every side. The radiance pierced in a moment through the folds of sadness and despondency which had accumulated over my heart, and flooded it with this universal light." [2]

Swami Dayananda Saraswati, the founder of the Arya Samaj, was in his fourteenth year when his spiritual awaken-

---
[1] Quoted by P. C. Mozoomdar in his *Life and Teachings of Keshub Chunder Sen* (2nd ed., Calcutta, 1891), 61. See also 11 and 56.
[2] Rabindranath Tagore, *My Reminiscences*, 217. Tagore adds that the insight then gained " has lasted all my life."

ing took place. On the night of the Sivaratri festival he had accompanied his father to the temple, where they joined other devotees in observing the fast, keeping the vigil and singing hymns in honour of the deity. But by midnight the temple-keeper, the lay devotees and the lad's father, overcome with fatigue, were asleep. The boy, who had all along striven to overcome drowsiness by bathing his eyes in water, stood up and looked toward the lingam. A mouse appeared, attracted by the offerings spread before the symbol. It helped itself to the good things, and in its hurry to retreat desecrated the sacred emblem by impudently running over it. But the deity showed no sign of resentment. Many reflections crowded into the lad's mind. Torn with doubt, he woke his father, whose stock arguments carried no conviction to his inquiring mind. He went home and broke the fast, only to be censured by his father the next morning. The members of the Arya Samaj now celebrate the night of Sivaratri as the anniversary of Dayananda's enlightenment, and, rightly enough, see in it the beginning of their founder's lifelong crusade against idolatry.[1]

The Egyptian king, Akhnaton, stands out among the adolescents who have passed through a conversion experience. He was not more than nineteen when he broke away from orthodoxy, and changed his name to signify his change of faith; and he was not more than twenty-three when he gave sublime expression to that faith in his hymn to Aton. Some Egyptologists think it impossible for a boy in his teens to have been the leader of so vast a movement, and they suppose that the king was a tool in older hands.[2] When, however, we remember the rapid development of body and mind in Egypt, their supposition is needless. Moreover, Akhnaton's passion for truth, his dislike of half-measures, and the thoroughness with which

[1] Dayananda tells the story in his autobiography, which was republished as an introduction to the English translation of the *Satyarth Prakash* (Lahore, 1908), 2 f. It is quoted in full in Farquhar's *Modern Religious Movements in India*, 102 ff. There is also a good account in Lajpat Rai's *The Arya Samaj* (London, 1915), 7-10.

[2] The latest discussion on this topic is ably summarized by Prof. T. Eric Peet in the *Journal of the Manchester Egyptian and Oriental Society*, No. ix. (1921). See also Weigall's preface to the 1922 edition of his *Life and Times of Akhnaton*.

he sought to carry out the reformation, are all marks of the adolescent mind.

At the risk of extending unduly a chapter already lengthy, we may point out that the Japanese Buddhist, Dengyo (A.D. 767-822), was not quite eighteen when he retired to a mountain near his native village, from the fastnesses of which he emerged nine years later to effect a reformation in the monasticism of his day akin to that wrought by Bernard of Clairvaux in Western Christendom.[1]

Professor Anesaki has shown that a significant feature of the intellectual ferment in Japan at the end of the nineteenth and beginning of the twentieth century was "l'aspiration spirituelle chez les jeunes hommes et les femmes." In this connection he gives a most interesting sketch of the spiritual pilgrimage of modern Japanese like Takayama, Kiyozawa and Tsunashima, which is too long to reproduce here.[2]

The data we have gathered together in this chapter, when taken in conjunction with the fact that the initiatory rites among primitive peoples and the rite of confirmation in the Churches which practise it are fixed so as to fall normally within the period of adolescence, seem to warrant the conclusion that there is a close connection between the ripening of the mental and physical powers at adolescence and religious awakening. This conclusion is further strengthened when we remember that confirmation, first communion, and tribal initiation sometimes produce a genuine religious awakening. Our wider survey disposes of the too facile generalization of Thouless that adolescent conversions " are, in the main, merely products of the conventions of the community in which they were produced, and not (as we might easily have supposed) evidences of a deep-seated uniformity in human nature." [3]

---

[1] Anesaki, *Quelques pages de l'histoire religeuse du Japon*, 33. Dengyo's younger contemporary, Kobo, was twenty-four when his conversion occurred.
[2] Op. cit. 146-169.
[3] *An Introduction to the Psychology of Religion*, 17.

CHAPTER XI
EXPERIENCES PRECEDING CONVERSION

THE causes which render the soul divided and unhappy and in need of unification by conversion are varied. The sense of sin is a very common cause in Christianity, Judaism and Islam. As the sense of sin varies in intensity, so also will the feeling of disharmony which it induces in the soul. Where it has brought with it a poignant sense of guiltiness in the eyes of God, and caused a man to cry, " Against Thee only have I sinned," the feeling of unhappiness and division will be acute. Where, however, there is no sharp consciousness of divine disapproval, but simply a disturbing realization of the cleft between ideals and conduct, the conflict will probably not take so agonizing a form. It would, however, be a complete mistake to think that the sense of sin is the only cause of the soul's disharmony, even in Christian circles, where the doctrine of sin receives so much emphasis. Starbuck goes too far in saying that the central fact in the pre-conversion state is the sense of sin.[1] What has disturbed the inward peace of many Christian adolescents has not been their sense of sin, but their inability to discover an adequate scale of values and a system of satisfying loyalties which would correspond to their expanding outlook and ambitions. Further, in many of the conversions to Christianity in the mission-field to-day the sense of sin is by no means a marked feature of the pre-conversion state. One of the most scholarly missionaries in India to-day writes : " I think it is true to say that a deep sense of their sinfulness has seldom been a power constraining Hindu seekers to submit themselves to Christ. Mr. N. V. Tilak, one of the most notable converts of recent

[1] Starbuck, 58

Experiences preceding Conversion

times in Western India, frankly admits that in his own case there was no keen sense of sin in his heart impelling him to Christ, and that he knows it was similarly absent in the case of many others. He was drawn to Christ in the first instance by his patriotism and by his belief that only Christ could lift up his people and make them great again."[1] Johannes Warneck, in his fine psychological study of the impact of Christianity upon the animistic Battaks of Sumatra, shows how these people almost invariably accepted Christ as the deliverer from the power of demons, and only later did they come to see in Him the deliverer from sin; and he also shows that the conversion of these animists cuts deeper into life and produces a more profound transformation than does many a conversion taking place in Christendom to-day.[2] Moreover, an examination of the remarkable cases of Christian conversion recorded in Begbie's *Broken Earthenware* will show that what led the converts to the Salvation Army penitent form was not their sense of sin, but their desire to escape the misery, mental and physical, to which their vices had brought them. Their sense of sin was a post-conversion development.

When we turn to the conversions which took place in Early Buddhism we find this sense of sin conspicuous by its absence from the pre-conversion state. What made the soul of Gotama Buddha and his followers divided and unhappy was not their sense of sin, but the appalling prospect of an unending line of lives.

The best way, however, to discover the causes which have placed men and women in need of unification by religion is to examine the motives which have driven and led them to conversion. But before we can do this effectively, it is necessary to define the sense in which we here use the term motive. Both in common speech and by writers on psychology and ethics it is used with a good deal of ambiguity. If, for example, we say that the motive of the conversion of the animistic Battaks mentioned above was security or their desire to escape from fear, we use the term motive in

[1] Dr. Macnicol in the *Expositor* for July, 1918.
[2] 263, 266 f., 246.

the sense of end-motive. We make it almost, though not quite, equivalent to intention. This is the usage to which writers on ethics incline. We may, however, with equal truth say that their motive was fear. In this case we indicate the emotion or feeling dominant at the time and which impelled them to turn from their ancestral faith to Christianity. This is the use of the term favoured by writers on psychology.[1] At bottom the two ways of using the term are not so different as might seem at first sight. It is the thought of the end which arouses the emotions; and it is the emotions thus aroused which supply the driving force which makes the realization of the end possible. To rule out any possibility of ambiguity we propose to use the term end-motive to denote that which induces men to make the reaction we know as conversion, and to use the term instinctive-motive to denote that which impels them to it. Some of our witnesses reveal the end-motive which induced them to seek conversion; many more, however, reveal the instinctive-motive that lay behind their action. In some cases the one can be inferred from the other, so inextricably are they linked.

Fear often supplies the instinctive-motive of conversion. It may be either the fear of God and the penalties of the divine wrath, or it may be fear of the consequences of continued indulgence in some vicious habit. Among the earliest Sufis " an overwhelming consciousness of sin, combined with a dread—which is hard for us to realize— of Judgment Day and the torments of hell-fire so vividly painted in the Koran, drove them to seek salvation."[2] How real it was in the conversion of such a saint as al-Ghazali, the following quotation from his *Confessions* will show: " I perceived that I was on the edge of an abyss, and that without an immediate conversion I should be doomed to eternal fire."[3]

Fear has often impelled men to conversion in Christianity. In New Testament times we find it at work in the con-

---

[1] E.g. McDougall, *Outline of Psychology*, 125, and all who expound the " New Psychology," otherwise their much-used phrase, " unconscious motive," would be meaningless.
[2] Nicholson, *Mystics of Islam*, 4.   [3] Claud Field's trans., 43.

versions of the dying malefactor and the Philippian jailor. Professor Stalker rightly calls attention to this element in the conversion of Paul: "When St. Paul heard himself accused of persecution by an Interlocutor addressing him from above, and was told ... that He whom he was persecuting was Jesus, and when thereupon there flashed into his soul an overwhelming sense of guilt, because the transactions of the foregoing months of his life were suddenly revealed as odious crimes, he anticipated that the next step must be the pouring out on his devoted head of the divine wrath in some indescribable form."[1]

In A.D. 387 the mob in Antioch, to show their resentment of an edict of the Emperor Theodosius, smashed the public baths and statues of the imperial family. Their rage soon gave way to a feeling of terror at the prospect of the emperor's condign punishment. Chrysostom seized the opportunity their alarm afforded to urge them to amendment of life. "Let us take refuge," he said, "with the King who is above all, and summon Him to our aid." The churches were soon thronged; many an intemperant man sobered; many indolent Christians quickened into zeal; and a large number of pagans entered the Christian fold.[2]

In later Christianity dread of the lurid fires of hell and purgatory was a powerful motive in driving men to repentance. It entered into the conversion of Luther,[3] while Theodore Beza, who was converted as he recovered from an illness in which his life was despaired of, says, "I saw nought before me but a terrible judgment of God."[4] To come to modern times, the well-known missionary, Mary Slessor of Calabar, was converted through fear of the flames of hell.[5]

Revivalists, like Jonathan Edwards and Wesley, often appealed to the emotion of crude fear. The former went so far as to complain of the weakness of those who shrank from throwing children in paroxysms of fear by talking of

[1] D.A.C. ii. 152.
[2] The story is told in full in Stephen's *Life of St. Chrysostom*, chap. xi.
[3] Lindsay, *History of the Reformation*, i. 198 f.
[4] Baird's *Theodore Beza*, 364.   [5] *Life*, 3.

136 *Conversion : Christian and Non-Christian*

eternal damnation.[1] As late as the middle of the nineteenth century General Booth could write: " Nothing moves people like the terrific. They must have hell-fire flashed before their faces, or they will not move." Forty years later, in his instructions to his field officers, he insists that " at death probation ends, the day of mercy closes, and there is no hope for evermore."[2] James does not exaggerate when he says: " Old fashioned hell-fire Christianity well knew how to extract from fear its full . . . conversion value."[3]

Fear of death motived the conversion of a number of troops during the Great War. One of my pupils writes:

" I never really discovered the power of God within my own life until one day in France, when I was brought face to face with what seemed certain death. It was then that I prayed to God with my whole soul to bring me out alive and to give me another chance to work for Him. By a miracle I was spared, and since then my life has been changed. I understood what it meant to be born again."

Fear of malignant spirits is the motive underlying many conversions among animistic peoples in the mission-field to-day. For the animist Christ is " the light that shines amid the darkness of his fears ; it assures him that he is not in the power of nature spirits or fetishes, and that no human being has any sinister power over another, since the will of God really controls everything that goes on in the world."[4]

The same holds true of the Mediterranean world for, roughly speaking, two or three centuries, both before and after the dawn of the Christian era. Fear of the assaults of demons and the relentless tyranny of Fate drove men and women into both Christianity and the Mystery-Religions. In the case of Early Christianity, the fear of demons was reinforced by the fear of the imminent end of the world, for chiliastic expectations did not cease with the Apostolic

---

[1] *Thoughts on the Revival of Religion*, 203.
[2] *Life*, i. 228 ; ii. 162.   [3] James, 264 n.
[4] Schweitzer, *On the Edge of the Primeval Forest*, 154. Cf. Warneck, *passim*.

Experiences preceding Conversion

Age. Such passages as 1 Cor. viii. 5, x. 20 f., Eph. ii. 2, vi. 12, Col. ii. 15, 1 Jn. iii. 8, Heb. ii. 14 show that in New Testament times conversion brought a real deliverance from the dread of demonic powers.

In all these cases the instinctive-motive is fear; and we are pretty safe in inferring that the end-motive was the desire for security. Al-Ghazali was drawn to Sufism because it promised him security from the divine wrath; Mary Slessor into personal faith in Christ for the same reason; the believers in demons into Christianity because it promised them security from these malignant powers; many of the mob of Antioch into the Church, because it had been known on former occasions to have abated the emperor's wrath.

Strong feelings of repugnance and loathing, amounting almost to nausea, turned Raymond Lull, the greatest, perhaps, of missionaries to the Moslem world, to the feet of Christ. Born in 1235, he lived for thirty years a life of pleasure and indulgence. A married man himself, he cherished an adulterous passion for the beautiful and pious wife of a rich Genoese. Exasperated by her silent resistance, he wrote her some flaming verses, to which she replied bidding him place his homage at the feet of Christ. About this time he had several visions of Christ on the Cross, but, blinded by passion, he waited for the lady to come to church on the Feast of the Conversion of St. Paul, and followed her and even allowed himself to cross the threshold of the church on horseback. Some hours later she sent a message to him to say she would see him that night at her house. Thinking she was about to yield to his desires, he hastened thither. Bidding him contemplate the despicable thing for which he had forgotten his duty and his faith, she bared her chest, and showed him her breasts eaten away by cancer. He staggered home, threw himself on his knees in agonizing prayer to God. He had another vision of the Crucified Christ, and heard the Saviour say, "Raymond, follow me." Before the morning broke, he had given himself to God in complete surrender.[1]

In other cases the tender emotions motive the struggle

[1] I have abridged the account given by Marius André in his *Le Bienheureux Raymond Lulle* (Paris, 1900).

towards the new life. The thought of a divine love, ever persistent towards men, in spite of their neglect and scorn of it, gives rise to feelings of remorse and gratitude. Thus we find evangelists like Moody and Evan Roberts emphasizing the love and tenderness of God. During the Welsh Revival all the hymns that were sung with such fervour tended to rouse the tender emotions. The love of God manifest on Calvary was Evan Roberts's almost exclusive theme. " The special note of the revival was ' The Lamb '—the bleeding Lamb. His redeeming love was commemorated in song, but not in sacrament."[1] The Welsh gatherings never tired of singing " Dyma gariad fel y moroedd," the first verse of which has been rendered into English thus :

> " Wondrous love, unbounded mercy !
> Vast as oceans in their flood :
> Jesus, Prince of Life, is dying—
> Life for us is in His blood !
> Oh ! what heart can e'er forget Him ?
> Who can cease His praise to sing ?
> Wondrous love for ever cherished
> While the heavens with music ring." [2]

Such song will arouse gratitude in the heart of man. It was gratitude for the kind treatment he had received from Jesus that impelled Zacchæus into the new life. In some cases this gratitude will merge into a feeling hardly to be distinguished from love. Thus was the woman who was a sinner converted through her love for Him who condescended to sinners. What the end-motive was in these two cases is not stated.

The instinctive-motive that carried over the dacoit Namdev into the religious life was the feeling of remorse that filled his mind when he realized that his selfish wrong-doing had robbed the widow of all her means of subsistence.[3]

When the soul has been divided by grief, this emotion

[1] Vyrnwy Morgan, *The Welsh Religious Revival*, 86.
[2] Ibid. 83. For the deep impression made on the animistic heathen by the story of the Passion of Our Lord, see Warneck, 227, 230, 257, 306.
[3] Supra, 54 ; cf. the conversion of Omar recorded above, 81

may supply the instinctive-motive that drives it to seek unification in the religious life. A good case in point is that of the Buddhist mother, who was crazed with grief at the loss of her child, and whose psalm has been cited above.[1]

Grief mingled with remorse moved Jacoponi da Todi to amend his life in a striking and sudden fashion. He was about forty years of age when he was converted. An experienced man of the world, " at once sensual and keenly intelligent," he had been married for a year to a young, unsullied and deeply religious girl. He had sought to fill her life with that gaiety which he himself so deeply prized. At a marriage festival, a balcony, on which there was dancing, collapsed; and, though many were injured, Jacoponi's wife alone was mortally hurt. " And when they took off those garments of vanity which she had upon her, in order to make her ready for the grave, they found at last next to her bare flesh a harsh shirt of hair." The beautiful girl had been an ascetic at heart. The shock nearly drove him out of his mind, but he emerged a reborn soul. He gave up his establishment, distributed his goods to the poor, exchanged his beautiful clothes for the Franciscan habit, made poverty his bride, and so became one of Italy's greatest mystics, and a typical singer of the Franciscan movement.[2]

In these last two cases the end-motive is not clearly stated, but it is not too hazardous to suggest that it was the desire for consolation and the thought that adequate consolation could be found only in religion. Conversions of this type abound. Tukaram and Chaitanya had both been bereaved of near relatives just before their conversion.[3]

Something very like chagrin drove the blacksmith, Govinda Das, to devote himself for the rest of his life to the service of Krishna. One day his wife quarrelled with him, and called him an illiterate fool. Greatly hurt, he left home. Hearing that a great saint had appeared in Navadipa,

---

[1] Supra, 75.
[2] I have taken these details from Miss Underhill's *Jacoponi da Todi*, 48 ff.
[3] See above, 54, 56.

he made his way thither, and fell in with Chaitanya. He wrote:

> "The very sight was wonderful to me. I cannot describe the feelings that came upon me. A thrill of joy passed through me, and my hair stood on end through joy like the spikes of the Kadamva flower. I stood lost in wonder and delight. I was spell-bound and transfixed to the spot; my limbs trembled and I perspired till my garments were wet. What I felt I cannot exactly describe—I wished I could wash the dear feet of the Lord with my tears." [1]

Chaitanya granted his request that he would take him as his body-servant, and he was the saint's sole companion on his journey to the south. Perhaps it is idle to try to divine the end-motive that operated in this case, but the suggestion may be hazarded that, as the blacksmith's self-esteem had been wounded, he was drawn into the religious life by the desire to be "somebody."

Here, possibly, we light upon the reason why slaves were conspicuous among the early Christian converts, and why the depressed classes in India to-day are much more responsive to the Gospel than the high-caste peoples. They may not completely understand the message that is brought to them, but they dimly apprehend that it means salvation for them from the miseries of their lot in life. Self-regarding motives may drive them into the new faith, while the end-motive in many cases will be the desire to improve their conditions, and to join a religion in which they will be received and treated as men, and not as chattels. Lest such a statement may seem to invalidate the worth of their conversion, we may point out that Jesus Christ never dictated to men the needs of which they should be *conscious* in coming to Him. Further, many of these people go on to find in Him more than they sought.

Some who have undergone the experience of conversion say nothing explicitly of the emotion dominant at the time, but they reveal very plainly their end-motive. Often it is the desire to get right with God and to adjust themselves to the scheme of religious realities in which they believe.

[1] *Kadcha* of Govinda Das, trans. from Sen, H.B.L.L. 448.

Experiences preceding Conversion

But it need not be so. One of Starbuck's correspondents declared that what she wanted was "to get the approval of others." "The wish to please my minister," says another, "counteracted my negative attitude."[1] In both these cases the end-motive is clearly stated, and in all probability we are right in thinking that the submissive instinct urged them forward.

Cases abound in which the subject's conception of duty has supplied the end-motive in conversion. Professor Stalker says:

> "Again and again instances of such conversions have come within the range of my own experience. I have seen a man elected to an office in the church, who only then awoke to the full claim which religion had upon him, and thenceforward lived up to his new conception of duty. I believe it is very far from uncommon for parents first to become earnestly religious when their children are born, because they feel how unfit they are to train these young immortals for their destiny unless they be decided themselves. . . . Instances will occur to every reader of ministers who have entered on their office without being themselves earnest Christians, but who, by the solemnity of their position, have been made aware of their own deficiencies, and have, thereupon, turned to the proper quarter for their removal. Synesius was called upon to be a Christian bishop while he was still a heathen and unbaptized; there were strong reasons of a public and philanthropic nature which made it desirable that he should occupy this position of authority, and the sense of responsibility carried him over the line of decision."[2]

In these cases it would be worse than useless to conjecture what the instinctive-motive was. If we could ask these people what it was, they would all probably say that, if a conception of their duty was their end-motive, the instinctive-motive was their sense of duty—a statement that would not take us very far. If they placed themselves in the hands of a psycho-physician, he would probably find that their unconscious motives were somewhat different. It is not impossible that he would discover that their sense of self-importance, their regard for their own reputation, and their desire for the approbation of others unconsciously affected their conduct.

[1] 49 f. [2] *Expositor* for July, 1918.

142 Conversion : Christian and Non-Christian

The foregoing discussion might be almost indefinitely extended, but sufficient has been said to make it clear that the causes which render the self consciously inferior, divided and unhappy, and in need of conversion are extraordinarily diverse, as are also the motives which drive and lead men to conversion. It should also be said that we have kept separate in our discussion causes and motives that might in actual experience closely interlace. In some cases the religious motive is difficult to trace, but if we possessed a full knowledge of the convert's life we should probably be justified in asserting its presence.

CHAPTER XII

TYPES OF CONVERSION

VARIOUS attempts have been made to classify conversions. At one time two main types were thought of—the gradual and the sudden. Then it was discovered that sudden conversions were sudden in appearance only; the abrupt break through to the new life being the sudden irruption of forces that had long been maturing in the subconscious. Pratt [1] opposes the volitional type (in which the steady effort of the person concerned is never relaxed until the new life is won) to the type in which feeling predominates. Many follow Starbuck and James in differentiating between the volitional and the self-surrender type of conversion. In the former type, conversion is the culmination of long striving for a better self, for unification of character. In the latter type strenuous endeavour seems to accomplish nothing. Unification comes only when all effort is given up. In extreme cases these two types can be clearly marked off from one another, but in milder cases they tend to become indistinguishable. A combination of the two is readily conceivable, for there is some surrender even in volitional cases, while in surrender cases an act of volition of a high order may be necessary in order that the surrender may be made.

Every attempt at classification has its perils, for every case of conversion is, in a sense, unique, the factors which enter in being exactly identical in no two cases. Types do exist, however, and may be distinguished, provided we do not take our classification too seriously. We propose to mark off three types, according as the change is predominantly intellectual, moral, or emotional.

[1] *The Religious Consciousness*, 122 ff.

144 *Conversion : Christian and Non-Christian*

In cases where the change is mainly intellectual, conversion takes the form of a clarification of thought, by means of which new insights are gained and a new system of values framed. The subject is divided and unhappy, because he is unable to win a satisfying view of the universe —a view that shall reveal to him the ultimate drift and meaning of life. Thus what Gotama Buddha wanted was a more satisfying view of the world process, as he conceived it in terms of the karma doctrine. For him, therefore, the moment of unification was the moment of illumination. Here we touch upon the characteristic feature of Early Buddhist conversions. The phrase most frequently used in the Pali texts to mark the moment of a man's conversion is, "He obtained the pure and spotless Eye of Truth." This means that the convert had come to realize the truth of the central Buddhist doctrine of the impermanency of all things. "The Pali phrase," says Dr. J. E. Carpenter, " describes the rise within the mind of a new way of looking on the world, and is constantly figured as the appearance of light in the midst of darkness."[1]

The authors of the *Thera-theri-gatha* often describe their achievement of this new insight in almost lyrical strains:

> " And first as novice, virtuous and keen
> To cultivate the upward mounting way,
> I cast out lust and with it all ill-will,
> And therewith, one by one, the deadly Drugs.
> Then to the Bhikkhuni of ripening powers
> Rose in a vision mem'ries of the past.
> Limpid and clear the mystic vistas grew,
> Expanding by persistent exercise.
> Act, speech and thought I saw as not myself,
> Children of cause, fleeting, impermanent.
> And now, with every poisonous Drug cast out,
> Cool and serene I see Nibbana's peace."[2]

> " While passed the first watch of the night, there rose
> Long memories of the bygone line of lives ;
> While passed the second watch, the Heavenly Eye,
> Purview celestial, they clarified ;
> While passed the last watch of the night, they burst
> And rent aside the gloom of ignorance."[3]

[1] *Theism in Mediæval India*, 21, n. 2.   [2] *Therigatha*, 99–101.
[3] *Therigatha*, 120. Written of thirty Sisters. See also 172 f., 179 f.

Types of Conversion

> " In fivefold concentrated ecstasy,
> My heart goes up in peace and unity,
> Serene composure have I made my own ;
> My vision as a god's is clarified.
> I know the destinies of other lives—
> Whence beings come and whither they do go ;
> Life here below, or otherwhere of life—
> Steadfast and rapt, in fivefold Jhana sunk." [1]

> " In trust and hope forth from my home I came
> Into the homeless life. And there in me
> Have mindfulness and insight grown, and tense
> And well composed my heart and mind. Make thou
> Whatever shams thou list, thou'lt harm me not." [2]

In this respect, as in others, Buddha made his own experience normative. He analysed the states through which he himself had passed, and then formulated them into a system of self-culture to be prescribed for all whom his teaching had awakened. " What justification by faith was to Luther that the perception of *bodhi* was in Buddha's own spiritual life, and in the religious reformation that he initiated." [3]

Another excellent non-Christian case, in which conversion was mainly a clarification of thought, is that of Dayananda Saraswati. It led him from the traditional polytheism in which he had been brought up to a lifelong crusade in favour of monotheism. [4]

Among the New Testament conversions that of Paul stands out as a conspicuous example of the intellectual type. It turned on the acceptance of the proposition that the crucified Jesus of Nazareth was the Messiah. [5] There is no sufficient evidence that Paul knew Jesus or was present in Jerusalem at the Crucifixion, but his active persecution of the Christians shows that he was early conversant with their claim that Jesus of Nazareth was the promised Messiah. Their assertion that the crucified Jesus was to be identified with the Messiah called forth from him a

---

[1] *Theragatha*, 916 f. [2] Ibid. 46. Addressed to the tempter Mara.
[3] Macnicol, *Indian Theism*, 68.
[4] See above, 130, where the story is told in full.
[5] Cf. Sanday and Headlam's *Romans*, 186.

passionate and indignant protest. The bare idea was to him unspeakably shocking (Deut. xxi. 23). In the course of the persecution, his knowledge of the Christian faith would grow, and he would hear the shameful death on the cross explained and justified in terms of vicarious suffering (1 Cor. xv. 3). Probably in this way doubts would soon arise in his mind as to whether, after all, the Christians were not right in maintaining that some divine purpose lay behind the shame of Calvary. The triumphant death of the martyr Stephen would, almost certainly, fix these doubts more firmly in his mind. May not Stephen's dying prayer, uttered in Paul's hearing, " Lord, lay not this sin to their charge," have haunted his imagination for days and weeks ? It is no objection to this to point out that there is no evidence that Paul had any misgivings with regard to the persecution of the Christians, and that in this matter he verily thought he did God a service. It would be a natural reaction of his mind to plunge further into fanaticism as soon as doubts suggested themselves. Then came the long ride to Damascus, with the enforced cessation from action that it brought. Suddenly the tired traveller, who was posting forward at midday, when he should have been taking his siesta, saw a light from heaven brighter than the sun, and heard a voice in the Aramaic tongue : " Saul, Saul, why persecutest thou me ? It is hard for thee to kick against the goad." " Who art thou, Lord ? " cried the astonished Saul ; and in answer came the voice, " I am Jesus whom thou persecutest." Stunned and blinded and a changed man, Saul was brought by his companions into Damascus, and the local Christians, to their intense surprise, found that the lion had become a lamb. The capital hour of Paul's life had arrived. Henceforth all whispered doubts and obstinate questionings were laid aside, and he devoted his life to the propagation of the faith of the crucified Messiah.[1]

In certain circles Christianity has often been so presented as to bring about conversions, the conspicuous element

[1] This account of Paul's conversion presupposes the settlement of an exegetical problem connected with Rom. vii. 7–25. I take the view that the crisis described in this passage is not the experience on the Damascus road. See further Chapter XIV, below.

Types of Conversion 147

in which was a kind of intellectual insight into the plan of salvation. The need of salvation, it is said, arose with the sin of Adam. This need God Himself met in the death of His Son, which is a perfect expiation and an entire satisfaction for the sin of the world. The work of Christ is a finished work. Naught remains for man to do but to accept it. When Christianity is thus presented it does not surprise us to hear that an unsophisticated fisher-boy announced his conversion with the cry, "I see it! I see it!"[1] Similarly, one of Starbuck's correspondents wrote: "I could fairly see the Gospel truths which had been misty."[2] Conversions of this type were frequent under the ministry of Finney, who himself remarks: "It was a fact that often interested me that lawyers would come to my room, when pressed hard . . . for conversation and light, on some point which they did not comprehend; and I observed again and again that when these points were cleared up, they were ready at once to submit. Indeed, they take a more intelligent view of the plan of salvation than any other class to whom I have preached."[3]

In the second type of conversion the change is moral rather than intellectual. The subject has been living a depraved and sinful life, but at his conversion, not only do the shackles of sinful habits fall off from him, but he is cured of his very love of sin. Cases of this type abound in all religions. The best-known case in the annals of Christianity is that of Augustine. A slave of lust, as he calls himself, he was set free from all propensity to sensual indulgence after his conversion in the garden in Milan. Similarly, Raymond Lull was cured by his conversion of his guilty passion for a married woman, and won for himself new moral ability. We refrain from giving other illustrations of this type of conversion, for it is difficult to choose from the wealth of available material; and it is the type of conversion that has attracted the most attention. In all soberness, we may say that there is no moral malady that conversion has not been known to cure.

In the third type of conversion the prominent change

---

[1] Clow, *The Cross in Christian Experience*.
[2] Starbuck, 87.
[3] Finney, 304.

is emotional. Conversion is the birth of a new and dominating affection. In brief, the subject falls in love. The primary thing in such conversion is not a clarification of thought, nor an accession of moral ability, but the reorganization of the emotional life round a new centre. Naturally, such conversions occur with most frequency in Christianity and in the *bhakti* sects of Hinduism, where loving devotion to the Deity is a central tenet. They are also found among the Sufis, who regarded love as the essence of all creeds. As is well known, a deep religious meaning underlies the constant references of Sufi poets to love, wine, roses and beautiful women. The Beloved, the Mistress, whose lovely cheeks and perfumed tresses are described, is none other than the Divine Lover, who elsewhere is the Wine or Cupbearer, while the intoxicated one is the lover of God.

A number of the conversions which took place during the ministry of Jesus were due to this personal affection for Him. " The Church originated," says Wernle,[1] " in a hero-worship—the theologians call it faith—the truest and purest that has ever been."

Many of the mediæval mystics appear to have fallen in love with Christ at their conversion. Some, indeed, are very like the Sufis and Hindu *bhaktas* in their use of the language of human love to express their affection for the Divine Lover. Putting aside extreme cases, we may here note that the conversion of St. Francis of Assisi was a plighting of his troth to Christ, who satisfied all the romantic aspirations of a soul filled with the ideas characteristic of an age of chivalry. This passionate affection for Christ, which was poles apart from the *amor intellectualis Dei* of Spinoza, controlled him throughout his life.

Francis would have found a kindred spirit in the Sufi poet who wrote:

> " Love thrilled the chord of my soul's lute,
> And changed me all to love from head to foot.
> 'Twas but a moment's touch, yet shall Time ever
> To me the debt of thanksgiving impute." [2]

[1] *Beginnings of Christianity*, i. 127. [2] Nicholson, *Mystics of Islam*, 84.

Similarly, Jalaluddin sang:

> "When first the Giver of the grape my lonely heart befriended,
>   Wine filled my bosom and my veins filled up,
> But when His image all my heart possessed, a voice descended,
>   'Well done, O Sovereign Wine and peerless Cup!'" [1]

The conversion of most, if not all, of the *bhakti* saints of India was a falling in love with the Deity on whom they lavished their devotion. Chaitanya's love for Krishna amounted to a passion. Sometimes he would imagine he was Radha, Krishna's favourite mistress. "I make my heart imagine her emotions," he said,[2] "and thus I taste the delicious sweetness of Krishna." Govinda Das quotes him as saying: "As the young man yearns for his beloved, so the soul yearns for God; it is for the want of a better object of comparison that the Vaishnavas worship the Lord under this form." [3]

Known over all India is the following story of Mira Bai, the Rajput Queen and devotee of Krishna. When she visited Brindaban, a famous *bhakta* refused to see her because she was a woman. Hearing this she asked: "Is he then a male? Does he not know there is but one male in existence, my beloved Krishna?"

Two stanzas must suffice to indicate Tukaram's passionate love for Krishna:

> "Now Pandurang I've chosen for my part,
>   None, none but his to be.
> In all my thoughts he dwells, dwells in my heart,
>   Sleeping and waking he.
>
> "Bound with cords of love I go,
>   By Hari captive led,
> Mind, speech and body, lo,
>   To him surrendered." [4]

Even in Early Buddhism conversions, which were equivalent to a falling in love, were not unknown. Many were due, as we have seen, to the expulsive power of a new system of ideas, but often it was a system of ideas quickened

---

[1] Nicholson, *Mystics of Islam*, 107.
[2] Sarkar, 80.   [3] Sen, H.B.L.L. 536.
[4] Macnicol, P.M.S. 70 and 72. Pandurang and Hari are other names for Krishna.

by devotion to Buddha's own winsome personality. Of the women who wrote the *Therigatha*, Mrs. Rhys Davids says: "In practically every case the breaking out of the groove of habit or convention was proximately caused by a personal influence—that of a ransomed sister or brother, or to the greatest brother of them all."[1] The following citation must suffice to illustrate this point:

> "Lo! from Benares I am come to thee—
> I, Sundari, thy pupil, at thy feet,
> O mighty Hero, see me worship here.
> Thou art Buddha! thou art Master! and thine,
> Thy daughter am I, issue of thy mouth,
> Thou very Brahmin! even of thy word."[2]

What Mrs. Rhys Davids has said of the Sisters is equally true of the Brethren, as the following quotations make clear.

> "The Master hath my fealty and love,
> And all the Buddha's ordinance is done.
> Low have I laid the heavy load I bore,
> Cause for rebirth is found in me no more."[3]

> "When first I saw the Blessed Master, Him
> For whom no fear can anywhence arise,
> A wave of deep emotion filled my soul
> At sight of Him, the peerless man of men.
> Had a man erst on hands and knees besought
> Favour of Fortune's goddess hither come,
> And won the grace of Master such as this,
> Still might he fail to win (the thing he sought).
> I for my part (all hindrance) cast away—
> (The hope of) wife and children, coin and corn,
> And let my hair and beard be shorn, and forth
> Into the homeless life I went from home.
> The life and training practising, all faculties
> Well held in hand, in loyalty to Him,
> Buddha supreme, master of self I lived."[4]

> "Sluggish and halt the progress that I made,
> And therefore was I held in small esteem.
> My brother judged I should be turned away,
> And bade me, saying: 'Now do thou go home.'

[1] *Psalms of the Sisters*, p. xxxii. See also Rhys Davids, Hibbert Lectures, 4th ed., 170, and Rhys Davids and Oldenberg in S.B.E. xiii., p. xvii.
[2] *Therigatha*, 335 f.   [3] *Theragatha*, 1088.   [4] Ibid. 510–513.

> So I, dismissed and miserable, stood
> Within the gateway of the Brethren's Park,
> Longing at heart within the Rule to stay.
> And there he came to me, the Exalted One,
> And laid his hand upon my head ; and took
> My arm, and to the garden led me back.
> To me the Master in his kindness gave
> A napkin for the feet and bade me thus :
> ' Fix thou thy mind on this clean thing, the while
> Well concentrated thou dost sit apart.'
> And I who heard his blessed Word abode
> Fain only and always to keep his Rule,
> Achieving concentrated thought and will,
> That I might win the crown of all my quest.
> And now I know the where and how I lived,
> And clearly shines the Eye Celestial ;
> The Threefold Wisdom have I made my own,
> And what the Buddha bids me do is done." [1]

In concluding this chapter we recur to a remark made early in it. No classification of conversions is entirely satisfactory, as one type so easily shades off into another. We have taken Augustine's conversion as a typical case in which the change was moral. Granger and Thouless, however, treat it as though it were mainly intellectual.[2] They trace his movements from Manicheeism to the New Academy, to Neo-Platonism and to the Pauline Epistles, and show how he was all the time seeking a satisfactory world-view. There is some truth in such a presentation, but we are confirmed in our view that the main change was moral. Augustine's real malady, of which his conversion wrought the cure, was sensual lust. Again, we have taken Paul's conversion as a case in which the change was mainly intellectual. It would be easy to treat it also as a case of falling in love with Christ. As soon as he realized that the death which Christ had endured was out of love for sinful men, and in order to free them from the burden of sin, there arose in the soul of Paul a passionate love for the One Who had laid down His life for him, and Whom in his blind fury he had persecuted and hated. This love could not but be deepened by the apostle's feeling that

---

[1] *Theragatha*, 557–562
[2] *The Soul of a Christian*, 89 f. ; Thouless, op. cit. 197 ff.

he had been guilty of the basest ingratitude and had repaid love with hate. Once generated in his heart, this love acted with all " the expulsive power of a new affection." It broke the bonds of habit and prejudice, and carried him away on a tide of emotion into a new life, which it henceforth dominated and controlled. Christ's love for him and his love for Christ bound Paul and his Lord so closely together that it is no longer Paul that lives, but Christ lives in him, and whatever Christ does he does, and whatever he does Christ does.

CHAPTER XIII

THE IMMEDIATE ACCOMPANIMENTS OF CONVERSION

WILLIAM JAMES claims that "the most characteristic of all the elements of the conversion crisis" is "the ecstasy of happiness produced."[1] He quotes at length the cases of Finney and the Methodist evangelist, Billy Bray. We shall now proceed to show that this joy is a marked ingredient of the experience of all converts, whether Christian or non-Christian.

Within Christian circles the evidence for the joy of the converted man is amazingly rich; but owing to considerations of space we must confine ourselves to the New Testament and to two other cases. Dean Church has spoken of the joy and exultation that throb through Early Christian literature as "one of the most singular and solemn things in history." As he points out, the rapture of the New Testament converts was due to the fact that their conversion convinced them "that at last the routine of vice and sin has met its match, and that a new and astonishing possibility has come within view, that men, not here and there, but on a large scale, might attain to that hitherto hopeless thing to the multitudes, goodness."[2]

There is a great contrast between Paul, the over-anxious Pharisee, and the jubilant Christian apostle. The despairing cry, "O wretched man that I am, who shall deliver me from the body of this death?" is replaced by the song of victory, "Thanks be to God, who giveth us the victory through our Lord Jesus Christ." The new and buoyant

---
[1] 254; cf. Starbuck, 120 ff.
[2] *The Gifts of Civilization*, 156. Cf. Harnack, *Acts of the Apostles*, Excursus iii., "Luke and the Christian Joy."

sense of moral ability is an unfailing spring of joy to the apostle, and to the other New Testament converts. After Pentecost the disciples "take their food with gladness and singleness of heart, praising God." (Acts ii. 46). After his conversion the Ethiopian eunuch goes "on his way rejoicing" (Acts viii. 39; cf. viii. 8). Likewise the Philippian jailor "rejoiced greatly" (Acts xvi. 34). Naturally, this joy figures largely in the epistles of Paul (1 Thess. i. 6, v. 16; Rom. xii. 12, xiv. 17, xv. 13; 2 Cor. i. 24, vi. 10, viii. 2; Gal. v. 22; Phil. i. 25, iii. 1, iv. 4). If further evidence be needed of the prevalence of joy among the New Testament converts, mention may be made of such passages as Eph. v. 4, 20; Phil. iv. 6; Col. i. 12, ii. 7, iii. 17, iv. 2; 1 Thess. iii. 9 and v. 18, in all of which thanksgiving is referred to as a normal Christian occupation. The other writings of the New Testament reflect the same experience. The Christians addressed in the First Epistle of Peter "rejoice greatly with joy unspeakable" (i. 8; cf i. 6, iv. 13). A prominent point in the parable of the Hidden Treasure is the joy of discovery (Matt. xiii. 44).

Professor A. Caldecott's examination of the religious experiences of Wesley's helpers led him to the following conclusion: "In these cases we see a joy unequalled, so far as they can testify, by any other which they knew; some of them had tried other sources, not a few, being men of warm nature and strong natural passions, and affections, and high moral tone. But now they found, as one of them says, not only occasional ecstasy, but a fund of 'solid happiness.'"[1]

We permit ourselves one other example of the joy of the Christian convert. The Japanese, Kanso Utschimura, writes:

"I was now taught there was only one God and not many over eight millions, as I had formerly believed. Christian monotheism laid its axe at the root of my superstition.... My conscience and my reason said Amen to it. One God, not many—that was a glad message to my soul. I was no longer under the necessity of making a long prayer every morning to the four groups of gods

[1] *The Religious Sentiment: Illustrated from the Lives of Wesley's Helpers*, 26.

in the four parts of heaven and to the god of every temple that I passed. . . . I now marched proudly past the temples with head erect and conscience unburdened. No god of that temple could punish me for prayers that had been omitted, for I knew that I was protected by the God of gods. My friends soon noted my changed mood. Formerly, as soon as I came in sight of the temple, I was dumb, for I had to say my prayers in my heart. Now, I chattered and laughed joyously all the way to college. I did not regret that I had entered into the covenant, for belief in one God made me a new man." [1]

To some it will come as a surprise to find with what rapture the early Buddhist converts celebrated the joy of their conversion. They strike the lyrical note again and again, and frequently their poems become veritable psalms of triumph as they celebrate the joy they have found :

> " Buoyant in sooth my body, every pulse
> Throbbing in wondrous bliss and ecstasy.
> Even as cotton-down blown on the breeze,
> So floats and hovers this my body light." [2]

> " Abundantly this brother doth rejoice,
> For the blest truths the Buddha hath revealed
> Are his, and he hath won the Path of Peace,
> And his the bliss where worldly cares are stilled." [3]

> " In fivefold concentrated ecstasy,
> My heart goes up in peace and unity.
> Serene composure have I made my own ;
> My vision as a God's is clarified.
> I know the destinies of other lives :
> Whence beings come and whither they do go ;
> Life here below, or otherwhere of life—
> Steadfast and rapt, in fivefold Jhana sunk. " [4]

At the time of the Great Enlightenment the Buddha burst forth into a psalm of thanksgiving, and spent twenty-eight days at the foot of the tree, in enjoyment of the bliss of emancipation.[5] When he was on the road from thence

---

[1] Cited by Warneck, 211 f. See also 233 f., 242 f., 251 for the joy of the animistic heathen when freed from the fear of demons by conversion to Christianity. Cf. also Campbell N. Moody, *The Mind of the Early Converts*, 105 f.
[2] *Theragatha*, 104.   [3] Ibid. 11.   [4] Ibid. 916 f.
[5] So the *Maha-Vagga*. Later books extend the period to forty-nine days.

to Gaya, a naked ascetic, named Upaka, remarked on the serenity and brightness of his face.[1] About the middle of his career, he said :

"Ay, young sir, I verily am of those who fare happily, even though you see me exposed in this hut to the chilly nights of winter. Your well-housed citizen, happy after his kind, nay, the king himself with all his pleasures, is not so happily at ease as I. They may be smitten with torments through greedy desire, enmity, or blunders. But one who has cut off at the root all those sources of suffering dwells at ease, for he has won peace." [2]

The *Dhammapada* thus describes the happiness of those who have accepted the *dhamma* :

"We live happily, indeed, not hating those who hate us ! among men of hatred we dwell free from hatred !
We live happily, indeed, free from ailments among the ailing ! among men who are ailing let us dwell free from ailments !
We live happily indeed, free from greed among the greedy ! among men who are greedy let us dwell free from greed !
We live happily indeed, though we call nothing our own !
We shall be like the bright gods feeding on happiness ! " [3]

The *Udana* tells of one Bhaddiya, who had once enjoyed the comforts of a royal home, but who, after his conversion, roamed through the forests and sat at the foot of trees, repeating in his new-found gladness : " Ah, Happiness ! Ah, Happiness." [4]

Often this intense joy sprang out of the self-mastery gained in conversion :

" Good fight he made, and made good sacrifice,
And in the battle won : now by such war,
The fervent following of the holy life,
In happiness he resteth (evermore)." [5]

" In me the senses have been hushed to calm,
Like horses well tamed by the charioteer,
In me no vain conceits are found, nor aught
Of poison-fumes survives—one such as I
May stir up envy e'en among the gods." [6]

[1] *Maha-Vagga*, i. vi. 7.
[2] Cited by Mrs. Rhys Davids in E.R.E. vi. 512.
[3] S.B.E. x. 54. [4] *Udana*, ii. 10. Strong's trans., 24.
[5] *Theragatha*, 236. [6] Ibid. 206.

Immediate Accompaniments of Conversion 157

In other cases it arose out of the new intellectual insights then won :

> " When by insight he sees the happy-omened Path,
> Twice fourfold, ultimate, that purifies from all
> That doth defile, and seeing, dwells with mind intent,
> Rapt in an ecstasy of thought : no higher bliss
> Is given to men than this.

> " When work of thought makes real and true the way of peace,
> From sorrow free, untarnished and uncorrelate,
> Cleansing from all that doth defile, and severing
> From every bond and fetter, and the brother sits
> Rapt in an ecstasy of thought : no higher bliss
> Is given to men than this." [1]

But more often it was rooted in the blissful knowledge that, the religious goal having been attained, there was no further possibility of rebirth :

> " Oh ! but 'tis long I've wandered down all time,
> Living as mother, father, brother, son,
> And as grandparent in the ages past—
> Not knowing how and what things really are,
> And never finding what I needed sore.
> But now my eyes have seen th' Exalted One ;
> And now I know this living frame's the last,
> And shattered is th' unending round of births.
> No more Pajapati shall come to be." [2]

> " The Seven Factors of the awakened mind—
> Seven ways whereby we may Nibbana win—
> All, all have I developed and made ripe,
> Even according to the Buddha's word.
> For I therein have seen as with mine eyes
> The Bless'd, the Exalted One. Last of all lives
> Is this that makes up Me. The round of births
> Is vanquished. Ne'er shall I be again ! " [3]

> " O free, indeed ! O gloriously free
> Am I in freedom from three crooked things :
> From quern, from mortar, from my crook-back'd lord !
> Ay, but I'm free from rebirth and from death,
> And all that dragged me back is hurled away." [4]

---

[1] *Theragatha*, 520 f.
[2] *Therigatha*, 159 f. Pajapati is the name of the woman who wrote in verse.
[3] Ibid. 21 f.   [4] Ibid. 11.

Conversion : Christian and Non-Christian

> " A traveller I these long, long ages past,
> And round about the realms of life I've whirled ;
> One of the many-folk and blind as they,
> No Ariyan truths had I the power to see.
> But earnestly I strove for light and calm ;
> And now all shattered lies the endless way.
> All future bournes abolished utterly,
> Now cometh never more rebirth for me." [1]

Accustomed as so many are to think of Buddhism as fundamentally pessimistic, it is difficult for them to appreciate the throbbing joy of these early converts. But the seeming paradox of joy in a pessimistic *milieu* is explained when we keep in mind the fact that the transmigration-karma doctrine was accepted by the Early Buddhists.[2] It is difficult for a Westerner to accustom himself to the strange psychological climate of the Early Buddhist literature, but one does not need to live long in India to find out the extent to which this doctrine has permeated the thinking of the people—even the simple, illiterate villagers. Buddha's message was a gospel to which many of India's karma-haunted millions turned for comfort and hope. Many were appalled at the prospect of endless migration, and to them Buddha came with his message of release.

" ' Even as the ocean has everywhere but one taste—that of salt—so my doctrine has everywhere but one essence—that of deliverance,' said Gotama."

This is why the lives of those whom his teaching had awakened were filled with joy when they reached the end of the quest he had set before them for inner self-unification. The fact that they use different religious idioms from ours ought not to blind us to the reality of their unruffled joy.

Sometimes the feeling of these early converts is less rapturous and intense, and is more fitly designated peace than joy. It is not, however, the peace that springs from reconciliation with God, but rather intellectual repose, deliverance from perplexity of mind, the state that Paul calls " peace in believing " (Rom. xv. 13).

---
[1] *Theragatha*, 215 f.
[2] The Buddhist refinement of the Brahmanical doctrine does not concern us here.

Immediate Accompaniments of Conversion 159

It was the calm and peace of Assaji that drew the attention of Sariputta and ended in his conversion.[1] It manifests itself frequently in the *Thera-theri-gathas*, but the following quotations must suffice:

> "Sleep softly, little Sturdy; take thy rest
> At ease, wrapt in the robe thyself hast made.
> Stilled are the passions that would rage within,
> Withered as pot-herbs in the oven dried."[2]

> "Happily rest, thou venerable dame!
> Rest thee, wrapt in the robe thyself hast made.
> Stilled are the passions that have raged within.
> Cool art thou now, knowing Nibbana's peace."[3]

> "Home have I left, for I have left my world!
> Child have I left, and all my cherished herds!
> Lust have I left, and ill-will, too, is gone,
> And Ignorance have I put far from me;
> Craving and root of Craving overpowered,
> Cool am I now, knowing Nibbana's peace."[4]

The *bhakti* saints of India rarely strike this minor key. Theirs is much more the spirit of St. Francis of Assisi. Like him, they are *jongleurs* of God. Chaitanya, for example, would sing and chant Krishna's name for hours, till he became delirious with *bhakti*. Whole nights and days would be spent by him and his companions in singing Vaishnava songs in *sankirtan*. In his transports of emotion he would often dance till he fell down exhausted by the intensity of his joy and love. He would ask in song:

> "How shall I speak of my bliss to-day?
> The Beloved has entered my temple for ever."[5]

The Maratha *bhakta*, Namdev, sings:

> "Now all my days with joy I'll fill
> Full to the brim,
> With all my heart to Vitthal cling
> And only him.

---

[1] See above, p. 71. [2] *Therigatha*, 1.
[3] Ibid. 16.   [4] Ibid. 18.
[5] *Chaitanya Charitamrita*, Sarkar's trans., 4.

"He will sweep utterly away
   All dole and care;
And all in sunder shall I rend
   Illusion's snare. . . .

"Lo, all the sorrow of the world
   Will straightway cease,
And all unending now shall be
   The reign of peace." [1]

Tukaram, who belongs to the same school as Namdev, expresses his joy thus:

"Before my eyes my dead self lies;
   O, bliss beyond compare!
Joy fills the world, and I rejoice,
   The soul of all things there." [2]

From the *Tiruvachakam* we cull the following lines as evidence of the ecstatic joy which accompanied Manikka's conversion:

"He called, in grace He made me His,
He as a Brahman showed His glory forth,
Then, while undying love dissolved my frame, I cried:
I raised enraptured voice above the billowy sea's loud waves;
In utter wilderment I fell, I rolled, I cried aloud,
Madman distraught, and as a maniac raved;
While those who saw were wildered, who heard it wonder'd sore,
More than the frenzy wild of raging elephant
Bore me away beyond endurance far. 'Twas then through
All my limbs a honeyed sweetness He infused, and made me blest.
He filled me full with honeyed sweetness;
Ambrosial drops most marvellous
He caused throughout my being to distil;
With tender soul, as though He'd made me as Himself,
He formed for me a frame where grace might flow.
And as an elephant explores fields of sweet cane, at last
He sought, and found, and made even me to live. In me
Mercy's pure honey while he mixed,
He gave in grace supernal food—
Ev'n He Whose nature nor Brahma knows nor Mal." [3]

[1] Macnicol, P.M.S. 47.
[2] Ibid. 79. A small point noted by Carpenter (*Theism in Mediæval India*, 428 n.) is worth mentioning. Ananda (joy) is a frequent element in the names of the *bhaktas* and is a significant indication of their inward joy.
[3] Pope's trans., 27 ff.

Immediate Accompaniments of Conversion 161

> " Soon as I thought upon His sacred form
>   Which every thought of man transcends,
> The Lord of mercy's flood of purest joys,
>   That ne'er delude swept o'er my soul.
> My Lord revealed Himself that He might make
>   Me ever fully His alone.
> To Him, the Lord of Lords Supreme, go thou
>   And breathe His praise, O humming-bee." [1]

> " In love, Thy servant's soul and body thrilling through,
>   And melting all my heart with rapturous bliss,
> Thou hast bestowed sweet grace beyond my being's powers—
>   And I for this have no return to give ! " [2]

> " The mother's thoughtful care her infant feeds : Thou deign'st
>   With greater love to visit sinful me—
> Melting my flesh, flooding my soul with inward light,
> Unfailing rapture's honeyed sweetness Thou
> Bestow'st—through my every part infusing joy !
>   My Wealth of bliss ! O Civan-Peruman ! " [3]

Another Tamil Saivite, Tirunavukkarasu Swami, whose conversion experience we have noticed above, sings of his joy in less ecstatic tones :

> " No man holds sway o'er us,
>   Nor death nor hell fear we ;
> No tremblings, grief of mind,
>   No pains nor cringings see.
> Joy, day by day, unchanged
>   Is ours, for we are His." [4]

Kabir thus describes his joy in feeling that he is saved :

> " My dread of transmigration is at an end
> Since God displayed His love for me.
> The light hath dawned, the darkness is dispelled ;
> I have obtained the jewel, God, by meditation on Him.
> When He conferreth happiness sorrow fleeth away ;
> The jewel of my heart is absorbed in God's love." [5]

---

[1] Pope's trans., 149.   [2] Ibid. 220.   [3] Ibid. 296.
[4] Trans. from Kingsbury and Phillips's *Hymns of the Tamil Saivite Saints*, 51.
[5] Trans. from Macauliffe, op. cit. vi. 276.

Conversion: Christian and Non-Christian

"He has awaited for me countless ages, for love of me He has lost His heart.
Yet I did not know the bliss that was so near to me, for my love was not yet awake.
But now my Lover has made known to me the meaning of the note that struck my ear." [1]

"O Sadhu ! the simple union is the best.
Since the day when I met with my Lord, there has been no end to the sport of our love.
I shut not my eyes, I close not my ears, I do not mortify my body.
I see with eyes open and smile, and behold His beauty everywhere.
I utter His name and whatever I see, it reminds me of Him—whatever I do, it becomes His worship.
The rising and the setting are one to me ; all contradictions are solved.
Wherever I go, I move round Him,
All I achieve is His service :
When I lie down, I lie prostrate at His feet.
He is the only adorable one to me : I have none other.
My tongue has left off impure words, it sings His glory day and night ;
Whether I rise or sit down, I can never forget Him ; for the rhythm of His music beats in my ears.
Kabir says : My heart is frenzied, and I disclose in my soul what is hidden. I am immersed in that one great bliss which transcends all pleasure and pain." [2]

Debendranath Tagore has described the uprush of joy at his conversion in the following moving words :

"My mind could scarcely contain the unworldly joy, so simple and natural, which I experienced at the burning *ghât*. Language is weak in every way : how can I make others understand the joy I felt ? It was a spontaneous delight, to which nobody can attain by argument or logic. . . . With this sense of joy and renunciation, I returned home at midnight. That night I could not sleep. It was this blissful state of mind that kept me awake. Throughout the night my heart was suffused with a moonlight radiance of joy." [3]

We may now turn to another very common accompaniment of conversion, namely, the feeling of newness. Not only does the convert feel that he himself is a new man,

---
[1] Poem 86 in Rabindranath Tagore's translation.
[2] Ibid., Poem 41.   [3] *Autobiography*, 39.

Immediate Accompaniments of Conversion 163

but the whole of the objective world frequently appears to undergo a change, and to become invested with a beautiful newness and glory. James and Starbuck have given many examples of this feeling from Protestant evangelical circles.[1] One of Starbuck's correspondents says, "My horses and hogs and everybody became changed." With greater felicity of expression Masefield, in his poem *The Everlasting Mercy*, describes with psychological exactness this feeling in the words he puts into the mouth of the converted poacher :

> " O glory of the lighted mind,
> How dead I'd been, how dumb, how blind !
> The station brook to my new eyes,
> Was bubbling out of Paradise ;
> The waters rushing from the rain
> Were singing Christ has risen again.
> I thought all earthly creatures knelt
> From rapture of the joy I felt.
> The narrow station-wall's brick ledge,
> The wild hop withering in the hedge,
> The light in huntsman's upper storey
> Were parts of an eternal glory,
> Were God's eternal garden flowers,
> I stood in bliss at this for hours."

The apostle Paul, no doubt, had this feeling in mind when he wrote: " If any man be in Christ, there is a new creation : old things are passed away ; behold all things are become new " (2 Cor. v. 17). Rabindranath Tagore, in a passage we have already quoted,[2] thus describes it : " All of a sudden a covering seemed to fall away from my eyes, and I found the world bathed in a wonderful radiance, with waves of beauty and joy swelling on every side."

It is a far cry from the Bengali poet to Dwight L. Moody, but at this point they are one. The American evangelist writes :

> " I remember the morning on which I came out of my room after I had first trusted Christ. I thought the old sun shone a good deal brighter than it ever had before. I thought that it was just smiling upon me ; and as I walked out upon Boston Common and

[1] James, 248 ff. ; Starbuck, 119 f.   [2] Supra, p. 129

164 *Conversion : Christian and Non-Christian*

heard the birds singing in the trees, I thought they were all singing a song to me. Do you know, I fell in love with the birds. I had never cared for them before. It seemed to me I was in love with all creation."[1]

Rabindranath Tagore apart, I have not been able to find in the religions of India any clear examples of the discovery at conversion of new beauties in the external world. In view of the subjective bent of the Hindu mind this is not surprising. We do, however, find a very remarkable interest taken in Nature by the authors of the *Thera-theri-gatha*. In that work there are quite a number of passages which depict the *arahat* " listening in his cave to the music of the rains and to the crash of the storm, joying in the beauty of crag and cloud, of verdure and blossom, of bird-life and the cries of forest-creatures."[2] Unfortunately for our purpose, the poems do not make it clear whether this feeling for the beauties of Nature was an accompaniment of the conversion-experience or the outcome of solitary meditation in the upland caves and woods, to which awakened spirits often betook themselves to practise the system of mind-culture laid down by Buddhism for all who sought unification of the divided self.

A similar doubt attaches to Chaitanya's new attitude to the external world after his conversion. After it, he saw God in everything. The blue sky reminded him of Krishna's complexion, the singing of the birds of his lute, and every shady bower of the groves of Brindaban, where the Lord had sported with the milkmaids. But we cannot say for certain whether this new attitude came to him at his conversion, or whether it is more reasonably explained as due to his psychopathic temperament.[3]

Some converts report that their conversion was accompanied with a vision or a voice, or both. In some cases a great blazing light (photism) is also reported. The American revivalist, Finney, and the Japanese prophet, Nichiren, are one in reporting simply the vision. Nichiren's

[1] *Life*, 40.
[2] Mrs. Rhys Davids's *Buddhism*, 205.
[3] For Chaitanya's psychopathic temperament see *Chaitanya Charitamrita*, Sarkar's trans., xiii. 20, 30 f., 216 ; and Sen's *Chaitanya and his Companions*, 159, 238, 249, 251, 253, 263, 268, 278.

Immediate Accompaniments of Conversion 165

vision was of Kokuzo,[1] the god of wisdom; Finney's of the Lord Jesus Christ. "As I went in and shut the door," says the latter, "it seemed as if I met the Lord Jesus Christ face to face. It did not occur to me that it was wholly a mental state; it seemed that I saw Him as I would see any other man. He said nothing, but looked at me."[2]

Augustine heard a voice saying, "Tolle lege," but makes no mention of a vision. He himself throws out the suggestion (only to reject it), that what he actually heard was the formula of some game uttered by a child playing in a neighbouring house. The great probabilities are that we have here a characteristic audition.[3]

In his earlier days the famous Sufi, Ibrahim ben Adham, was a prince in the city of Balkh. "One day he went to the chase, and having become separated from his suite was pursuing an antelope. God caused the antelope to address him in elegant language and say: 'Wast thou created for this, or wast thou commanded to do this?' He repented, abandoned everything, and entered upon the path of asceticism and abstinence."[4]

Cases in which the vision and voice are conjoined abound. At the crisis of his life the prophet Isaiah not only saw Yahweh lifted up in majesty, but heard His voice.[5]

The apostle Paul's conversion was accompanied with a photism as well as with a vision and voice. He describes the light as "above the brightness of the sun, shining round about me and them which journeyed with me."[6]

In some cases the photism occurs without any accompanying voice or vision. Henry Nicholas (b. 1501-2), the founder of the "Family of Love," was suddenly surrounded, as he lay in bed, by a great light, "in shape like a mountain rising from his bed up into heaven, wrapping

---

[1] Anesaki, *Nichiren, the Buddhist Prophet*, 14.
[2] *Autobiography*, 17. This took place on the same day as the struggle in the wood referred to below, 184. The photism mentioned by James (*Varieties*, 252) did not, as a matter of fact, occur at the time of Finney's conversion, but some months later. See his *Autobiography*, 29.
[3] *Confessions*, viii. 10.
[4] Hujwiri, 103. The Sufis were particularly liable to auditions. See on this Nicholson, *Mystics of Islam*, 63 f.
[5] Isa. vi.   [6] Acts xxvi. 13.

him wholly about, and illuminating him in mind and spirit through and through, until he was absolutely one being with the shining mountain. He felt himself penetrated with the divine Spirit, and, to use his later phrase, raised to be 'a begodded man.' "[1]

After Pascal's death in 1662 a paper bearing the following words was found over his heart. They obviously refer to his conversion, which led him to abandon the world and put himself under the direction of the Port Royalists:

" The year of grace 1654.
Monday, 23 November, the day of St. Clement, Pope
and martyr, and others of the martyrology,
the eve of Saint Chrysostom, martyr and others,
from about half-past ten in the evening until
about half an hour after midnight,
Fire.
God of Abraham, God of Isaac, God of Jacob,
not of the philosophers and savants.
Certitude. Certitude. Feeling. Joy. Peace."

There is here no suggestion of any voice or vision, but I cannot but think that the word " Fire " refers either to some photism or to another well-known automatism—the sensation of heat or fire which burns in the breast of some mystics at times of special exaltation. It has been described by the English mystic, Richard Rolle, in the prologue to his *Incendium Amoris*.

I have been unable to discover evidence for any photism in connection with non-Christian conversions, but allowance must be made for the fragmentary nature of the available evidence. The nearest approach to a photism is the experience of Moses of the burning bush. The dazzling play of light on the desert sands in his case, as in Paul's, would help to produce it. Among the Hindus the Yoga praxis naturally led to disturbances of the auditory and other nerves and to a variety of subjective effects. Here lay its supposed superiority to the method of pure meditation. There are frequent references in the Upanishads to

[1] Rufus M. Jones, *Studies in Mystical Religion*, 431.

a light flashing and shining.[1] The following passage gains in coherence if we may assume that the writer was referring to some photism he had experienced at the moment he won the insight which assured him that the long agony of life was ended :

"The body is the bow, the syllable Om is the arrow, its point is the mind. Having cut through the darkness, which consists of ignorance, it approaches that which is not covered by darkness. Then, having cut through that which was covered (the personal soul), he saw Brahman, flashing like a wheel on fire, bright like the sun, vigorous, beyond all darkness, that which shines forth in yonder sun, in the moon, in the fire, and in the lightning. And having seen him, he obtains immortality."[2]

Nor were auditions wanting:

"Other teachers of the world (as Brahman) think otherwise. They listen to the sound of the ether within the heart, while they stop the ears with the thumbs. They compare it to the seven noises, like rivers, like a bell, like a brazen vessel, like the wheels of a carriage, like the croaking of frogs, like rain, and as if a man speaks in a cavern."[3]

Nor have I been able to discover a case parallel to Paul's, in which temporary blindness ensued at conversion, though cases of psychogenic blindness are well known. The Great War produced a crop of them. Dr. Jung says: "Unable to conceive of himself as a Christian, and on account of his resistance to Christ, he became blind, and could only regain his sight through submission to a Christian—that is to say, through his complete submission to Christianity. Psychogenic blindness is, according to my experience, always due to an unwillingness to see—i.e. to understand and to accept—what is incompatible with the conscious attitude. This was obviously the case with St. Paul. His unwillingness to see corresponds with his fanatical resistance to Christianity."[4]

[1] *Kath Up.* ii. 5. 14 f., *Svet.* vi. 14, *Mund.* ii. 2. 10, *Prasna* v. 5, *Maitr.* vi. 20 and 26, vii. 11. It will be noted that all these citations are from later Upanishads. I am not aware of any similar passages in the older ones.
[2] *Maitr. Up.* vi. 24 (S.B.E. xv. 322).
[3] Ibid. vi. 22 (S.B.E. xv. 321).
[4] Quoted by Thouless, op. cit. 190.

168 Conversion : Christian and Non-Christian

Psychology no longer attributes to these visions, voices and photisms an objective reality, but regards them as sensorial automatisms, psychically caused and conditioned. They are by no means confined to the conversion-crisis, but occur at any period of the religious life, as the lives of Paul, St. Teresa, George Fox, Blake, Evan Roberts, Rabi'a, Chaitanya, Nichiren, and Honen (to mention only a few names) show. As is well known, parallel phenomena occur in secular life. A libertine and murderer like Benvenuto Cellini saw visions of angels when he was imprisoned in St. Angelo.[1] The appearance of these automatisms is not due to the Spirit of God, but to the subject's physical and mental condition.

Perhaps the most outstanding feeling accompanying conversion is that which most subjects have of being under a higher control. They are convinced that some influence from without has taken possession of them, and, triumphing over all opposition, has done for them what they could not do for themselves. This experience of an external dynamic raises important theological questions relating to the operations of divine grace, but at this point we need only set out the psychological evidence for this feeling of an external power impinging on the personality at conversion.[2]

In New Testament times this sense of a divine power operative in conversion is everywhere present. Paul, for example, is convinced of nothing so much as that in the full tide of his career as a persecutor he was apprehended by Christ (Phil. iii. 12), and his life forced into a new channel. In the following passage, which is evidently biographical, the same idea comes out: "For God who said, ' Light shall shine out of darkness,' has shone within my heart to illuminate men with the knowledge of God's glory in the face of Christ " (2 Cor. iv. 6, Moffatt). The apostle has here in mind more than the contrast between the darkness of his pre-Christian life and the light of his Christian life. He is also thinking of the moment when God said, " Let there be light : and there was light " (Gen. i. 3),

[1] Granger, *Soul of a Christian*, 161.
[2] For James on this feeling, see 226, 228, 243 ff.

Immediate Accompaniments of Conversion 169

and he chooses the figure of light bursting forth out of darkness to bring out the idea that his conversion was analogous to a creative act of God.[1] Precisely the same idea underlies 2 Cor. v. 17 (καινὴ κτίσις).[2]

Further, for Paul the vision of the Ascended Lord, the photism and the voice that accompanied his conversion, would be indisputable evidence of the presence and working of divine power. Whenever such automatisms find a place in conversion, they tend to heighten the subject's feeling of being under divine control. Hence, when a New Testament convert broke out into the glossolalia, he was called a πνευματικός, by which term was meant a man possessed by a πνεῦμα other than his own, and which had come to him from without. To speak with tongues was at one and the same time undeniable proof of true conversion and of possession by the Holy Spirit (see Acts x. 44-47; cf. ii. 14-21, xi. 15-18). As Principal H. Wheeler Robinson finely says: "A man who is converted in the New Testament sense is one who has surrendered to forces immeasurably greater than anything he has of himself; one who has awakened to an overwhelming consciousness of a spiritual world brought to focus before him in the Person of Christ; one who finds the little bay of his individual life, with all its little pebbles and little shells and little weeds, flooded by a tide of a great deep, over which the very Spirit of God broods."[3]

The *Tiruvachakam* of Manikka Vachakar time and time again ascribes his conversion to the all-sufficient grace of Siva. As the poet looks back on his past life, he is filled with wonder that Siva ever visited in grace such a one as he was. His tongue never tires of celebrating the divine grace that wrought the miraculous change, when "He came and made me His." The stanzas, quoted above (pp. 59 ff.) from Hymn XLI, will be sufficient proof of this, though we venture to add the following striking lines :

---

[1] Cf. Feine, *Gesetzesfreie Evangelium des Paulus*, 67.
[2] On this passage there are some good remarks in Gennrich's *Die Lehre von der Wiedergeburt*, 15-17. The passage presupposes, he says, "ein schopferisches eingreifen des allmachtigen Gottes."
[3] *Christian Doctrine of Man*, 322.

170 Conversion : Christian and Non-Christian

"To me, mean as I was, with no good thing, Thou didst grant grace,
That I, with mind erewhile embruted—pure One !—should Become commingling love, in soul-subduing rapture melt !
Thou camest in grace on this same earth, didst show Thy mighty feet.
To me, who lay mere slave—meaner than any dog—
Essential grace more precious than a mother's love !"[1]

"Thou only One, to Whom can none compare ! Thou light Shining within the very soul of me, Thy slave !
On me who knew not the true goal—of merit void—
O Love unique—Thou hast choice grace bestowed,
O radiant Form Whose splendour bright no tongue can tell !
My Wealth of bliss ! O Civan-Peruman !"[2]

"Afflicted sore by glancing eyes of silly damsels, soft of foot—
I stood, my mind with sorrow pierced ; and then Thy grace I gained—was saved—
Ev'n I. O Master mine ! Thou bad'st Thy servant come ; ' Fear not ! ' Thou said'st.
'Twas thus that grace was given to me : O Rapture ! Who so blest as I ? "[3]

The Maratha poet Tukaram thus sings :

"My selfish bonds are loosed, and now
I reach forth far and free.
Gone is the soil of birth and death,
The petty sense of ' me.'

"Narayan's grace gave me this place,
Where I in faith abide.
Now, Tuka says, my task I've done,
And spread the message wide."[4]

In her Introduction to the *Autobiography* of Debendranath Tagore, Miss Underhill has called attention to the presence of this feeling of divine control in the life of the Maharshi. She says : " That consciousness of an Infinite Life and Love pressing in on the soul, desiring it and soliciting it, which Christians call ' grace ' . . . runs like a thread of fire

---

[1] Pope's trans., 5.   [2] Ibid. 294.   [3] Ibid. 353.
[4] Macnicol, P.M.S. 80. Narayan is another name for Vishnu.

Immediate Accompaniments of Conversion 171

through these pages. We are made to feel with the Maharshi the inexhaustible generosity of the Divine Life pouring like a torrent into the surrendered soul."[1]

It is greatly to be regretted that, owing to the tantalizingly fragmentary nature of the records of non-Christian conversions, we are unable to cite further psychological evidence for the presence of this feeling of being under the divine control at the time of conversion. If, however, we turn from the documents which enshrine the personal experience of the converts to the doctrinal statements in which they formulated their faith, we find great stress laid on the doctrine of divine grace. Since the other sources fail us, we may here be allowed to argue from doctrine back to the religious experience which created it.

The notion of divine grace is one of the regnant ideas of the Mystery Cults of the Græco-Roman world. Those who submitted to the rites of initiation were held to be reborn by the divine power. The god had entered into them, had endowed them with a fresh supernatural strength, and had conferred on them a new personality. Even the Stoics, with all their stress on the duty of every individual to seek with unremitting endeavour his own moral perfection, felt the need of divine grace. "No man," says Seneca, "is good without God. Can anyone rise superior to fortune save with God's help?"[2]

In India the Vaishnava theologians have always made the grace of the deity one of their central doctrines. As Siva's theophanies are due to his grace and his desire to aid human weakness, so also are the incarnations of Vishnu. Among the Vaishnavas there has been much controversy as to the relation between divine grace and human freedom. Some have held that the grace of God is irresistible, and the soul remains passive till the grace of God comes to its aid, as the kitten waits for its mother to come and lift it up and carry it away out of danger. The other school holds that the soul co-operates with the grace of God, by seizing hold of God, as the young monkey escapes from

[1] P. xii.
[2] Ep. xli. 2. I owe the quotation to C. H. Moore in *The Beginnings of Christianity*, pt. i., vol. i. 252.

danger by clinging to its mother's side.[1] That such a debate should have arisen testifies to the Vaishnavas' abundant feeling of the divine dynamic impinging on their souls at the religious crises of their lives. We may surmise that some of them had had such an overwhelming experience of the pressure of divine power upon them that it cast their theology in a predestinarian mould, as it did the theology of Augustine.

Hujwiri tells us that the Sufis had a technical term, *Qahr* (violence), by which " they signify the reinforcement given to them by God in annihilating their desires and in restraining the lower soul from its concupiscence."[2] " According to high mystical theory," says Nicholson,[3] " repentance is purely an act of divine grace, coming from God to man, not from man to God. Someone said to Rabi'a : ' I have committed many sins ; if I turn in penitence towards God, will He turn in mercy towards me ? ' ' Nay,' she replied, ' but if He shall turn towards thee, thou wilt turn towards Him.' "

At the opposite extreme to the Sufi position is that taken up by the Early Buddhists. They set out to unify themselves without the help of any higher power. In this respect Buddha's own experience was made normative. The Pali books consistently represent him as attaining the Great Enlightenment by no wisdom or help higher than his own. His very last words were an exhortation to self-help :

" Behold now, brethren, I exhort you saying: ' Decay is inherent in all component things ! Work out your own salvation with diligence ! ' This was the last word of the Tathagata."[4]

His words a little earlier in the same *sutta* convey exactly the same idea even more forcibly :

" Therefore, O Ananda, be ye lamps unto yourselves. Be ye a refuge to yourselves. Betake yourselves to no external refuge. Hold fast to the truth as a lamp. Hold fast as a refuge to the truth. Look not for refuge to anyone besides yourselves."[5]

[1] On these two schools, see Barth, *Religions of India*, 226 f. ; J. E. Carpenter, op. cit. 417 ; and Macnicol, *Indian Theism*, 110.
[2] Hujwiri, 377. [3] *Mystics of Islam*, 31.
[4] *Maha-parinibbana Sutta*, vi. 10 (S.B.E. xi. 114).
[5] Ibid. ii. 33. See also iii. 66.

Immediate Accompaniments of Conversion 173

The testimony of the *Thera-theri-gatha* is all along the same line. Everything has come to its authors from their own exertions:

> " Happily rest, thou venerable dame !
> Rest thee, wrapt in the robe thyself hast made.
> Stilled are the passions that have raged within.
> Cool art thou now, knowing Nibbana's peace." [1]

> " And first as novice, virtuous and keen
> To cultivate the upward mounting Way,
> I cast out lust and with it all ill-will,
> And therewith, one by one, the Deadly Drugs.
> Then to the Bhikkhuni of ripening powers
> Rose in a vision mem'ries of the past.
> Limpid and clear the mystic vistas grew,
> Expanding by persistent exercise.
> Act, speech and thought I saw as not myself,
> Children of cause, fleeting, impermanent.
> And now, with every poisonous drug cast out,
> Cool and serene I see Nibbana's peace." [2]

Early Buddhism stands alone as the only great religion which has denied the need and possibility of divine grace. But the non-appearance of the feeling of a divine power impinging upon the soul, and the denial in Buddhist doctrine that men may expect to receive the help of divine grace in their endeavours after the higher life, present no difficulties to the Christian theologian. The Early Buddhist was prevented from recognizing its appearance by the axioms of his faith; for, in a matter like this, much depends on expectation and training. There is a natural tendency on the part of all converts to report what they have been taught to look for. These Early Buddhist converts shared the pragmatic agnosticism of the founder of their faith. Buddha freed his treatment of the sick soul from every trace of mysticism, and left no place in his system for prayer or divine grace. Though Early Buddhism is psychological through and through, it is satisfied with the bare facts ascertainable by psychology, and makes no attempt to go outside their range. Quite consistently, therefore, it took shape as a system of " self-salvation by means of psychology

[1] *Therigatha*, 16. [2] Ibid. 99–101.

without a deity."[1] It is curiously modern in its clear grasp of the truth that any advance in ethics must be based on psychology, and especially on a clear study and analysis of the nature of the mind in its intellectual, volitional, and emotional aspects. But it claimed that unaided human nature is capable of working out its own restoration. " It surpassed almost all other ethical systems in enumerating human weaknesses and vices,"[2] but it nevertheless continued to hold that human nature was sufficient for its own moral progress, and that every man could be his own saviour. In a word, its agnosticism and its psychology unite in the declaration that divine grace neither exists nor is needed by man.

There is no need, however, to doubt that these Early Buddhists were actually recipients of the divine grace whose existence they denied. God is everywhere present in grace, and the gift of His grace is never conditioned by man's race, logic, or creed, but by his ethical states and moral needs. " Whenever, therefore, the soul aspires beyond the commonplace it shares in the life of the Spirit."[3] In this connection it should be pointed out, as a fact of profound significance, that Buddhism has survived as the faith of millions only in its Mahayana form, the central feature of which is a most elaborate doctrine of divine grace.

This feeling of being under some external control is always very strong in a revivalistic *milieu*. Writing of the conversions which took place in the Welsh Revival of 1904–5, Fursac says [4]:

" The subject witnesses the storm without taking part in it, or rather he submits as a victim, who feels and suffers, but who cannot and will not resist. The force which determines conversion seems foreign to the individual and acts unexpectedly and without participation of the will; hence this appearance of the marvellous and the supernatural which arises from the phenomenon and the unshakable faith of the believers in the action of a superior power."

[1] Söderblom, E.R.E., Art. " Communion with Deity (Introductory)." Cf. also Mrs. Rhys Davids's statement: " Buddhism preached a doctrine of a regenerate personality, to be sought after and developed by and out of the personal resources of the individual through a system of intellectual self-culture " (*Buddhist Psychological Ethics*, p. lxiv).
[2] Prof. Anesaki in E.R.E. v. 449.
[3] Granger, op. cit. 54. Cf. John i. 9; Acts xvii. 26 f.
[4] *Un Mouvement Mystique Contemporain*, 66.

Immediate Accompaniments of Conversion 175

At this point the psychologist rightly claims that the suggestive power of an excited revival meeting is very liable to be mistakenly attributed to a higher power. Thus, during the Welsh Revival, every suggestion that came to the different members of the crowds then assembled was accepted as a prompting of the Holy Spirit; and, since one of the axioms of the revival was instant and absolute obedience to the promptings of the Spirit, some queer scenes were witnessed. In one meeting the same Holy Spirit which prompted one man to pray prompted Evan Roberts to suppress him.[1] Here, as elsewhere, we need to bear in mind that the intensity of any feeling is no criterion of its worth. It must be judged, not by its intensity, but by its fruits.

We have now seen this feeling of a higher help coming with a strange compelling and enabling power upon the soul at conversion in almost every religion, with the exception of Early Buddhism. The psychologist is naturally tempted to evaluate it. There are those who maintain that the feeling has nothing to correspond with it in objective reality. It is an illusion, beginning with the subject's need of a higher help and ending with the sense that such help has been given. In other words, it is a self-originated feeling, mistakenly attributed to outer causes—the feeling of "otherness" being due to the irruption into consciousness of forces that have long been incubating in the unconscious.

Strictly speaking, however, the right to evaluate this feeling lies outside the scope of psychology. All that psychology can with justice claim to do is to marshal the evidence for its incidence. The question whether there is an objective reality corresponding to the subjective impression belongs rightly to the sphere of metaphysics; and the answer we shall return to the question depends upon our *weltanschauung*, or view of the universe. Those who accept the Christian view of the universe will find no difficulty in answering in the affirmative. For them the psychological explanation does not rule out the religious one; for, as William James allows, it is open for theology to claim that

[1] Vyrnwy Morgan, *The Welsh Religious Revival*, 50 f.

the subconsciousness is one of the avenues through which the grace of God draws near to the soul.

Religious thinkers, who prefer to approach the problems of theology from the standpoint of the reality and pragmatic value of religious experience, will find in this experience of an external dynamic impinging upon them at what they feel to be the most august moment in their lives much to support their faith. They will never accept any explanation which explains away the most real thing that they know—an experience that is for them self-authenticating. Entrenched behind this experience they are invulnerable to all sceptical attack. On the other hand, however, there will always be a large body of Christian thinkers to whom no psychological feeling, however satisfying in itself, will ever give the assurance of epistemological validity.[1]

[1] See Galloway's *Philosophy of Religion*, 251–270, for some good remarks on the psychology of religion and the problem of validity.

CHAPTER XIV

THE PSYCHOLOGICAL MECHANISM OF CONVERSION

THE best method of studying the psychology of conversion is to examine individual cases that are more or less representative. We may take Paul as a representative of the type in which the crisis is sudden and the subject is entirely unaware of any preparation for the change. Paul describes his conversion as an abortion—an unnatural and violent change, due to a revelation of God's Son in him (1 Cor. xv. 8). He was in no way conscious, before the crucial moment came, of any leaning toward Christian discipleship or of any relaxation in his efforts to stamp out the obnoxious teaching. In the full tide of his career as a persecutor he was apprehended by Christ (Phil. iii. 12) and his life forced into a new channel. For him, as Feine says,[1] there are no bridges between the old and the new. But the modern mind, which is determined to minimize the catastrophic and to seek for continuity in every phase of life, discovers in Paul's pre-Christian experience the psychological antecedents of his conversion. "The lightning of Damascus strikes no empty void, but finds plenty of inflammable material in the soul of the young persecutor."[2] The crisis was sudden and unexpected by Paul, because it came with one of those sudden uprushes into consciousness of thoughts and feelings long incubating in the subconscious mind.

Such an explanation of the psychology of Paul's conversion might have been offered twenty years ago. To-day, how-

---

[1] *Das Gesetzesfreie Evangelium des Paulus*, 70.
[2] Deissmann, *St. Paul*, E.T. 123.

178 Conversion : Christian and Non-Christian

ever, we are able to go much further than this and to explain in greater detail the psychological mechanism [1] by which the change was brought about. In brief, what took place was a sudden irruption into consciousness of a complex which had been thrust into the unconscious by repression.[2] Before he became acquainted with the Christian faith, the dominating complex in the mind of Paul was what we may call a Pharisee-complex. His Pharisaic zeal is evidence of this. From the first day that he heard of the Christian faith what we may call a Christian-complex began to develop. All that he subsequently heard of the Christian faith only served to further its growth and to make it more closely knit. Since this Christian-complex was in antagonism to his cherished beliefs, a painful conflict was set up, during which the offending Christian-complex was repressed—that is, unwittingly separated from the rest of the mind and driven into the unconscious. Repression, so far from destroying the complex, enhanced its potential energy by cutting it off from the rest of the mind. This energy manifested itself in further feverish persecution of the Christians. In a state of tension, the apostle journeyed to Damascus, and on the way thither the power of the Pharisee-complex to resist the Christian-complex reached its limits. An explosive change took place in which the Christian-complex rose from its burial in the unconscious and became the dominant factor in the conscious life of Paul. The new orientation was bound to take place if the mind was to preserve its equilibrium; for no intensely painful complex, that is strongly repressed, can be kept permanently quiet in the unconscious. Sooner or later the imprisoned psychic energy breaks out and results either in some pathological state or in a complete rearrangement

---

[1] Though the term "mechanism" is used, no suggestion is intended that in the life of the mind an involuntary automatism rules as in Nature as such.

[2] At present there is some lack of agreement among psychologists as to the use of the term "complex." In these pages I have followed the usage of Hart and Tansley. The latter defines a complex as any "well-defined system of ideas and emotions created in the mind by the play of experience upon the primary forces of the mind—the instincts" (*The New Psychology*, 178). Other writers—for example, McDougall—restrict the term to acquired conative trends and settings of the mind, which are in some degree morbid.

of complexes, which restores unity and equilibrium to the mind.[1]

An exactly similar psychological mechanism appears to have operated in the conversion of Dayananda Saraswati.[2] In his case, however, the actual outbreak of the repressed complex into consciousness was helped by an external event, whereas in Paul's case it broke into consciousness when its development was complete. Brought up in a Hindu home, the founder of the Arya Samaj possessed what we may call a polytheism-complex. But all unknown to him a monotheism-complex had been developing through what he had heard of the Sthanakavasi Jains. This monotheism-complex, contradicting as it did his inherited beliefs, would be repressed, but it needed only some stimulus for it to break out into consciousness and dominate it. The needed emotional stimulus came when he saw the unclean mouse impudently running over the sacred emblem of Siva. From that moment he had broken with polytheism and idolatry for ever.

Cases similar to the two just considered abound. The subject is conscious of no leanings to religion, when suddenly the whole course of his life is changed by the adoption of religion. In all these cases careful investigation would reveal that the convert at some point in his career had been influenced by religious ideas, which left indelible traces on his mental life.[3] In the following case the subject had doubtless received many religious impressions in childhood and youth, and even in his manhood had continued to receive them, for he lived in a Christian land. When he went to church, he was led there, we may well believe, by the influence of a religious-complex, of which he was unconscious because it had been repressed.

"Once in an American Church, the clergyman, yielding to some sudden impulse, recited, much to the scandal and indignation of

[1] This explanation of how the change comes about is not essentially different from James's explanation of it as a change in the habitual centre of a man's personal energy. See *Varieties*, 196 f. The doctrine of complexes enables us to work it out more precisely.
[2] See above, 129 f.
[3] Coe (*Psychology of Religion*, 168) quotes S. H. Hadley as saying that the down-and-outs converted at the Water Street Mission in New York were men who were under the influence of religion in their childhood homes.

his congregation, 'The Charge of the Light Brigade.' Some days later a man called on him, and said : ' Sir, I am one of the survivors of the Balaclava charge. I have led a wild, bad life, and haven't been near a church till, by accident and from curiosity, I went into your church last Sunday. I heard you recite that great poem, and it has changed my life ; I shall never disgrace my cloth again ! ' " [1]

Other cases might easily be examined, but the conclusion seems clear that all cases of conversion, in which the subject is entirely unaware of any preparation for the change, are due to some complex, buried in the unconscious by repression, steadily developing till it overcomes all resistance and bursts forth into consciousness and becomes the dominant factor therein.

We may take the conversion of Augustine as representative of another type. In these cases the subject is keenly aware of a painful conflict, which ends in a sudden crisis, in which he makes a deliberate choice between two conflicting lines of conduct. Augustine's soul was divided and unhappy because of the struggle within his soul between two major complexes—the religious- and the sex-complex. This made the conflict much more dramatic than it was in the case of Paul. It is easy to trace in the case of Augustine the building up of the two constellations of ideas and emotions that we call complexes. The religious-complex began with the impressions he had received from his mother of the power and beauty of the Christian life. It was strengthened when at the age of nineteen he read, in the course of his studies at the University of Carthage, the *Hortensius* of Cicero. Philosophy came to him, as to many young men of the age, as a call to abandon vice and folly. Then came his mother's earnest entreaties that he should live a chaste life. " The loss of a friend at Tagaste gave him the first vivid realization of death, which marks an epoch in most men's experience, and he himself passed through a dangerous illness." [2] Next came the influence of Ambrose and his studies in Neoplatonism and the Epistles of Paul. These impressions were further deepened when

[1] Lord Tennyson's *Life* of his father, 717. I owe the reference to Jackson, *The Fact of Conversion*, 125.
[2] Montgomery, *Saint Augustine*, 55.

Psychological Mechanism of Conversion 181

he heard of the conversion of the famous rhetorician, Victorinus, and the story of the life of Antony and the two young courtiers who had renounced the world.

Augustine has spoken so freely of his sexual life that it is an easy matter to trace the development of his sex-complex. He fell into evil ways before he left home for the University of Carthage, where he lived a dissipated life, taking a mistress, who bore him a son. About a year before his conversion he put his mistress away, not because he was moved by any compunction, but in order to prepare the way for an advantageous marriage. "But unhappy I . . . impatient of delay, inasmuch as not till after two years was I to obtain her I sought, not being so much a lover of marriage as a slave to lust, procured another."[1]

Thus were the two complexes built up, and how acute the conflict between them was is known to every reader of the *Confessions*, and is revealed by Augustine's famous prayer, *Da mihi castitatem et continentiam sed noli modo*. Such acute conflict cannot be continued indefinitely, and the mind will use various means to put an end to the great emotional tension involved. The conflict may be avoided by thrusting the offending complex into the unconscious, or by the segregation of the two complexes into separate logic-tight compartments.[2] Augustine, however, chose another method. He brought the conflict to an end by choosing a course of action which meant the definite victory of the religious-complex. To this he was helped by the additional stimulus provided by the voice "as of a boy or girl" saying, *Tolle lege, tolle lege*, and by the verse of scripture which met his eyes as soon as he opened the codex of the apostle Paul : " Not in rioting and drunkenness, not in chambering and wantonness, not in strife and envying ; but put ye on the Lord Jesus Christ, and make no provision for the flesh." There and then he made the personal surrender of himself to God.[3]

---
[1] *Confessions*, vi. 25.
[2] The phrase is Hart's. See his *Psychology of Insanity*, 56.
[3] Thouless has a good study of the conversion of Augustine (op. cit. 197-200). He speaks of Augustine's religious-complex bursting into consciousness at the moment of conversion, but, surely, what we have here is not a conflict between a complex in consciousness and another

Augustine's conversion is sometimes regarded as an example of the self-surrender type, in which the subject relaxes all his efforts before unification comes to the divided soul. But the *Confessions* give us no hint that their author abandoned all his strivings for an attitude of pure receptivity. His conversion was a surrender to God, but his own view was that the surrender was made by a decision of his will, which decision was made possible by an accession of strength suddenly imparted to the will by the grace of God. He habitually, in after-life, regarded grace as an *auxilium Dei*, and a regenerate will as one of the chief blessings conferred by Christ. Candour, however, compels us to admit that psychology has something to say even on this point. It produces evidence of the existence of resources of power that are normally not called into use, but which are released when some exceptionally strong stimulus is forthcoming.[1]

From the purely psychological point of view, the conversions of Paul and Augustine resemble one another in that we have in both cases a struggle between two antagonistic complexes. There is, however, this difference. Whereas in the case of Paul the offending complex was repressed into the unconscious, in the case of Augustine both complexes were present to consciousness. Augustine brought the conflict to an end by the choice of a line of conduct which made the religious-complex supreme in his life; but Paul's soul was unified by the sudden uprising of the buried complex into his conscious life.

Many other cases could be cited in which the psychological mechanism resembles that which operated in the case of Augustine. In general, what happens is that two growing complexes in more or less acute conflict with one another render the mind divided and unhappy. Unification is

repressed into the unconscious, but an acute conflict between two complexes both present to consciousness. Nor can I follow Thouless in making Augustine's conversion primarily an intellectual one. It is much more likely that the great African's intellectual difficulties were what the New Psychology calls a rationalization of the conflict between his moral and religious ideals and his unclean life. Thouless recognizes this alternative, but rejects it.

[1] See James's striking essay, " Energies of Men," in his *Memories and Studies*

Psychological Mechanism of Conversion 183

brought about by a voluntary choice, which lifts one complex into a dominant position in the mind. The additional stimulus needed for making the choice often comes from some external event, but it need not do so. It did in the conversion of John Parenti, who was Minister-General of the Franciscan Order from 1247 to 1257. Before his conversion he was a magistrate in the neighbourhood of Florence, and had heard of the religious reformation going on in the Umbrian country and had begun to reflect upon it. The additional stimulus, which led him to the choice of the religious life, came in a strange manner. One evening, when walking in the country, he met a swine-herd in difficulties with his herd. The pigs refused to go into the sty and were running hither and thither. The man lost his patience and cried out : " Go in, you beasts ; go in, as lawyers and judges go to hell." This chance speech went straight to the onlooker's heart, and he at once abandoned his profession and entered the Order.[1]

Almost any external event may precipitate the crisis and help the choice. The following story is told by a man of education and gentle birth. He had been brought up in an agnostic home, but coming into contact with the Salvation Army had been greatly troubled about the state of his soul.

> "My conversion was brought about by the contrast presented to me between the General (Booth) and Bradlaugh, both seated in the same train . . . but one comfortably settled down to reading a *Daily Telegraph* and the General, having a care-worn look, scrutinizing everything passing up and down, as if they one and all (including myself) were objects of interest to him, and he was wanting to do them good."[2]

Here, obviously, the contrast between General Booth and the well-known rationalist was not the cause but the occasion of the narrator's conversion. His Christian-complex had been forming for some time, and was in conflict with his agnostic-complex. The contrast between the two leaders helped forward the choice between the antagonistic complexes.

[1] Father Cuthbert, op. cit. 180 f.
[2] Begbie, *Life of William Booth*, ii, 228 n,

184 Conversion : Christian and Non-Christian

Sometimes, however, the choice has to be made without the help of any such external stimulus. The conversion of the American revivalist, Finney, is a case in point.[1] He had long been labouring under a conviction of sin, and in great distress of mind went to a solitary place in a wood. " I was brought face to face," he says, " with the question whether I would accept Christ as presented in the Gospel, or pursue a worldly course of life. As I turned to go up into the wood, I recollect to have said : ' I will give my heart to God or I never will come down from there.' " The struggle went on for some time, and he exclaimed that he would not leave the place if all the men on earth and all the devils in hell surrounded him. At last the long conflict came to an end, and he walked home in a perfectly quiet frame of mind. Thus only after long mental agony, and without the help of any stimulus from without, was he able to make the choice which made the Christian-complex the governing one in his life.

We may now turn to an interesting type of conversion, common in Evangelical circles, in which the conflict between two opposing complexes is brought to an end, not by an act of volition, but by the surrender of all effort. In these self-surrender cases, as they are often called, strenuous endeavour seems worse than useless to bring the conflict to a close. It " only makes them twofold more the children of hell than they were before," says James [2] in a characteristic phrase. The inward change comes as soon as the subject relaxes all effort. Can we describe the psychology of this experience ? Various explanations have been given, but none of them are wholly satisfactory.[3]

In attempting another explanation, it should be noticed that two separate questions are involved. Why does voluntary effort defeat itself ? Why does the surrender of effort accomplish what volition fails to do ? The first question is not difficult to answer. Every time the subject makes a voluntary effort against his besetting sin, he calls forth the spontaneous suggestion that he will fall again into that sin. And since every suggestion tends to realize itself

[1] *Autobiography*, chaps. i and ii.   [2] James, 110.
[3] James, 209 ff. ; Starbuck, 113 ff. ; Thouless, op. cit. 172.

Psychological Mechanism of Conversion 185

in conduct, and since, moreover, "when the will and the imagination are at war, the imagination invariably gains the day,"[1] the subject soon realizes his fears. Hence voluntary effort, instead of freeing the mind from its evil habits, binds them more closely by repeated indulgence. With each relapse the subject falls deeper into the mire, for the memory of past lapses and fruitless resolves gives rise to the further suggestion that any cure of the evil is impossible. Thus the subject is increasingly paralysed by the suggestion of failure.

The second question is not so easily answered. It may be tentatively suggested that the psychological mechanism is as follows. When the direct assault on the besetting sin is abandoned, the noxious suggestion of inability begins to languish. The field of consciousness is now taken up with thoughts of Him to Whom the surrender may be made. Thus, instead of the suggestion, "I am doomed to failure," the dominant suggestion comes to be: "My success is assured, for the invincible power of God is on my side." This suggestion of power releases psychic energy that the will had been impotent to stir so long as the suggestion of inability operated. Before, however, the new suggestion can do its work, the mind must be freed from all tension by the abandonment of voluntary effort. In Evangelical circles the suggestion is rendered the more potent by its strongly marked emotional affect, since the surrender is made to a Person and not to a mere force; and, above all, to a Person thought of as One not only able, but also eager to save, and Who has shown His eagerness by an act of redemptive love. This suggestion may come to the convert in various ways. He is frequently told that those who want the new life can do nothing themselves to get it, but there is nothing God cannot do as soon as the surrender to

---

[1] Baudouin, *Suggestion and Autosuggestion*, 125. This is the Law of Reversed Effort, as formulated by the New Nancy School. It is stated more fully thus: "When an idea imposes itself on the mind to such an extent as to give rise to a suggestion, all the conscious efforts which the subject makes in order to counteract this suggestion are not merely without the desired effect, but they actually run counter to the subject's conscious wishes and tend to intensify the suggestion" (ibid. 116). The keen psychological insight of Paul had given him insight into this peculiarity of the working of the mind (Rom. vii. 7 ff.). Cf. Augustine's *Confessions*, viii. 10, 20-28.

186 Conversion : Christian and Non-Christian

Him is made. He also hears the repeated testimony of men and women who have undergone this change by trusting God to do for them what they could never do for themselves.

The psychological mechanism of these self-surrender cases appears to be similar to that which comes into play in cases where the psycho-physician uses re-association to cure a patient of some nervous habit, pain, phobia or moral disorder. A morphino-maniac, for example, is unable to pass a chemist's shop without going in and buying chlorodyne. The more he exerts his will in the attempt to cure himself the worse he gets. He is obsessed by the suggestion of failure. Under medical hypnosis he is made to picture himself victoriously passing certain shops where he gets the drug. Thus in his mind the idea of a chemist's shop, instead of being associated with the thought, " I cannot keep out," becomes re-associated with the idea, " I can easily pass the shop by." The psycho-physician accomplishes his cure by re-associating the morbid complex with thoughts of power, confidence, ability. He does for his patient exactly what Bishop Gore advises us to do for ourselves, when he says : " Act against sin, in Christ's name, as if you had strength, and you will find you have." [1]

It should, however, be noticed that before the psycho-physician can do anything in such cases, the mind of the patient must be calm and free from anxiety. " To attempt to stimulate a restless and worried mind with energetic suggestions," says a well-known practitioner, " is as futile as whipping a dying horse. When the mind is quiet and rested, only then do I suggest thoughts of vigour of mind, strength of body, determination of will." [2] Here we see the reason why all effort and tension must be given up in the surrender type of conversion.

In some self-surrender cases the subject is not enchained by any vice, but is divided and unhappy because of his fear that he may fall into some devastating sin, that will rupture his right relations with God. Bunyan and Brain-

---

[1] In a University Sermon printed as Appendix II to the later editions of *Lux Mundi*. For re-association in psychotherapy see Hadfield, *Psychology and Morals*, 148 ff.
[2] Hadfield in *The Spirit*, 108.

Psychological Mechanism of Conversion 187

herd are cases in point. The former had long given up his youthful habits of lying, cursing and swearing. Brainherd had been brought up in a pious home and no grave moral disorders had disfigured his life. Yet both were obsessed with the fear that they might sin and incur eternal damnation. In neither case was any effort of their own able to remove the great depression. In both cases the black cloud lifted as soon as they ceased their strivings, repudiated completely the notion that anything they could do would secure their right standing with God, and accepted the view that God Almighty in Christ had done all that was necessary for the salvation of any sinner. To use phraseology of their day, they accepted the finished work of Christ, " the righteousness of God without law," and passed at once into a state of " assurance."

It was a word of scripture that brought Bunyan's long conflict to an end. He had found many passages that suggested to him that he might commit the unpardonable sin. At last he found one that brought the right suggestion and filled his mind with the feeling of assurance:

"One day, as I was passing into the field, and that, too, with some dashes on my conscience, fearing lest yet all was not right, suddenly this sentence fell upon my soul, ' Thy righteousness is in heaven.' And methought withal I saw, with the eyes of my soul, Jesus Christ at God's right hand; there, I say, was my righteousness; so that wherever I was, or whatever I was doing, God could not say of me, He wants my righteousness, for that was just before Him. I also saw, moreover, that it was not my good frame of heart that made my righteousness better, nor yet my bad frame that made my righteousness worse; for my righteousness was Jesus Christ Himself. . . . Now did my chains fall off my legs indeed; I was loosened from my afflictions and irons; my temptations also fled away; so that from that time those dreadful scriptures of God left off to trouble me: now went I also home rejoicing." [1]

The apostle Paul's case was very similar to that of Bunyan. The crisis of the Damascus road needed to be supplemented

[1] *Grace Abounding*, Sections 229 f. Pratt (op. cit. 140 ff.) has an interesting but unsympathetic analysis of the cases of Bunyan and Brainherd. It is wanting in psychological insight through Pratt's antagonistic attitude to Puritanism in general and his inability to appraise a religious experience he has not himself shared—a disability to which every student of the psychology of religion is more or less exposed.

by another before final unification and happiness came. From his Jewish ancestry and training the apostle had inherited a deep sense of sin. Deissmann thinks [1] that in Rom. vii. 9–11 we have a record of the boy Saul's first recognition of the fact of his own sin and guilt; and that the law, death and sin early cast a shadow on the soul of the sensitive lad, driving him to the strictest school of Phariseeism. The only way he knew of winning the divine favour was by devoting himself to the keeping of the law. This he did with the energy of a nature that did nothing by halves (Gal. i. 14). In course of time he made the discovery that, try as he would, it was impossible for him to keep the law in all its requirements. He has described his struggle in an autobiographic chapter (Rom. vii.). It was an incessant and unequal struggle which always ended in humiliating defeat. This sense of moral failure appears to have turned into one of moral impotence soon after he had realized that the demands of the law had reference, not merely to overt acts, but to an inward moral and spiritual purity. Rom. vii. 7 points to a time when he realized that the law demanded an inward conquest of all unworthy thoughts and desires, and that was completely beyond his unaided power. In this moral *impasse* there was wrung from his heart the cry: "O wretched man that I am, who shall deliver me from this body of death?" (Rom. vii. 24). How long this state of tension continued we cannot say; nor is there evidence available to fix the exact point in his career when it came to an end. It may have ended with his surrender to Christ on the Damascus road, but it is rather more likely that it ended at some date subsequent to his conversion, as in the case of Bunyan. The absence of the doctrine of justification by faith from his earliest letters points in this direction. Rom. vii. 25, however, makes it clear that, after a period of great effort and strain, the apostle suddenly relaxed his efforts, with the result that spiritual equilibrium and peace came with equal suddenness. The entire futility of seeking to establish a righteousness of his own came home to him, and with it the recognition that the righteous shall live by faith; and by faith he means

[1] Op. cit. 93 ff.

that a man ceases from his own works that God may work in him and for him.

It might make for clearness if we kept the term "conversion" for the first decisive turning to the religious life, and called the subsequent experience, which brought the sense of assurance, the discovery of the way of faith. The two experiences often coincide, but need not. They did not coincide in the case of men like Paul, Luther, Bunyan, Wesley and General Booth.[1] It is, however, a matter of terms, for in no case did unification and permanent happiness come to the soul till the second discovery had been made.

In other conversions we have yet another set of psychological factors. There is no repression of a painful complex into unconsciousness, and no painful conflict between two antagonistic complexes both present to consciousness, but the psychological mechanism seems to be that a complex blurred and indefinite in outline suddenly becomes, by subconscious incubation, closely knit and sharply defined. Here again the development may take place gradually or it may be precipitated by some external event. The former seems to have been the case with Gotama Buddha. He was conversant with a number of systems put forward by different teachers as means of crossing the ocean of *samsara*. Some of them he had tried and found wanting, but during long years of patient meditation and inquiry he gradually built up for himself a new construction of the world, which, as he sat under the peepul-tree, suddenly became so sharply defined that he was able to allow it to take possession of his mind and drive out all opposing systems.

Similar is the case mentioned above of a group of lawyers converted by Finney. They had been brought up as Christian men. Some of them held office in their church, but they needed the revivalist's teaching about the plan of salvation to make their Christian-complex clear and definite. The preaching of the early Christian missionaries did much the same thing for Cornelius, the Ethiopian eunuch and Lydia. Many adolescent conversions are of

[1] Begbie, op. cit. i. 159, for the case of General Booth.

this type. Religious teaching has built up a religious-complex, and their religious awakening dates from the time when the complex became so definite as to become the ruling one in their mental life.

Here we light upon the explanation of the mental growth of those religious people who cannot date their conversion and are incapable of saying when they first became devoted to religion. These " once-born " souls have a well-marked religious-complex, but it has never been in conflict with any other complex. Its development under religious nurture has been so gradual that no crisis has occurred in their religious history. In them the kingdom of spiritual values has come " without observation."

As we saw in an earlier chapter, some conversions are best explained as a falling in love with the Divine Being. This is probably the case in many adolescent conversions. Are we, therefore, forthwith to declare that in these cases there is a sublimation of the sex libido into religious channels? Thouless thinks that this is so. The conversion of the adolescent is the sudden solution of the conflict due to a repressed sex-complex " by the sublimation of the repressed love instinct into religious channels."[1] Curiously enough, the only adolescent conversion Thouless examines in any detail is that of General Booth. But the General's conversion was of the volitional type. He had a gift for business, and meant to get on in the world and retrieve the family fortunes. The conflict in his case was between these ambitions and the feeling that he ought to dedicate himself to God. He settled the conflict in characteristic manner by deciding one day " to go in for God," as he said.[2] He was fifteen at the time, and there is not the slightest trace of a repressed sex-complex. His sex life was entirely normal. He fell in love with Catherine Mumford when he was twenty-three, married her at twenty-six, and had a family of children. Yet there are, undoubtedly, many adolescent converts who fall in love with Jesus Christ; but it does not follow that there is a sexual element in their love, unless we are prepared to go all the

[1] Op. cit. 223. Cf. 134 and 224
[2] Begbie, op cit. i. 54 f.

Psychological Mechanism of Conversion 191

way with the Freudians and maintain that all love is sexual.[1]

Are there, then, no cases of conversion in which the sex libido is diverted into religious channels? There are, but such cases generally possess pathological features. It can hardly be questioned that there was a sublimation of the sex instinct in the conversion of Madame de Guyon and Henry Suso; and, possibly, also in the conversion of Catherine of Genoa. Both Madame de Guyon and Catherine of Genoa were unhappy in their married lives at the time of their conversion. That the sublimation was complete in the case of the French mystic may be doubted. Her friendship with her director, P. la Combe, is a curious feature in her life. Of him she says that Our Lord made her know that " I was his mother and that he was my son." Suso's erotic phantasies are proof enough in his case.[2]

When we find celibate saints of either sex using the luscious language of the *Song of Songs* to describe their intimacy with Christ,[3] or the *Gita Govinda* and the lyrics of Vidyapati, with their full and unblushing delineation of every process in the commerce of the sexes, to depict their intimacy with Krishna, we may rightly suspect a sublimation of the sex libido into religious channels. We may also conjecture that, when a man or woman who has been living a life of free sexual indulgence is suddenly converted, the sex libido is sublimated. Varamukhi, the courtesan converted by Chaitanya, is probably a case in point. I summarize the account of her conversion given by Govinda Das:

"In the course of his travels Chaitanya came to Ghoga, near Ahmedabad. He performed his accustomed *kirtan* with the usual accompaniments of profuse tears, laughter, sweating, shouts of Krishna's name. He rolled over and over in the dust in his frenzy, and finally fell into a hole in the road. A wealthy courtesan, named Varamukhi, who lived in a gorgeous style with many attendants, had been watching through the window of her house.

[1] On this see a pungent note by McDougall, *Outline of Psychology*, 431 n.
[2] Delacroix, op. cit. 311.
[3] Cf., e.g., the saying of Richard of St. Victor on the Spiritual Marriage: In primo gradu fit desponsatio, in secundo nuptiæ, in tertio copula, in quarto puerperium." Cited by Miss Underhill, *Mysticism*, 165 n.

192   Conversion : Christian and Non-Christian

'Woe is me!' she cried, and came down, followed by her maidservant Mira, to whom she said: 'To-day I make over to you all my property. I have much wealth, but despise it all. To-day I become a beggar on the streets.' Then she let down her hair, which reached beyond her hips. The crowd was spellbound at the sight of her beauty, but Chaitanya, as became a *sannyasi*, closed his eyes. With clasped hands she begged him to cut asunder the ties that bound her to the world, and cried: 'Very sinful am I, a worm of hell. . . . Tell me how I shall get salvation; how shall I escape the fear of Yama ? There is no more use for this sinful body.' So saying she cut off her long hair, and, protecting herself from shame with a minimum of clothing, she stood before the Master with clasped hands. Chaitanya said: 'Varamukhi, I speak a few words to you. Keep them always in mind. In this place make a *tulsi* garden, and in the midst of it stay, worshipping Krishna.' The crowd then began to praise the courtesan, but her maidservant began to weep bitterly. With a smile on her face, Varamukhi said to her: ' Whatever wealth I have I give to you. Serve well all strangers that come. Keep in mind Hari's name and sit in seclusion. Commit no sin. Serve Radha Krishna with fond devotion. To love is good, but not illicit love. Make love with Krishna, Mira. Your body, mind, soul, all make over to Krishna. Then will you get Krishna's endless wealth. Keep no one's company but Krishna's.' So saying Varamukhi left all her possessions and her sinful life and went and made the *tulsi* garden." [1]

Varamukhi's counterpart among the Franciscans would be St. Margaret of Cortona, who, however, was content with one lover.

From what has been said it will be seen that the psychological mechanism of religious conversion is the same as in " counter-conversions," and in the secular life of the mind. From the purely psychological point of view, the same mental machinery was at work both in the conversion of Paul and the " counter-conversion " of the Italian philosopher, Roberto Ardigo, from Roman Catholic orthodoxy to freethought.[2] A prebendary of Milan Cathedral, his mind was early assailed by doubts about his inherited faith. These

---

[1] *Kadcha* of Govinda Das. Bengali text in Sen, V.S.P. ii. 1151 ff
It is worth pointing out that a Bengali Vaishnava work, *Premabhakti Chandrika*, advises sublimation. "The passions of the soul are to be employed for service to Krishna. . . . Flowing in material channels they bring misfortunes in their train, but in the heart of a truly spiritual man the so-called evil passions only bring ardour to the soul and heighten its religious felicities" (Bengali text and Eng. trans. in Sen., V.L. 231).
[2] See Pratt, op. cit. 126 f.

Psychological Mechanism of Conversion 193

doubts were suppressed, and the conflict manifested itself in a closer study of Thomas Aquinas and in polemical writings against the Protestants. One day, as he sat in his garden, the last thread that bound him to orthodoxy snapped, and he declared himself a Positivist. Here we have the formation of a scientific-complex, which in conflict with the religious-complex was repressed into the unconscious, from whence it suddenly arose and became the ruling factor in the subject's life.

No comment is necessary to bring out the psychological kinship between many a sudden conversion and the experience which led Sir Henry Jones, so long Professor of Moral Philosophy in the University of Glasgow, from shoe-making to a lifelong quest for learning. He left the village school at a very early age, and his mind was soon mastered by two ambitions—to become a first-rate shoe-maker like his father, and to become an elder in the little Calvinistic Methodist Chapel. A wealthy farmer's wife, and a Scot to boot, saw the lad's ability, sent for him and told him that he was not meant to be a shoe-maker, but should go to college and become a minister. But for a long time nothing she could say moved him from his fixed ambitions. Sir Henry writes:

"I continued to visit Mrs. Roxburgh week by week for some years, holding to my own views and sticking to my own purposes. . . . A time came, sudden as lightning, when my purposes went to the winds and hers held. . . . One memorable day Tom (a friend of his own age) was allowed by the schoolmaster and I by my father to have a holiday. Wombwell's menagerie had come to Llanrwst . . . and neither Tom nor I had ever seen a lion, or tiger, or elephant, or camel. . . . We went to Llanrwst early in the day, arriving long before the show opened. Then we took a walk along the streets of Llanrwst with one of my second cousins, called Sam Roberts, son of a tailor and draper in the town. Looking up the street, Sam saw a group of disreputable loungers hanging round the door of a tavern. Then he turned round to me and said: 'Look at your shop-mates, Harry. . . .' It was a perfectly casual remark on his part, but to me it was by far the most startling event in my whole life. I was stunned and helpless. The things that Mrs. Roxburgh had told me were true ! My shop-mates were disreputable. . . . Shoe-making held no future that could be respectable. Such were the thoughts that crowded in

194   Conversion : Christian and Non-Christian

upon me. Distrust and deep repugnancy at the very thought of spending my life at shoe-making took immediate and full possession of my mind. The views which Mrs. Roxburgh had been pouring into my soul week by week and year by year had accumulated like dammed waters. And now the dam had broken, and I was swept away as by a flood. . . . My whole life seemed to me to have been a mistake. . . . Only one thing remained. I would become 'something better than a shoe-maker,' or I would die in the attempt." [1]

It is significant that Sir Henry adds : " No one can pass through an experience like mine and deny either the reality or the bitterness of sudden and complete conversion."

There is a clear psychological kinship between the conversion of Buddha and Professor Hilprecht's discovery of the correct translation of an Assyrian text. " He went to bed on one occasion after a hard spell of work on the translation of an Assyrian stone, of which he had assumed a false interpretation, and woke in the morning with a new translation in his mind which turned out to be correct." [2] In both cases the final solution of a baffling problem came in an unexpected manner, after long-continued effort which had apparently been fruitless, but which had contributed to the building up of that constellation of ideas and emotions which modern psychology calls a complex.

The question is certain to be raised whether the psychological explanations here advanced are prejudicial to the religious view of conversion. In some quarters they may be keenly resented as implying that conversion is not an act of God. On reflection, however, it will be seen that they leave untouched the problem of the ultimate causation of conversion. It is not necessary to think of divine grace as independent of the laws of the mind in its operations. The laws which govern the working of the human mind are just as much God's laws as those by which the planets revolve in their orbits. It is surely a mistake to see the action of God only in the unusual and catastrophic, and to refuse to see it in ordered processes. Psychology can

[1] *Old Memories*, 70–73.
[2] See *The Spirit*, 207 f. Another better-known case is Hamilton's sudden discovery of the theory of quaternions.

Psychological Mechanism of Conversion 195

only demonstrate how God works; but it is not less God Who has done a thing when we have come to understand how He has done it. The confident assertion of the alienist, Fursac,[1] that we may look forward to the day when psychology will have proved that there is no more need of the grace of God to explain conversion than of Jupiter to explain thunder, will impress only those who accept his *weltanshauung*. The Christian Theist will remind himself of a kindred claim made not so long ago in certain quarters that the theory of evolution had given the *congé* to the Creator of the universe.

The term " suggestion," however, is one at which some minds take alarm, because it carries with it the suggestion of self-deception. There is no need for any such disquiet, for it " may be only another way of saying that God and man are conjunct, and that in the deeps of the soul, beyond our power of knowing how, divine suggestions come to human consciousness." [2]

As to those seeming reservoirs of energy which are stored up in the soul of man, psychology can do no more than describe their presence and their manifestations. The question of their *ultimate* source lies outside its province. There is much to " suggest that we are not merely receptacles, but *channels* of energy. Life and power is not so much contained in us; it *courses through us* . . . What may be its relation to divine immanence in Nature it is for other investigators to say." [3] It is a fact fraught with great significance that religion abolishes conflict in the soul of man and liberates its energies as nothing else can. Moreover, conversion can do instantaneously for the victims of vice what psychotherapy can accomplish only by protracted treatment. There is no vice that conversion has not been known to cure. Above all, " it is only a religious force which, in the twinkling of an eye, can so alter the character of a man that he not only then and there escapes and stands utterly free from tyrannical passions, but is filled full of a great enthusiasm, desires to spend his whole

---

[1] *Un Mouvement Mystique Contemporain* (Paris, 1907), 68.
[2] Rufus M. Jones, *Studies in Mystical Religion*, p. xxxiii.
[3] Hadfield in *The Spirit*, 111.

life in working for righteousness, and feels as if he had been fed on honey-dew and drunk the milk of Paradise."[1]

I have set down these psychological explanations with some hesitation, knowing that they will be resented in certain quarters. For myself, I am convinced that they are in no way prejudicial to the religious explanation, and do not prevent our seeing in conversion what Henry Drummond once called "the contemporary activities of the Holy Ghost." To attempt a purely psychological explanation of the poignant rebirth of some souls has been rather like carrying out a vivisection on the body of a friend. At the same time, it has often caused my heart to rejoice at the redeeming grace of God, and encouraged me to pursue with renewed vigour my work as a minister of the Gospel of Christ.

[1] Begbie, *Broken Earthenware*, 59.

CHAPTER XV

CONVERSION DURING REVIVALS

WE have hitherto dealt with cases of conversion in which the experience seems to have been original and unborrowed. When, however, we turn to conversion taking place in a time of revival, we are confronted with a different state of affairs. At such times conversions occur not sporadically, but in epidemic form, one following another in rapid succession as though by contagion. The Christian Church was born in an atmosphere of revivalism, and from time to time revivals have marked the course of its history ever since; but the revival is by no means an exclusively Christian phenomenon. Various religions have from time to time nourished the faith of their adherents by meetings with a strong emotional colouring. Davenport [1] has described such meetings among the North American Indians. The worshippers of the Thracian Dionysos induced in themselves a state of religious frenzy by their wild dancing, excited cries and savage rites. The Mystery-Religions of the Græco-Roman world, as we have pointed out already, used various means to produce a profound emotional effect upon the minds of their initiates. Bengal and Orissa in the sixteenth century were swept by a revival headed by Chaitanya, the apostle of salvation by devotion to Krishna. The Brahma Samaj in 1868 enjoyed a wonderful uplift and refreshing when Keshab Chandra Sen introduced into its worship the enthusiastic methods of the Vaishnavas.[2] The closing phases of the pilgrimage to Mecca, which gathers together crowds of Moslems, produce scenes full of religious

[1] *Primitive Traits in Religious Revivals*, chap. iv.
[2] See above, 65

emotion and comparable in many respects to those witnessed at camp meetings among negroes.[1]

In the present chapter no attempt will be made to discuss all the psychological features of revivals. We must confine ourselves to those features which bear upon conversion. Nor will it be necessary to consider at length the psychology of the crowd, though the conversions which take place in a time of revival are necessarily modified by crowd conditions. It is sufficient to say that modern psychologists are agreed that presence in a crowd involves all who are genuine members of it in the loss to some extent of their normal powers of inhibition. Their emotional tension is heightened, and they are more readily influenced by suggestion. The ability of the conscious mind to select and criticize is to some extent in abeyance, and the subconscious tends to take control. As a result, the crowd tends to hurry forward its members along a common path.

Investigation has shown that it is not possible for a revival to break out in any *milieu*. Every spontaneous outbreak of revival is preceded by a period of incubation. Where the conditions are not ripe for such an outbreak, the technique of the professional revivalist is designed to produce appropriate conditions. Before we examine this technique, the preparedness for the outbreak in the case of four spontaneous revivals may be briefly indicated.

The parallel between the conditions prevailing in the Roman Empire, into which the first Christian missionaries carried their message, and the conditions in England during the Commonwealth, when George Fox set in motion the Quaker Revival, is so close that they may be taken together. In both cases the times were times of religious ferment. Men and women in large numbers had broken free from their religious moorings and were sailing troubled seas with little to guide them to the haven of spiritual peace. They were dissatisfied with their inherited faith, and from it many had gone out. Some had gone out not knowing

---

[1] These scenes are well described in *With the Pilgrims to Mecca* (London, 1905). The name of the author of the book is not given, but it professes to be written by a Persian Moslem who has received an English education. An admirable account of negro revivals will be found in *The Souls of Black Folk* (London, 1903), by W. E. B. Du Bois, who is himself a negro.

whither they went, but all were mindful of a better country. In both cases there was the same medley of religious cults and sects. In almost all the fields of his labour Paul would meet with initiates into the different Mystery-Religions. In England during the Commonwealth there were the Independents, the Baptists (both Particular and General), the Presbyterians, the Fifth Monarchy men, with their millenarian ideas, the Muggletonians and the Seekers or Waiters. Modern research helps us to see in most of them, in spite of certain excesses, men and women of honest heart, filled with unsatisfied longings for a vital religious experience.

It cannot be doubted that Paul and Fox would find in these groups many whom long seeking had left in an expectant and suggestible state of mind. The conditions were therefore ripe for the outbreak and rapid spread of a revival. The preaching of Paul and the message of Fox and his Publishers of Truth came to men and women prepared for it, and in both cases the first converts came from companies of men and women in whose hearts religious feeling was already aglow. Paul seems to have won most of his Gentile converts from the "God-fearers," whose religious cravings had formed them into a fringe around the Jewish synagogues. George Fox won his first successes among the Seekers, who had banded themselves together in a fellowship of prayer to wait for a new outpouring of the Spirit. In both cases it was the existence of these prepared souls that made the outbreak of the revival, psychologically speaking, possible, and caused the preacher's message to fall like a spark on gunpowder.

In both cases, too, there was a creative moment when the revival broke out, followed by a period of rapid expansion. The creative moment in Quakerism falls in June, 1652, when at Preston Patrick whole congregations of Seekers went over to Fox *en masse*,[1] and, to use Oliver Cromwell's phrase, became "happy finders." Three and a half years later the Quaker message had spread through all the counties of England and was being carried into Scotland and Ireland.

[1] The story is told by Braithwaite in his *Beginnings of Quakerism*, chap. iv.

The cause of this rapid spread is to be found in the wide diffusion of companies of Seekers throughout the land.

In the history of primitive Christianity, Pentecost seems to have been the creative moment when the revival first broke out. Luke's account of Pentecost presents several difficulties, but it is clear that he intends his readers to feel that the movement, whose history he is recording, entered upon a new phase that day. The historical kernel of the narrative seems to point back to some memorable occasion when the little company, met for prayer in Jerusalem, first became conscious of the strange phenomena of the glossolalia. It is not difficult to see how highly suggestible the hundred and twenty souls then gathered together would be. Not long before they had gone through those wonderful experiences which had created their resurrection faith. Heterogeneous as they would be in other respects, a common direction given to their thoughts by united prayer would go a long way in fusing them into a psychological mass. Nor would the crowd of Jews from the countries of the Dispersion, and the "devout persons" who listened to Peter's speech, be in a less suggestible frame of mind, for not only was their attention focused in a common direction, but their emotional condition had already been heightened by the festivities of the Pentecostal season.

Pentecost was followed by a period of rapid expansion. A stay of three weeks in Thessalonica was sufficient for Paul to gather a considerable number of converts. This lightning success is sometimes compared with the much slower work of modern missionaries among heathen peoples. But the comparison is beside the mark. Paul did not preach to men well satisfied with their faith, nor was it his business to convince minds not specially interested. In most of his audiences the "God-fearers" and women would form the majority. He spoke, therefore, to men who were dissatisfied with their own position and were conscious of a clearly felt want. His message fell on a prepared soil. And when we remember that women as a rule are more suggestible than men, some light is thrown on the prominence of women among the apostle's converts

The same holds true of the Welsh Revival of 1904-5. Though the form in which it broke out was unexpected, it had been prepared for long before any outbreak was recorded. Many little groups of Christians had been united for years in earnest prayer for a revival. Evan Roberts, the leader of the revival, had himself been praying for thirteen years for a " baptism of the Holy Spirit." From the psychological point of view, no better means than long-continued, earnest prayer could be devised for charging the subconscious mind in preparation for the day when the revival would break out. Fursac rightly says: " Le Réveil n'est pas l'œuvre d'un Revivalist, mais de la population revivalisée." [1]

It is more difficult to demonstrate the preparedness of Bengal and Orissa for the Chaitanyite revival, as the available data are more scanty. But it is clear that Chaitanya appeared at a time when the people were weary of the prevailing monistic philosophy, and were longing for a personal deity and a God of grace. The degenerate Buddhism of the day was a spent force in Bengal. The horrors of Tantricism were to be found in many places, and the spiritual life of the people was at a very low ebb. Chaitanya's three chief disciples—the elderly scholar, Adwaitacharyya, the *sannyasi*, Nityananda, and the Moslem convert, Haridas —seem to have been pious souls who were waiting, so to speak, for the consolation of Israel, and, when the revival came, they responded gladly. Adwaita had long been grieved by the materialistic tendencies of the age. Himself a conspicuous scholar in a city of learning, he had long been troubled about the religious condition of Navadipa, where zeal for learning seemed to have excluded a vital religious faith.[2]

Conversely, the absence of a prepared *milieu* helps to explain the failure of some French pastors to transplant the Welsh Revival into France.[3] In the winter of 1857-8

[1] Op. cit. 176. Cf. Bois, *Le Réveil au pays de Galles*, chap. i. and pp. 71-73, and Morgan, op. cit. 41. Finney always laid great stress on prayer as an essential means of promoting revival. See his *Autobiography*, 38 f., 302, 363 ; and his *Lectures on Revivals of Religion, passim*.

[2] Sen, *Chaitanya and His Companions*, 30.

[3] Bois, *Quelques Réflexions sur la Psychologie des Réveils*, 94 ff., 17 n., 37, 67.

a revival swept with great power through the Northern States of America, but, in spite of anticipations to the contrary, it left the Southern States untouched. Finney somewhat naïvely gives his reasons for this:

> "This revival became almost universal throughout the Northern States. A divine influence seemed to pervade the whole land. Slavery seemed to shut it out from the South. People there were in such a state of irritation, of vexation, and of committal to this peculiar institution, which had come to be assailed, that the Spirit of God seemed to be grieved away. There seemed to be no place found for Him in the hearts of the Southern people." [1]

Finney's theological explanation may, or may not, be correct. The psychological explanation is that opposite interests kept the revival out of the Southern States. The minds of the people there were dominated at that time by thoughts which did not touch religion.

Turning now to the technique of the professional revivalist, we notice that it aims at three things: (1) Securing a suggestible audience by the creation of crowd conditions; (2) still further heightening the suggestibility of the audience by raising its emotional tone; (3) securing from the audience the desired response.

The process of obtaining a suggestible crowd may begin long before the revivalist faces his hearers. His reputation as a "soul-saver" will itself work wonders, especially if in these modern days it is spread abroad by the Press. Men like Finney, Moody and Torrey came before their audiences with all the prestige attaching to men who were known to have won thousands of souls. Their hearers were in a mood of expectancy. We select a striking incident from the life of Finney to illustrate this point. He preached one evening in a village school-house to a crowded congregation, and greatly impressed the young people who worked in the local cotton-mill, of which his brother-in-law was the manager.

> "The next morning," he writes, "I went into the factory to look through it. I observed there was a good deal of agitation among those who were busy at their looms and their mules and

[1] Finney, 370 f.

other implements. On passing through one of the apartments, where a great number of young women were attending to weaving, I observed a couple of them eyeing me and speaking very earnestly ; and I could see that they were a good deal agitated, though they laughed. I went slowly towards them. They saw me coming, and were evidently much excited. One of them was trying to mend a broken thread, and her hands trembled so that she could not mend it. I approached slowly, looking at the machinery as I passed ; but this girl grew more and more agitated and could not proceed with her work. When I came within eight or ten feet of her, I looked solemnly at her. She was quite overcome, sunk down, and burst into tears. The impression caught almost like powder, and in a few moments nearly all in the room were in tears. This feeling spread through the factory. . . . The revival went through the mill with astonishing power ; and in the course of a few days nearly all in the mill were hopefully converted." [1]

Obviously these young women expected something to happen as soon as Finney appeared. The most suggestive among them soon realized their expectations, though Finney, apparently, did not utter a word.

In some revivals absurdly extravagant claims have been made for the leader, all of which served to enhance his prestige. After his successes among the Westmoreland Seekers in 1652, George Fox passed on into the Furness district, and was the means of convincing the mistress of Swarthmore Hall, Margaret Fell, and her household. He was received into the family almost as a new Messiah. " There is extant a letter to him from Margaret Fell and other members of the household which shows the excesses of language into which ardent devotees might be led. It is in substance a plea for the return to Swarthmore of the young prophet, but contains passages of perilous rhapsody." [2] The following phrases addressed to Fox are specially noteworthy : " O thou bread of life, without whom our souls will starve." " O thou fountain of eternal life, our souls thirst after thee, for in thee alone is our life and peace." " O thou father of eternal felicity." In a letter written by Margaret Fell in 1656 to James Naylor, and intended to bring him back to allegiance to Fox as the prophet of the new movement, she speaks of Fox as " him to whom all

[1] Finney, 154. [2] Braithwaite, op. cit. 105.

nations shall bow," " him who is the promise of the Father to the seed." [1] Nor must it be thought that Margaret Fell and her household stood alone in this matter. Fox received several letters couched in this strain from other men and women.[2] It was the same tendencies, in their acute form, that brought about the disaster of James Naylor's fall. He allowed himself to be pushed by devoted admirers into extremes from which Fox's sturdy common sense saved him.[3]

The wildest reports about Evan Roberts were implicitly believed by thousands in Wales. People held that he could read their thoughts and knew the details of their past lives. Some thought he had the power of life and death. By many he was regarded as inspired, and it was deemed a sin to disobey his commands. In a chapel at Cwmavon he asked for the windows to be broken down, and was immediately obeyed.[4]

Bearing in mind India's fluid conception of deity, we need not be surprised to find that those who saw Chaitanya's ecstasies said: " Such beauty and such devotion can never be human. Verily, he is an incarnation of Krishna." " His power shows that he is God." [5]

During the revival at Monghyr some of Keshab Chandra Sen's more enthusiastic followers " prostrated and abased themselves before him most utterly ; they began to talk of him in extravagant phraseology, such as ' Lord,' ' master ' and ' saviour.' "[6] " From this point onward there was always in Samaj a party who honoured their leader almost to the point of worship." [7]

In all of these cases the appearance of a leader, for whom such extravagant claims were made and upon whom the seal of divine favour was believed to rest, would induce an attitude of expectancy in the minds of those who flocked to hear him.

[1] Braithwaite, 249 f., for the full text of the letter. Braithwaite's comments on it should be read to understand fully the situation.
[2] Ibid. 105, n. 1.
[3] Naylor's case has often been discussed. The most balanced treatment is in Braithwaite, op. cit. chap. xi.
[4] Morgan, op. cit. 57–61. See also Fursac, op. cit. 149.
[5] *Chaitanya Charitamrita*, Sarkar, 193, 211.
[6] Mozoomdar, op. cit. 111. [7] Ibid. 114.

When at length the revivalist confronts his audience, his first business is to transform it from a mere aggregate of individuals into a psychological mass—into a genuine crowd with its interest and attention fixed in a common direction. At first the audience is not homogeneous. Many may be in a mood of expectation, but not all. Some are preoccupied, some indifferent, some prejudiced or even antagonistic. The revivalist's efforts will fall short of full success if these people are not welded into a sympathetic unity. Singing in chorus is one of the chief means used for securing this unity. In the Torrey-Alexander mission in London in 1904, about twenty minutes before the meeting proper began, Alexander would appear and get the audience to sing. He was most insistent that everybody should sing. He would say, "Those who have never sung before in their lives must sing to-day." On one occasion he went so far as to point out two gentlemen who were not singing. Professor Bois, who was present, remarks that he was not a little alarmed lest he also should be pointed out. Others, doubtless, would share that fear and under its constraint would join in the singing. Psychologically viewed, this procedure was Alexander's method of breaking down the reserve of the unemotional members of his audience and of getting them to yield themselves to the influence of the crowd, so losing, in however slight a measure, their normal self-control. Singing in chorus was used to create a genuine crowd with the interest and attention of all its individuals focused in a common direction; and the audience was thus made ready for the preaching of Torrey.[1]

Alexander had to get his audiences to sing, but among a musical people like the Welsh the singing was spontaneous. Professor Bois points out that the Welsh revivalist leaders had a habit of coming late to a meeting at which they were expected. The meeting would spend the two or more hours of waiting in singing and prayer. Thus the leaders appeared only when the assembly was already excited, fused with a common, intense emotion into a crowd, and thereby made ready to profit by their intervention.[2]

[1] Cf. Bois, *Le Réveil au pays de Galles*, 150–154.
[2] Op. cit. 333.

Conversion : Christian and Non-Christian

Devices for capturing even the sensory attention have their value, since they help to fix the attention of the many on the same thing. Cutten [1] mentions an extreme case in which an American revivalist began his address with his coat, vest and collar off. In a few moments his shirt and undervest were gaping open to the waist. In the course of a special sermon on "Booze," he was in the habit of breaking to pieces a common kitchen chair. Similarly, it was a sound psychological insight which led General Booth to dress his followers in uniform and to send them through the streets in procession with bands playing and banners waving. But long before the Salvation Army had developed its characteristic methods Chaitanya had employed in Bengal and Orissa enthusiastic singing in chorus as a prime means of propagating his gospel of devotion to Krishna. His methods were essentially those of the revivalist, though preaching was not, as we shall see,[2] one of the methods used for spreading the new faith. He won men by a tempest of emotion and devotional praise. The *sankirtan* was the all-powerful instrument. The *sankirtan* is enthusiastic dancing and singing in chorus with instrumental accompaniment. It is difficult for a Westerner, who has never been to India, to form an accurate idea of a *sankirtan*, or to estimate its effects on those who take part in it. He needs to see one, either among the Vaishnavas themselves or among the Christians, for the *sankirtan* has passed into the Christianity of Bengal, and at one time Keshab Chandra Sen did his best to introduce it into the Brahma Samaj. We quote here a description from the *Chaitanya Charitamrita* : [3]

" At dusk the Acharya began a *sankirtan* ; he danced while the Master gazed on. Goswami Nityananda danced hand-in-hand with

---

[1] *The Psychological Phenomena of Christianity*, 190 f.
[2] Infra, 240.
[3] Sarkar, 4. See p. 130 for a description of a great *sankirtan* held at Puri by Chaitanya. For an account of the modern *sankirtan* from the pen of a Hindu scholar, see Dinesh Chandra Sen, H.B.L.L. 579 f. The parallel between Chaitanya's methods and those of certain of the Sufis is obvious. For Sufi ideas on music and dancing as a means of grace, see Hujwiri, 171, 416, 420 ; Nicholson, *Mystics of Islam*, 63 ; and Jalaluddin in the *Acts of the Adepts*, an English trans. of which is prefixed by Redhouse to his trans. of the *Mesnevi* (London, 1881), 27 f.

the Acharya, and Haridas behind them. This song accompanied their dance:

> ' How shall I speak of my bliss to-day?
> The Beloved (Krishna) has entered my temple for ever!'

With perspiration, thrills, tears of joy, shout and roar, they turned and turned, touching the Master's feet now and then. . . . So the Acharya continued dancing and singing for three hours after nightfall."

It was a frequent thing, during this enthusiastic singing in chorus, for the singers to exhibit many external signs of deep emotion. Some would swoon away in rapture and roll on the ground; others would embrace one another and laugh and cry alternately. The sky was made to resound with shouts of "Hari," "Haribole." As the tide of feeling rose higher, the singers, in the contagion of their joy and rapture, would imagine that Krishna himself was with them, and all would become "immersed in a sea of divine *bhakti*."

When Chaitanya, accompanied only by Govinda Das, was touring South India, his methods were essentially the same. He would enter a town or village and begin to dance with arms uplifted and to sing Krishna's praises, either in the open road or in the courtyard of some friendly householder. A crowd would soon gather, and he would proceed to manifest extreme emotion, laughing, weeping, trembling, perspiring, and shouting Krishna's name. He would cry out: " O Govinda, where is my Krishna? Get him and bring him. Show me where is Krishna, my life!" The climax came when he fell down on the ground, and after rolling over and over would lie as though the life had gone out of him. A better means of organizing the onlookers into a psychological crowd could hardly be imagined.

Once the audience have been welded into a crowd and their suggestibility thereby heightened, the next step is to increase that suggestibility. This is done by rousing the emotions. The emotions most appealed to by revivalists are fear and love. The appeal is usually made by preaching and song. Of James McGready, a leader in the Kentucky Revival of 1796–1815, it was said that " he would portray hell so vividly that persons would grasp the seats to prevent falling into the burning abyss which they saw yawning at their feet."[1] With Finney the appeal to crude fear came to an end, though he insisted upon the certainty of endless punishment. Moody sought to rouse the tender emotions by dwelling on the love of God, though he did not omit the sterner aspects of Christian Truth. During the Welsh Revival the appeal was almost entirely to the tender emotions. The same was the case with the Chaitanyite Revival.

Since the days of Moody and Sankey singing has had an undisputed place in the technique of revivalism as a means of arousing the tender emotions. The revivalist preacher frequently has an accomplished vocalist as his assistant, unless, like Gipsy Smith, he is himself a vocalist of no mean order. How effective Sankey's singing was may be seen from the striking testimony of a distinguished man of letters. Mr. A. C. Benson, in his *House of Quiet*,[2] writes:

> "The meeting was held in a hall in a side street; we went smiling and talking, and took our places in a crowded room. The first item was the appearance of an assistant, who accompanied the evangelist as a sort of precentor—an immense bilious man, with black hair, and eyes surrounded by flaccid, pendent, baggy wrinkles—who came forward with an unctuous gesture, and took his place at a small harmonium, placed so near to the front of the platform that it looked as if both player and instrument must inevitably topple over; it was inexpressibly ludicrous to behold. Rolling his eyes in an affected manner, he touched a few simple chords, and then a marvellous transformation came over the room. In a sweet, powerful voice, with an exquisite simplicity combined with irresistible emotion, he sang 'There were Ninety-and-nine.' The man was transfigured. A deathly hush came over the room, and I felt my eyes fill with tears."

The words of the solo used by Alexander to stir the tender emotions are of interest to the psychologist. Their effect

[1] Cutten, op. cit. 180.
[2] 4th ed., 53 f. Few, if any, will doubt that the Master of Magdalene is here describing an experience of his undergraduate days, and that the evangelist and his assistant were Moody and Sankey. In Arnold Bennett's *Anna of the Five Towns* (chap. v) there is a clever, but unsympathetic, account of a modern revival meeting, in which the effects of music and singing are noted.

upon an audience, already moved, could not be other than profound:

> " Tell mother I'll be there,
> In answer to her prayer;
> This message, Blessed Saviour, to her bear.
> Tell mother I'll be there,
> Heaven's joys with her to share,
> O Saviour, tell my mother I'll be there."

We have already pointed out [1] that the hymns used in the Welsh Revival tended to arouse the tender emotions.

At his *sankirtans* Chaitanya used to sing the lyrics of Chandidas and Vidyapati. Chandidas was a Bengali poet of the fourteenth century, whose lyrics dealt with every phase of human love. Vidyapati was born in the same century and wrote in Maithili, the vernacular of the Darbhanga district. Chaitanya used a Bengali recension of his songs, which deal with the love of Radha and Krishna. They are full of erotic sentiment, but this was spiritualized by the Vaishnava, as the *Song of Songs* has been spiritualized by Christians of all ages. Krishna is the god of love, and Radha, his mistress, is typical of the human soul. As Radha is happy only when united to her lover, so the soul is happy only in union with the divine. When Krishna deserts Brindaban and leaves his mistress suffering the pangs of separation, it is a picture of the dark night of the soul left desolate by God. So interpreted, these lyrics have always made a great appeal to the Bengali people, and do so to this day. "From listening to and singing hymns," says the *Chaitanya Charitamrita*,[2] "one comes to love Krishna." "I have seen," says Dinesh Chandra Sen, "Kirtanyas creating a wild scene of emotion among the audiences by the irresistible appeal of these songs; not an eye that did not shed tears, not a heart that did not feel throbs of pain and joy alternately at the references to the divine cruelty and the divine love." [3]

---

[1] Supra 138.   [2] Sarkar, 98.
[3] Sen, V.L. 196. As far as I know, very few of the lyrics of Chandidas have been translated into English, though it is understood that Dr. Rabindranath Tagore has a translation in hand. Dinesh Chandra Sen has printed the Bengali text of many of the lyrics of Chandidas and

210 Conversion: Christian and Non-Christian

The preaching of revivalist leaders is generally of a clearly defined type. It is not marked by proof or argument, but by affirmations skilfully repeated in a variety of ways. "Affirmation, pure and simple, kept free from all reasoning and all proof," says Le Bon,[1] "is one of the surest means of making an idea enter the minds of crowds." Professor Bois has remarked [2] upon the "mathematical certainty" with which the revivalist Torrey preached. The effect thus produced was increased by the fact that, when Torrey cited a verse of scripture, he always gave the chapter and verse from memory. This works powerfully on a certain type of mind that aspires to that peace which certainty brings.

In like manner, Evan Roberts never argued with sceptics in his meetings, but called on the people to witness and pray. In one case, instead of replying directly to a sceptic, he cried out: "Will all those who believe that Jesus Christ is God, please stand up." The effect produced was incredible.[3] Evan Roberts had substituted for his own testimony the testimony of practically the whole crowd.

Testimony has always been one of the chief features of the meetings of the Salvation Army. It is usual for several converts to give their testimony. They do more, however, than simply affirm their faith. They tell the auditors their experiences, their joys and sorrows; they speak of their weaknesses, their besetting sins and failures, and of tempta-

---

Vidyapati in vol. ii. of his *Vanga Sahitya Parichaya* (Calcutta, 1914). He translates a few lyrics and gives their mystical interpretation in V.L. 203 ff.; see also 129–134. Grierson has translated twenty-two Vaishnava hymns in the J.A.S.B. of 1884, and has indicated the allegorical interpretation of each. He has also translated a few of Vidyapati's lyrics in his *Maithili Language, Part II., Chrestomathy and Vocabulary*. Beames translated six lyrics by Vidyapati and two by Chandidas in the *Indian Antiquary* for 1873, 37 ff. and 187 ff. In 1915 Dr. Ananda Coomaraswamy published a translation of more than a hundred of Vidyapati's songs under the title, *Vidyapati: Bangiya Padabali, Songs of the Love of Radha and Krishna*. The lyrics chosen for translation seem to be among the most erotic of Vidyapati's songs, and the average reader will be not a little puzzled as to how these poems could have played so great a part in a genuine religious revival. But before passing a final judgment, he should read the moving incident narrated by Dinesh Chandra Sen, which shows better than anything else I know how the pious Vaishnavas spiritualize these glowing lyrics. See H.B.L.L. 127 ff.

[1] *The Crowd*, 141. [2] Op. cit. 157–9.
[3] Ibid. 429. See also Finney, 116 f., for a good instance of the power of testimony.

tions hitherto irresistible, but now overcome by the grace of Christ. They speak of their loved ones, fathers, mothers, husbands, wives and children, who are not yet converted and for whose conversion their whole soul longs. As they speak, many a responsive chord is touched in the hearts of their hearers.

The preacher's affirmations are often repeated in the hymns that are sung, in which case the rhythm and the music to which they are set makes them even more effective. The repetition of musical refrains, such as, "For you I am praying," "Come, sinner, come," as the meeting was being "tested" in the Welsh Revival, must have had great suggestive power, especially when the audience accompanied the singing with joyous clapping of their hands.

Chaitanya, likewise, never argued with the monists and other opponents of *bhakti-marga*. He overwhelmed them with testimonies, both spoken and sung, to Krishna's grace.

The members of a crowd receive suggestions, not only from the leader, but also from each other. In a religious crowd there are generally some who give vent to their feelings by exclamations. The Welsh audiences often resounded with "Diolch Iddo"; English audiences with "Hallelujah," "Amen," "Praise God"; Vaishnava audiences with "Hari," "Haribole."[1] These exclamations are often taken up by others, and a general heightening of emotional tone results. The sight of tense, drawn faces around one and the noise of the applause tend in the same direction.

The suggestibility of the audience will be further increased if abnormal phenomena break out. Physical manifestations, beginning with the most suggestible persons present, and spreading by imitation and contagion, have been a frequent concomitant of revival meetings. In primitive Christianity the glossolalia was the most frequent automatism. In the Edwardian Revival in New England in 1734 weeping, crying, wailing, shrieking and fainting were common. During the early part of Wesley's ministry "fallings" frequently occurred. People would suddenly fall flat as if they had been shot, and suffered excruciating pain. The

[1] Hari is another name for Krishna. Haribole means "Cry Hari."

212 Conversion : Christian and Non-Christian

Kentucky Revival was remarkable for the jerks. Those who were affected jumped like frogs or bounded about like live fish out of water. The Society of Friends got the name " Quakers " from the quaking which attacked so many of Fox's converts. In the Welsh Revival physical manifestations were few, the most noteworthy one being the holy laugh. In the Chaitanyite Revival they were many, and included weeping, laughing, shouting, sweating, horripilation, trembling, falling on the ground, and rolling over and over in the dust. When a number were affected at one time, there were scenes of indescribable confusion.[1]

The rise of these automatisms is due to the breaking down of the ordinary powers of inhibition, and once they occur they influence all who see them and put them in a more suggestible frame of mind than ever, because in revivalist circles they have almost invariably been regarded as an indubitable sign of the Spirit's presence and power. More than once in his *Autobiography* Finney notices this. After one such outbreak he writes : " Everywhere I found a state of wonderful conviction of sin and alarm for their souls." " Many saw it and feared." After another outbreak he writes : " This . . . scattered conviction amongst the whole of them." [2]

When, by means of the methods we have just described, the audience has become extremely suggestible, the time is ripe for the revivalist to secure conversions. Repentant sinners are asked to show by some overt act that they have decided to commit themselves to the new way of life. This act is generally some quite insignificant reaction, such as raising the hand, rising to one's feet, answering a simple question in the affirmative, but sometimes it involves coming forward to the penitent form. Chaitanya was content if the convert uttered Krishna's name or a few words in his praise.[3]

The means used to secure this reaction are of interest

---

[1] *Kadcha* of Govinda Das. Bengali text in Sen, V.S.P. ii. 1147 ff., 1151 f., 1156 ff.
[2] Finney, 52, bis. 135.
[3] The *Chaitanya Charitamrita* says the name of Krishna ' is equivalent to Krishna's self. The name, the image, the self of a god are all one ; there is no distinction between them " (Sarkar, 209).

to the psychologist. The revivalist generally begins with a personal appeal. Sometimes he is commanding and authoritative, but more often he is tender and pleading, His confident, commanding tone and manner help to produce an effect over and above what he says; while pathetic, pleading tones induce the tender emotions. When Torrey had finished preaching he would ask all those who wished to accept Christ that night to stand up for a moment and show themselves to him. As each person stood up, he said : " God bless you, sir (madam)." Then he would continue in pressing monotones to ask : " Is there not yet another who wishes to accept Christ to-night ? " " The replies come, slowly at first, then more and more quickly and more numerous. Generally this crescendo is in its turn followed by a decrescendo. And when the people begin to rise more slowly and more sparsely and at longer intervals, Torrey redoubles his insistence and pressure. Alexander sings a solo in his beautiful baritone voice with such clear articulation that one does not lose a single word. And the number of conversions increases for a moment. When it beings to drop again, Torrey modifies his attack."[1] This Torrey did by dividing the assembly into groups and by taking these groups singly one after the other. He would appeal to those in the different aisles, those in the galleries and so on. At a meeting for young people, he successively appealed to those of eighteen years, then to those between fifteen and eighteen, then to those between thirteen and fifteen, and finally to those of twelve and thirteen years. Psychologically viewed, each step in the above procedure would tend to increase the pressure of the crowd on suggestible minds.

Torrey next sought to deepen the impression thus created by asking all those who had stood up to stand up again together. Most responded, but some did not. They were noticed by assistants scattered over the meeting, and in response to their pressure the defaulters rose. They went to the foot of the platform, where Torrey briefly exhorted them and got them to repeat in a loud voice : " I accept Jesus Christ as my Saviour and my King." Next the

[1] Bois, op. cit. 160.

Christian workers spread themselves throughout the hall and begged all to be converted. The first six benches became an inquiry room, while all over the hall might be seen little groups of twos and threes, kneeling and praying, struggling with troubled souls. Many of the latter were very much moved. This emotion communicated itself to others, and what was going on before the eyes of all acted powerfully on all who were present. At this point the attack was again modified, for Torrey now gave over the meeting to Alexander and the soloists.

Alexander stepped forward and asked all who had a mother in heaven to hold up their hands. When a large number had responded, a young man came forward and sang the lines quoted above (p. 209) as a solo. The effect was profound. Alexander then said: " Surely there are some who will wish to give their hearts to Jesus Christ while our brother sings the last verse again ? " Then, as the soloist sang, Alexander in a soft voice would ask at intervals : " Are there not some who wish to give their hearts to Jesus ? " As Professor Bois remarks, to many it came like an appeal from another world, like the voice of their beloved mother herself. Numbers, who had been able to resist the demands of Torrey, could not resist these touching recollections of their mother and of their early piety, and they stood up. " It is thus that Alexander supplements Torrey. He goes before him to prepare souls to listen to him ; he follows him to add emotional impression to the effect above all intellectual produced by Torrey." [1]

The methods adopted in the Welsh Revival were less deliberate and more spontaneous than those used by Torrey and Alexander, but from the psychological point of view they were the same. After the meeting had gone on for some hours and had, by continuous singing and prayer, worked itself into a state of great excitement, a pastor or deacon would " test " the meeting. He would ask all who were church-members to rise. A large number would do so and look around to find those who remained seated. The neighbours of the unconverted would then speak with them, kneel beside them and pray, while the occupant of

[1] Bois, op. cit. 154.

the pulpit urged all to prayer. As the conversion of one after another was announced, the "Diolch Iddo" sounded out. There were no inquiry rooms in which the troubled souls might be given guidance. They remained in their places in the midst of the meeting, and the whole assembly joined in the spiritual combat with its prayers and singing. "This is powerfully dramatic, sometimes more tragic than one can say, and at other times full of triumphant joy."[1]

At a meeting in Aberdare, at which Professor Bois was present, when believers were asked to rise, a young girl remained seated in one of the aisles. Her whole attitude and the expression on her face showed that she was much tormented. One of the revivalist ladies came down from the pulpit and sat beside her and exhorted her to give herself to Christ. At the same instant dozens of simultaneous prayers burst forth from every corner of the chapel demanding of God to convert this soul and give it peace. After the prayers the first verse of the hymn, "Who is a pardoning God like Thee?" was sung a dozen times or more. Emotion gripped every heart, and while the revivalist lady continued to supplicate the young girl, whose face was bathed in tears, the assembly repeated again its hymns and prayers. Before long the two women knelt on the floor to pray, and a delirious joy possessed the meeting. "Diolch Iddos" sounded out; some clapped their hands in their joy, others sang standing with their arms outstretched to the sky. In this case we have the whole suggestive power of an excited assembly centred on one poor soul. It does not surprise us to learn that some in similar circumstances took refuge in flight. The nervous tension was more than they could bear.[2]

In revivals where psycho-physical automatisms were a normal concomitant, it was not necessary for the leaders to resort to the elaborate procedure of the modern professional revivalist. The Holy Spirit Himself was thought to test the meeting,[3] and pointed out those who were in need of conversion by throwing them on the ground or rending them with strong cries and tears, etc. That many

[1] Bois, op. cit. 191. [2] Ibid. 193.
[3] Cf. Bois, *Quelques Réflexions sur la Psychologie des Réveils*, 121.

sinners so affected were genuinely converted need not be doubted, for they shared the accepted belief that what had befallen them was due to direct divine intervention.[1]

Similarly, Chaitanya never asked his hearers to show that they now desired to live a life of devotion to Krishna. He waited till the ecstasies of his own devotion had convinced them of the truth of his teaching and had aroused a like spirit of *bhakti* in them. So powerfully suggestive were his methods that he rarely had to wait long before many were so far carried away as to imitate him in song and dance. We have space to cite three cases only :

" In the course of his journey through the South, Chaitanya came to Travancore, whose Raja, Rudrapati, sent a messenger to him, saying that he desired to see him. The saint turned the messenger away, with the result that the king himself came to see him. Chaitanya greeted him with the words: ' You are very learned, but I know nothing but Radha and Krishna.' He then danced till he fell down in a swoon. The king picked him up and at once began to manifest in the highest degree all the usual signs of *bhakti*. He wept profusely, the hair of his body stood on end with intense delight, and he fell rolling in the dust till his body became grey with it. ' When,' says Govinda Das, ' my Nimai saw the king's *bhakti*, he said: "Come, brother. he is the very pupil of my eye, whose eyes flow with tears at the mention of the name of Hari. Know this for certain, O King, that my soul is satisfied on seeing your *bhakti* ! " ' "[2]

" At Chandipur, on the Northern Border of Mysore, Chaitanya fell in with a certain Iswar Bharati Gossain, who, disgusted with the world, had some years previously become a *sannyasi*. He was greatly puffed up with pride in his learning and began to ridicule Chaitanya, who, with characteristic humility, offered him a certificate of victory, at the same time urging him to give up his philosophy and take up with Krishna. Then the Master, says Govinda Das, closed his eyes and began to manifest all the usual signs of intense *bhakti*. ' O Krishna,' he cried, ' where are you ? O Merciful Lord, give us *bhakti* and purify our hearts.' Seeing a tamal-tree, he went and clasped it with his arms. When Iswar Bharati saw these manifestations, he fell at Chaitanya's feet and

---

[1] When Christians of good standing were affected, it was assumed that they were backsliders in need of conversion (see, e.g., the case recorded by Finney, *Autobiography*, 52). The perils of such an assumption are obvious. One has a good deal of sympathy with the lady mentioned by Finney. She was probably more suggestible than sinful.

[2] *Kadcha*, Bengali text in Sen, V.S.P. ii. 1147 ff. Nimai is another name for **Chaitanya.**

said: ' I do not want to reason with you. Now have I the thirst for Krishna. My prayer is that you give me this incomparable jewel of *bhakti*.' Chaitanya did not hear, but kept on weeping. Suddenly his body became rigid and he fell on the ground rolling in the dust. This was more than the philosopher could bear. He burst into tears. Then the Master showed him mercy and placed his hand on his back. At his touch Iswar Bharati became filled with the sentiment of Krishna *bhakti*." [1]

" Arrived at a wood near Poona, Chaitanya declared his intention of entering it. The people tried to dissuade him on the ground that it was haunted by dacoits. Paying no heed to their entreaties, he entered and sat at the foot of a tree. Soon Naroji, a Brahman, who had turned dacoit, arrived on the scene and asked Chaitanya to come to his house. The saint refused, whereupon Naroji ordered his men to bring food for the *sannyasi*. Great heaps of it were brought, which made the mouth of Govinda Das water, so he naïvely tells us. But the sight of the food had no such effect on Chaitanya, who became lost in the love of Krishna and in his dancing scattered the food in all directions. He was taken to task for this by two or three who were present. Naroji, however, said: ' I have never seen such a *sannyasi*, at the sight of whom I am greatly troubled. Who can say the sins I have committed ? Why have I to-day the desire to become a *sannyasi* ? ' At these words Chaitanya's tears began to flow, and, overpowered with his love for Krishna, he fell on the ground. Naroji exclaimed: ' What *mantra* have you uttered that it has produced this effect on me that I do not wish to live any longer in this forest in sin ? I am now sixty years old. I shall flee sin and renounce the world. I am wicked, though a Brahman's son. . . . Why should I commit any more sin ? . . . I will no longer be leader of this band of dacoits.' So saying he looked at his followers, threw away his weapons, and followed Chaitanya." [2]

At times the *sankirtan* swept whole crowds off their feet and they professed faith in Krishna. After once seeing the ecstasies of Chaitanya, many " could not return home, as they became almost mad, chanting Krishna's name, dancing, weeping and rolling on the ground." [3] At a great *sankirtan* held at Puri on the day of the Car Festival there were scenes of wildest excitement. When Chaitanya fell down in a fit and began to foam at the mouth, one of his followers, " mad with passion for Krishna, collected and

[1] *Kadcha*, Bengali text in Sen, op. cit. ii. 1156 ff.
[2] Ibid. ii. 1159.
[3] Sarkar, 193. See also 228, 56–59.

drank up that froth: highly fortunate was he."[1] The sight of this particular *sankirtan*, we are told, "drew the hearts of all; with the nectar of love, he moistened their minds. All the servitors of Jagannath, all the courtiers of the king, the pilgrims, the residents of Puri—all marvelled at the Master's dance and rapture, and all felt devotion to Krishna."[2]

At times the suggestive power of the crowd operates so strongly that even scoffers are converted. In 1652 George Fox spoke against steeple-houses in his usual strain in the church at Tickhill, in Yorkshire. Feeling ran high, and the parish-clerk struck him in the face with a Bible, causing the blood to gush forth. The people dragged Fox outside, and after beating him severely, threw him over a hedge. But he was nothing dismayed:

"So when I was got upon my legs I declared to them the word of life . . . and the priest and people coming by the house I went forth with friends into the yard and there I spoke to the priest and people. And the priest scoffed at us and called us Quakers, but the Lord's power was so over them all, and the word of life was declared in so much power and dread to them, that the priest fell a trembling himself, that one said to him: ' Look how the priest trembles and shakes. He is turned a Quaker also.' "[3]

Beside this entry from George Fox's Journal we may set the entry in Wesley's Journal for May 1, 1739:

"Many were offended again, and indeed much more than before. For at Baldwin Street my voice could scarce be heard amidst the groanings of some and the cries of others calling aloud to Him that is ' mighty to save.' A Quaker who stood by was not a little displeased at the dissimulation of those creatures, and was biting his lips and knitting his brows, when he dropped down as thunder-struck. The agony he was in was even terrible to behold. We besought God not to lay folly to his charge. And he soon lifted up his head and cried aloud, ' Now I know that thou art a prophet of the Lord.' "

During the Welsh Revival of 1904-5 it was no uncommon thing for mockers to be converted. At a meeting in a Welsh

---
[1] Sarkar, 152. Those who have seen the frenzy of the crowd at this festival will suspect no exaggeration here.
[2] Ibid. 154.
[3] *Cambridge Journal*, i. 36. I have modernized the spelling, etc.

Conversion during Revivals 219

chapel in London an Englishman was much amused by the gestures of the Welsh during their prayers. Two members of the assembly began to pray for him in a loud voice. This increased rather than diminished his amusement. Then one man present denounced him as a " mocker " and " no gentleman." Soon the whole assembly was at prayer demanding the conversion of the mocker, who in two minutes was on his knees. Amid indescribable enthusiasm and many cries of " Diolch Iddo," he said on rising that he gave himself to God.[1]

Side by side with these three Christian conversions of scoffers we may set the story of the conversion by Chaitanya of the famous Vedantic scholar, Prakashananda, who lived in Benares. A Maratha Brahman told him that Chaitanya had arrived in the city, on his way to Brindaban.

" The philosopher laughed much and scoffed at the Brahman, saying : ' I have heard that there is a *sannyasi* in Bengal, an emotionalist, a disciple of Keshav Bharati and a fraud on the public. He is named Chaitanya, and with his emotional band he roams over the country dancing. . . . He is *sannyasi* in name only, but really a great wizard. But his stock-in-trade of sentimentality will not sell at Kashi! Attend to Vedanta ; do not resort to him ! The companionship of the wild man will ruin you in life and death.' "[2]

Chaitanya and the Vedantist do not appear to have met until the former was again in Benares on his return journey from Brindaban. Moved, doubtless, by curiosity, Prakashananda came to the spot where Chaitanya was singing and dancing and manifesting the usual signs of ecstatic devotion. The scholar was soon carried away by contagion, and clasped the Master's feet, saying : " By touching your feet I have washed away all the sin of my former abuse of you."[3]

In each of the above four cases we have a man struggling against his suggestibility and in the end being compelled to yield. Wesley's picture of the Quaker's struggle is

[1] Bois, *Le Réveil*, 221. Very interesting are the instances on record in which the power of suggestion appears to operate outside the meeting, and by a kind of telepathic influence, to affect persons not present for whom the assembly is praying (see Bois, 225 f., and Fursac, op. cit. 40).
[2] Sarkar, 208. [3] Ibid. 309.

extraordinarily graphic. The Quaker was fearful lest he also should be attacked by the disorder, and his very fear acted as a powerful suggestion.

It has often been pointed out that the methods of the revivalist are essentially those of the hypnotist. As is well known, when a patient is in a state of hypnosis, the critical powers of the mind are inhibited and the mind is in such a condition of receptivity that almost any idea introduced into it is unquestioningly accepted and for the time being holds complete sway. Very similar is the state of all who are genuine members of an excited crowd. In their high suggestibility they resemble a patient in a state of hypnosis. Indeed, in a highly excited crowd suggestion operates with such force as to produce a state of hypnosis in a waking condition—a state in which almost any suggestion will be accepted. In popular speech, the crowd hypnotizes its members. It should further be remarked that the crowd is brought into this condition by precisely the same means that are used for inducing hypnosis, i.e. by narrowing down the field of consciousness. Hence the conclusion that the conversions which take place in a revival are due very largely to hypnotic suggestion. The first to make the reaction desired by the revivalist are, as a rule, the more suggestible members of the crowd. Their response causes a rise in the general level of feeling, and the power of suggestion and imitation soon overcomes a number of others. Their suggestibility, now heightened by many devices, compels them to do what others are doing. Professor Bois has given a good example of the quasi-hypnotic effect of the methods employed. At a meeting held by Torrey and Alexander in Liverpool, during the singing and before Torrey had begun to preach, Alexander asked how many wished to give themselves to Christ then and there. No less than one hundred and fifty persons stood up from every corner of the hall. Alexander began to count them in a loud voice. The number steadily mounted up and the people were so anxious that all should be counted that they cried to Alexander: "Here is one," "Here is another." That this numbering had a quasi-hypnotic effect on those who hesitated is seen by the fact that many, when they wrote down their names and addresses, also put down their numbers.[1]

The conclusion regarding the preponderating part played by suggestion in revivals is further supported by the fact that the less suggestible persons are left untouched. Torrey and Alexander found their work very difficult in Scotland. They were confronted with the characteristic reserve of the Scotch. Even the Welsh Revival did not affect the higher classes in the same way. Very few members of the learned professions were among the converts; and very few, if any, business magnates. The revival was practically confined to the working classes—to the miners, peasants, and petty shopkeepers.[2] The reason for this is not far to seek. Suggestion, it is true, exercises a great influence over the minds of all, but it rarely tyrannizes more developed and cultivated minds. " Within an educated mind no one idea or motor impulse is long without rivals for the control of attention. The rival ideas thus tend to inhibit each other, and either to prevent action altogether, or to give time for cool consideration of all relevant issues, before action is taken or adherence to belief finally given. In more primitive minds this inhibitive power is largely lacking." [3]

Finally, we notice that the enormous part played by suggestion in conversions in a revivalistic *milieu* explains why so many, who profess conversion at such times, soon backslide. It is the more suggestible ones who have been swept in by the tide of the movement, and not a few of them have undergone no radical change of mind. Many of them may even soon feel chagrined because they yielded to the pressure put upon them. Cutten calls attention to the large percentage of lapses after the Welsh Revival of 1904-5, and gives it as his judgment that " it takes two or three years for churches to get rid of the unsanctified riff-raff which is swept in with the tide of a revival." [4] Doubtless Cutten here speaks from his own experience, as he has served as the minister of several churches in America, where

[1] *Quelques Réflexions sur la Psychologie des Réveils*, 108 n.
[2] Ibid., 97, n. 2. Cf. Fursac, op. cit. 181.
[3] Pratt, op. cit. 170.
[4] Op. cit. 194. Cf. the table in Starbuck, 170.

revivals are more or less endemic. It is noteworthy that the Welsh people themselves say that a revival is like a tide, which at one and the same time covers the shore with weeds and treasures; and it takes time to collect and throw away the weeds and to pick up and arrange the treasures.[1]

Nevertheless, it would be foolish to rush to extremes and say that revivals bear no lasting fruit. Defenders of revivals rightly point to the residuum of those who remain steadfast and do not lapse. In out next chapter the lasting fruits of certain revivals will be noted. Moreover, though the emotionalism of revivals leads to some queer extravagances, it should not be denounced as entirely bad. In a crowd men not only suffer some loss of their powers of inhibition, but they are also conscious of a great accession of confidence, courage and moral power. Under the influence of a crowd they can do things of which they are incapable in isolation, and some are able thus to go far beyond their past attainments and to reach heights which in solitude they vainly struggled to win. Paul was far from being unaware of the value of emotional methods, but he was never content to begin and end in a tempest of emotion, nor did he think that high-strung emotion was the peculiar channel by which the Holy Spirit found access to the soul of man. In the self-portraiture of a passage like 2 Cor. x. 3–5 (R.V. Mg.) we see the apostle quite as anxious to convince the minds of men as to stir their emotions. In this regard he stands near to his Master, for, as Dean Inge says, though with a touch of exaggeration, " no religious teacher appealed less to excitement than did the founder of Christianity." [2]

[1] Quoted by Bois, *Le Réveil*, 606. The dangers of revivalist methods were never better put than by Catherine Booth, who was always fully aware of the perils inherent in her husband's methods (see Begbie's *Life of William Booth*, i. 175 f.).
[2] E.R.E. ix. 316.

CHAPTER XVI

THE FRUITS OF CONVERSION

THE most remarkable fruit of conversion is seen in the manner in which it has brought about complete and permanent deliverance from every known sin.[1] Indisputable evidence on this point is so abundant that we are embarrassed with a wealth of riches. We must content ourselves with setting down the evidence of the New Testament and of the non-Christian religions on this point.

No serious student of the New Testament can doubt that its converts were ushered at their conversion into an increasingly fuller moral and spiritual life. In the case of the evil-doers, it broke the chains of evil habit, freed them from the slavery of sin, and either completely destroyed their baser desires and inclinations or held them in check. "Fornicators, idolaters, adulterers, thieves, covetous, drunkards, revilers, extortioners—and such were some of you: but ye were washed, ye were sanctified," is Paul's amazing statement to the Corinthian Church (1 Cor. vi. 9 f.). Their conversion had meant an actual breach with a life that had

---

[1] For the converted man's unusual power to resist temptation see James, 220–228, 290–296. For further evidence of the permanent cure by conversion of alcoholics and other victims of vice see Begbie's *Broken Earthenware* and his *In the Hand of the Potter*, and Hadley's *Down in Water Street*. All three volumes, though popular in their treatment, are invaluable for the psychological study of conversion. Very remarkable is the case of O. B. D. (see *Broken Earthenware*, 63 ff.). Born of drunken parents, he had early acquired an insatiable appetite for drink. At the age of forty-five he was habitually in a soddened state. At a Salvation Army meeting he heard the assertion that the vilest and most shameful could become in an instant radiant with happiness and peace if they came in penitence to the penitent form. He came out, and "found God." He was instantly cured of his craving. Old companions offered him every inducement to break the pledge he had taken; one even flung a pot of beer in his face, with the remark, "Don't it smell good, daddy?" But O. B. D. never wavered.

been deeply stained with vice. A similar breach with an evil past is seen in the case of Zacchæus and the woman who was a sinner. Nor were these isolated cases. There must have been many who, in contact with Jesus, underwent a similar change. Many who were morally and spiritually blind He made to see, and many who were spiritually dead He must have raised up.[1] How profoundly Christianity affected the conduct of the Early Christians is seen by the peculiar designation it gained—the Way (see Acts ix. 2, xix. 9 and 23, xxii. 4, xxiv. 22).

But there were many of the converts of New Testament times who did not break through to Christ from a vicious past. Many of the "God-fearers" had, without doubt, been religiously minded before their conversion to Christianity. Like Paul, they changed their beliefs rather than their moral aims. But it would be a complete mistake to assume that in these cases there was no modification in character. As in the case of Paul, the new belief provided a new dynamic. The springs of their action were completely changed and so also was their estimate of all life's values. The New Testament throughout lays stress on the fruits of conversion. The First Epistle of John, for example, provides an "adequate set of criteria," by which its readers may satisfy themselves that they have undergone a genuine conversion.[2] When we come to the sub-apostolic age we find Justin Martyr in his *First Apology* (chap. xvi.) expressly stating that some of the heathen were converted by the honest way the Christians transacted business with them.

It is a far cry from Justin Martyr to George Fox, but the latter's robust sense of moral values gave a very definite bent to the Quaker movement, in spite of its many affinities with mystical religion. In the earliest days the Quaker tradesmen were boycotted and some were reduced to want, but their conversion had developed a type of ethical character that could not fail eventually to win admiration. They

[1] Matt. xi. 5. Some commentators, including Wellhausen and Loisy, hold that the language is here metaphorical and denotes the spiritual activity of Jesus. See Loisy, *Les Evangiles Synoptiques*, i. 663 ff.
[2] See Law, *The Tests of Life, passim.* For the abandonment of the grosser abominations of heathenism on conversion to Christianity on the mission field to-day, see Warneck, 268 f.

were among the first tradesmen in England to set a fixed price on their goods and to set their face against the current practice of bargaining. Says Fox in his Journal:

" For a time people that were tradesmen could hardly get money enough to buy bread, but afterwards, when people came to see Friends' honesty and truthfulness and yea and nay at a word in their dealing, and their lives and conversations did preach and reach to the witness of God in all people, and they knew and saw that they would not cozen and cheat them for conscience' sake toward God—and that at last they might send any child and be as well used as themselves at any of their shops, so then the things altered so that all the inquiry was where was a draper or shopkeeper or tailor or any other tradesman that was a Quaker: then that was all the cry, insomuch that Friends had double the trade beyond any of their neighbours: and if there was any trading they had it, insomuch that then the cry was of all the professors and others, If we let these people alone they will take the trading of the nation out of our hands. . . . And this was from the years 1652 to 1656 and since." [1]

The moral fruit of the Welsh Revival of 1904–5 was very striking. The revival, in spite of many undesirable features, was no mere debauch of unbridled emotionalism; it was accompanied by a real decrease in crime.[2] Family life was restored by the abandonment of drinking habits. In 1897, 1661 persons were arrested in Cardiff for drunkenness, but in 1904 the number fell to 213. Such an enormous drop is not to be explained entirely by the more effective application by the police of the licensing laws.[3] Long-standing quarrels were made up; enemies were reconciled;

[1] *Cambridge Journal*, i. 138. I quote from Braithwaite's *Beginnings of Quakerism*, 152, as he has corrected the orthographical and grammatical crudities. For fixed prices see Braithwaite, op. cit. 211, 523, and his *Second Period of Quakerism*, 560. The early date of the entry in the *Journal* should be noted. All the Quakers of the period were converted men and women.

[2] Bois, *Le Réveil au pays de Galles*, 582. Bois cites the testimony of the governor of Carnarvon Jail. For evidence of the decrease of crime after the revival in Rochester in 1830 see Finney, 250.

[3] I take these figures from Fursac (op. cit. 45), who must be adjudged a hostile witness, while disagreeing with his interpretation of them. The figures he gives for the county of Glamorgan are striking (ibid. 126). He admits that the evidence for the favourable effect of the revival on drunkenness is incontestable (ibid. 125).

ancient wrongs were repaired; bad debts paid; stolen property restored.[1] Cases were known in Swansea where people took their poor parents out of the Workhouse and supported them themselves.[2] Better work was done. Converted miners did not put stones with the coal when they filled the wagons, and the pit ponies were better treated.[3]

The ability of Early Buddhism to attract and heal those who were most sadly in need of moral renewal has already been demonstrated. Four of the authors of the *Therigatha* were, according to the Commentary, courtesans before their conversion.[4] No one who has read the *Thera-theri-gatha* can doubt that in its golden period Early Buddhism possessed the power to mend the broken earthenware of human lives. It lifted to a higher moral life, not only kings and Brahmans, but also the pauper and the outcasts of the streets. The ethical fruits of conversion were abundantly manifested in the life of Buddha himself. Hopkins does not exaggerate when he says of him: " No man ever lived so godless yet so god-like."[5] His calm patience and benign serenity would make him the idol, as well as the ideal, of Indian hearts.[6] His message, born out of his long struggle for unification, was ethical through and through. It was only the intensity of his moral passion that enabled him, while repudiating a permanent personality in man, to uphold the conception of recompense and retribution in an endless succession of births. He insisted on his converts showing the ethical fruits of righteousness in righteous lives. The Noble Eightfold Path is the surest proof of that. All metaphysical speculation was rejected in order to give more room to ethics. Nor did he consider sacrifice

[1] Bois, op. cit. 586–588.   [2] Ibid. 589.
[3] Ibid. 600. Howley points out that the Ulster Revival of 1859 caused the animosity between Catholic and Protestant to lie in abeyance for a time. " On the 12th of July not so much as an offensive coloured ribbon was displayed throughout the length and breadth of Durham Street (Belfast), nor, indeed, in any other locality in Ulster in which the people had become seriously impressed " (*Psychology and Mystical Experience*, 136).
[4] See Psalms xxii, xxvi, xxxix, lxvi.
[5] *Religions of India*, 325.
[6] India's exaltation of the passive virtues should here be borne in mind.

The Fruits of Conversion 227

and asceticism of any avail. Salvation comes only to him who has developed character, which is the only thing that counts.

> "Not matted hair nor heritage of birth
> Can prove the Brahman; nay, but sterling worth,
> And truthfulness and inward purity." [1]

Conversion meant a radical change of values. How radical in many cases that change was has already been indicated. It resulted in a moral life in Buddha's converts far above the average around them.

No one acquainted with vernacular literature of the Chaitanyite Revival in Bengal can doubt that the new teaching was able to win moral and spiritual victories in the lives of the sinful and the base. The conversion of ruffians like Jadai and Madhai, of dacoits like Naroji, of courtesans like Varamukhi, and of *devadasis* like Indira Devi, is proof of this.[2]

Manikka Vachakar's besetting sin was sensual passion, but his conversion gave him victory over it, as did Augustine's. He thus sings:

> "Poor servile worshipper—how many, many a time
> I've watered barren soil—not worshipping the Lord Supreme!
> The Eternal-First, th' imperishable flawless Gem, to me
> Came down; and bar of my 'embodiment' destroyed: and thus
>   Play we tonokkam!

> "The inner Light, past speech, the Worthiest entered within
> My soul, and brought me through lust's mighty sea that knows no shore,
> And then the craving senses' sateless vultures routed fled!
> Sing how a royal path in glory was made plain; and thus
>   Play we tonokkam." [3]

---

[1] *Dhammapada*, 393. Trans. from Saunders's *Heart of Buddhism*, 51.
[2] For details of the above conversions see supra, 191 f., 217. For Indira Devi see *Chaitanya and his Companions*, 257. Other similar cases may be found in Sen, V.L. 106 ff., 135, 151, 156.
[3] Pope, 189. Tonokkam is a South Indian game which ends by the hands of each opposing pair being placed on the shoulders of the other. It is here used as a symbol of the approach of the soul to Siva's feet.

"Foulness that heaves like billows of the sea He all destroyed;
   My soul and body enter'd—fills, and quits no more. He who
   In Perun-turrai dwells, with crown of spreading braided locks,
   Wreathed with the moon's bright beams, our Lord Supreme.
        This is His wile!"[1]

"Birth of this frame that burns and falls I took for true—did many deeds;
   In converse joy'd with maidens wreathed with flowers, with lustrous armlets decked.
   My bonds He cut, made me His own, cleansed foulness so no trace was left!
   'Twas thus the Last-One gave me grace: O Rapture! Who so blest as I?"[2]

Namdev, the robber, who at his conversion became a devotee of Krishna, thus testified to the annulment of his propensities to sin:

"One fast asleep can never know
   That to his chamber crawling in,
   There comes the snake—heedless so
   Am I to love of sense and sin,
   Since inward vision to bestow
   My Kesav has so gracious been.

"Alike are gold and dross to me.
   Jewel and common stone, the same.
   Now ne'er my soul can harmed be,
   Walk I in heaven or in the flame."[3]

Kabir emphasizes the moral fruit of his conversion in the following quaint allegory, in which the first wife is his "former manner of life" and the second wife his post-conversion life:

"My first wife was ugly, of low caste, and bad character, evil both in her father's house and mine.
   My present wife is handsome, sensible, of good character; I naturally took her to my heart.
   It turned out well that my first wife departed;
   May she whom I have now taken live for ever!
   Saith Kabir, when the young wife came I ceased to cohabit with the old one;
   The young wife is with me now, the elder hath taken another husband."[4]

[1] Pope, 280.   [2] Ibid. 353.
[3] Macnicol, P.M.S. 48.   Kesav is another name for Krishna.
[4] Trans. from Macauliffe, *The Sikh Religion*, vi. 213.

The Fruits of Conversion 229

Elsewhere he sings: " My tongue has left off impure words; it sings His glory day and night."[1]

As to the moral fruitage of conversions in the Brahma Samaj, we have the testimony of an eye-witness, the late Pundit Sivanath Sastri. He says that, when Keshab Chandra Sen joined the Samaj in 1857, " it entered upon a new career of spiritual activity and practical usefulness.... The lives of many were changed. Many who had gone far in the path of sin repented and gave up their evil ways."[2]

That conversion brings to those who experience it a more robust sense of moral values is evidenced by the manner in which converted men and women have carried out the difficult and distasteful duty of restitution. The classic New Testament case is that of Zacchæus. The autobiography of the revivalist Finney abounds in remarkable instances.[3] A very illuminating case of restitution by a converted Quaker is the following. Humphrey Bache, a London goldsmith, finding his trade falling off at the beginning of the Civil War, obtained employment under the Commonwealth as an overseer on the work of the City fortifications. He fell in with the common practice of concealing petty embezzlements in the wages sheets, and in this way took six pounds beyond his pay. He afterwards obtained a post at the Custom House, and was there the recipient of many bribes. He was converted, and at once determined to make restitution, though the amount involved was, as he says, " near if not full half I had in the outward, having a wife and five children to provide for, and not freedom to keep my employment any longer, being convinced it was oppression." But in the end he actually paid back ten pounds more than he had taken.[4]

When Chand Ray, a landowner in Bengal, was converted by Narottama, the Chaitanyite apostle, he at once sent to the Court of the Pathan king offering to pay all the Government revenue he had withheld for some time.[5]

---

[1] Trans. from Tagore, *One Hundred Poems of Kabir*, Poem 41.
[2] Op. cit. i. 119. See above, p. 64, for the case of Hazarilal.
[3] See 343, 359, 388–390.
[4] I have summarized Braithwaite's account, which is too long to cite in full (*Beginnings of Quakerism*, 517 ff.).
[5] Sen, V.L. 140.

230 *Conversion : Christian and Non-Christian*

Similarly, the notorious robber, Shaikh Sajjan, converted by Guru Nanak, the first *guru* of the Sikhs, showed the reality of his conversion by handing over to the poor all his possessions, most of which he had obtained by violence.[1]

The conclusion reached by Starbuck and James,[2] that among converted men and women the altruistic virtues are more developed, is borne out by a wider survey of the New Testament and non-Christian evidence. The disciples after Pentecost gave proof of their altruistic spirit in their attempt to live a communistic life, which had as its motive a desire to support the poorer members of the community. "All that believed were together, and had all things in common; and they sold their possessions and goods, and parted them to all, according as any man had need" (Acts ii. 44 f.; cf. iv. 34-37). The Gentile Churches founded by Paul showed a kindred spirit in their response to his request for a collection on behalf of the Church of Jerusalem. In Rom. xv. 28 the apostle refers to their generosity as "this fruit."[3] The New Testament term for the altruism of the converted man is "Love of the Brethren." This virtue, which receives frequent emphasis in the New Testament, is regarded as something distinctively Christian. In 1 Pet. i. 22 f. it is expressly connected with the new birth, and in 1 John iii. 14 it is one of the tests of conversion. In his suggestive essay, "What Happened at Pentecost," in the volume *The Spirit*, Professor C. Anderson Scott contends that the real and enduring result of the Spirit's coming was the *koinonia* of the believers. This *koinonia* he describes as "a community of sacred love, which freed humanity from all limitations of natural egoism."[4]

---

[1] Macauliffe, op. cit. i. 47.
[2] Starbuck, 127 ff.; James, 274, 278 ff., 369.
[3] Friedländer has some good remarks on the manner in which an almost incredible generosity continued after the close of the apostolic age (*Roman Life and Manners under the Early Empire*, iii. 199 f.). Campbell N. Moody maintains that the Christians of Formosa, who are mainly converts of the first generation, are at least twice as liberal as British Christians (*The Heathen Heart*, 143). Cf. Warneck, 283.
[4] 151. Harnack has a splendid study of the brotherly love and abounding charity of the early Church in his *Mission and Expansion*, i. 149-198. For the feeling of brotherhood among converts in the mission-field to-day see Campbell N. Moody, op. cit. 137 f., and Warneck, 270, 284.

The Fruits of Conversion

The Quaker refusal of " hat honour " and of the customary titles of the day, and their determination to " thou " all men, struck their contemporaries as intentional rudeness or capricious trifling. But in its essence it was an attempt to give expression, under the conditions of the age, to their new sense of brotherhood in Christ. Their common experience of conversion swept away differences of rank and position, and welded them into a fellowship such as had characterized the Church in the Apostolic Age. Among those who were equal in the sight of God, the use of flattery in any of its forms could have no place.

The brotherly love of the Friends often found another unique manifestation. Men and women would offer to take the place of those who had been thrown into prison, that the sufferers might have some respite.

"When I was in prison in Cornwall," says George Fox, "there was a Friend went to O(liver) C(romwell) and offered his body to him for to go and lie in Doomsdale prison for me or in my stead that he would take him and let me go at liberty, and it so struck him and came over him that he said to his great men and his Council, 'Which of you would do so much for me if I was in the same condition?'"[1]

From the characteristic altruism of the converted man sprang, not only the Quaker attack on social unrealities, but their equally stout attack on the social abuses of their day. Soon after his spiritual illumination Fox was led to speak out against the various forms of injustice and oppression then prevailing. He often wrote or spoke to the judges to do justly, and at Mansfield spoke to them of the oppression caused by fixing a legal wage for farm-labourers below what was equitable. He also protested against the iniquity of the criminal law, which put men to death for petty thefts. Zeal for social reform and philanthropic effort has never ceased to be a marked feature of the Quaker Community,

[1] *Cambridge Journal*, i. 245. In 1659 no less than 164 Friends made an offer to Parliament to take the places of brethren in bonds. This fellow-feeling was so noticeable that Fox had to write a paper to correct the statement of others that the Friends loved none but themselves. The paper was entitled "The People of God in Scorn called Quakers their Love for all Mankind."

but for its tap-root we must go back to the time when the Society of Friends was a community of converted men and women.[1]

How strong the altruistic spirit was among the converts of the *bhakti* movement in India is best seen by their polemic against caste. In view of the tyrannical hold the caste system has obtained on the Hindu mind, their repudiation of it is a remarkable phenomenon, explainable only by the religious experience through which so many *bhaktas* had passed. They may have been influenced at this point by Buddhist teaching, but it is much more likely that their conversion had filled them with altruistic impulses, and had led them to see that a man needs only to be a man to be able to exercise saving *bhakti*. Chaitanya said : " Be he Brahman, be he a hermit, be he even a Sudra, if he knows Krishna's mysteries, he is a *guru*." " God's grace defies caste and family distinctions."[2] When the tides of religious fervour were running strong in the Chaitanyite community, the caste rules were so much in abeyance that a Brahman accepted the Kayastha, Narottama, as his *guru*, to the scandal of the orthodox.[3]

Tukaram was himself a Sudra ; and the religious revival of the Maratha country, in which he is such a conspicuous figure, did much to break down, for a time at least, the acerbities of caste feeling. Tukaram sings :

" Our Lord knows nothing of high or low birth ; he stops whenever he sees devotion and faith.
A Vaishnava is one who loves God alone ; his caste may be anything at all."[4]

Frazer and Edwards give it as their considered judgment that " an unselfish desire to raise the world around him

[1] In his *Second Period of Quakerism* Braithwaite has a fine chapter on " The Church and Social Questions." He cites a number of German monographs which deal with this aspect of the life of the Early Quaker Community and gives a good account of the communistic proposals of that pioneer of modern Christian Socialism, John Bellers, whom Karl Marx described as " a veritable phenomenon in the history of political economy."
[2] Sarkar, 71, 113. [3] Sen, V.L. 125, 150 f.
[4] I take this citation from Frazer and Edwards's *Life and Teaching of Tukaram*, 162. For the polemic against caste among the Siva *bhaktas* of the South see J. E. Carpenter, *Theism in Mediæval India*, 369.

is the noblest feature of Tukaram's character, and, breathing as it does from so many of his poems in one form or another, remains the final impression."[1] We quote a representative poem:

" Whoso makes himself the friend of the oppressed, recognize him
   for a true saint.
Know that God dwells in him.
He who takes the unprotected to his heart,
Tuka says—how often shall I tell you ?
He is the very image of the Divine."[2]

The same altruistic spirit marks the Sufi converts. It is said of Abu Sa'id that his charity embraced all created beings. His purse was always open and he never quarrelled with any. "He seldom preached on Koranic texts describing the pains of hell, and in his last years, when reciting the Koran, he passed over all the 'verses of torment.' 'O God,' he cried, 'inasmuch as men and stones have the same value in Thy sight, feed the flames of hell with stones, and do not burn these miserable wretches!'"[3] Alongside this prayer we may place that of the Bengali *bhakta*, Vasudev Datta. "My heart breaks to see the sorrows of mankind. Lay thou the sins of the rest of mankind on my head; let me suffer in hell under the load of their sins, so that, Master, thou mayest remove the earthly pangs of all other beings."[4] No wonder Chaitanya's heart was melted when he heard this prayer.

Very striking is the altruism of Hallaj, who was put to death with every refinement of cruelty in Baghdad in A.D. 922 for the uncompromising pantheism of his assertion, " I am the Truth, or God." His hands were cut off and his eyes torn out. When they were about to cut out his tongue, he cried: "Wait a little, I have something to say." Then, lifting his face to heaven, he said: "My God, for the sake of these sufferings which they inflict on me because of Thee, do not inflict loss on them nor deprive them of

---

[1] Op. cit. 142.   [2] Op. cit., loc. cit.
[3] Nicholson, *Studies in Islamic Mysticism*, 56. Cf. the prayer of Abu 'l-Hasan Nuri in Hujwiri, 194.
[4] Sarkar, 177.

their share of felicity. Behold, upon the scaffold of my torture, I enjoy the contemplation of Thy Glory."[1] Hallaj was converted at the age of sixteen.

In searching the files of the contemporary press for material that might illuminate the inner life of the earlier stages of the Brahma Samaj, I came across the following contributed by a correspondent to the *Indian Mirror* of April 15, 1867. The reference is to the Brahmas of Eastern Bengal:

"I cannot in terms appropriate give utterance to the large-hearted charity which I have noticed in one of the Brahmos here. It is not directed to one particular object only. It stretches its hands on all sides, and with equal warmth embraces the orphan and the indigent, the educational as well as the religious department, the Hindoo and the Brahmo."

Another manifestation of the altruism of converted men and women is their missionary zeal—their burning desire to tell others of their experience that they may share its blessings. The apostle Paul is an outstanding case of this missionary zeal. It is said that he was filled with an irresistible and natural impulse to defend and propagate his faith, and that "the man who before his conversion to Christianity was a Jewish zealot and persecutor could not become a merely passive believer in the new religion."[2] But this does not adequately account for the inner compulsion laid upon him. "Necessity is laid upon me, for woe is unto me, if I preach not the Gospel" (1 Cor. ix. 16). "The question, however, as to the origin of this compulsion must not be avoided. St. Paul gives us a clear account. He became at once Christian and apostle—such is his answer to the question—through the vision on the road to Damascus."[3] This remark by Weinel is much nearer the mark than Cone's position cited above. Paul's new life and new vocation came together, and in referring to the one he often mentions the other. "God . . . revealed His

---

[1] Field, *Mystics and Saints of Islam*, 77.
[2] Orello Cone, *Paul*, 70.
[3] Weinel, *Paul*, 165. For the missionary zeal of converts in the mission field to-day, see Warneck, 272 ff.

The Fruits of Conversion 235

Son in me in order that I might preach Him among the Gentiles " (Gal. i. 15). The conversion was itself a summons to the apostolate.

The annals of post-apostolic Christianity abound in examples of the missionary zeal of converted men to such an extent that our difficulty is to make a selection from the many appropriate instances at our disposal. The tireless evangelism of John Wesley is too well known to need special emphasis here. George Fox, like Paul and Wesley, regarded the whole world as his parish. Nothing damped his missionary ardour, neither cold, nor hunger, nor the frequent assaults of enemies. In addition to his amazing labours in England, he gave two years in the prime of his manhood to a visit to America, traversing the American wilderness, and spending nights either in the open or in friendly Indian wigwams. After less than four years at home, he set out on his travels again, and went through Germany and Holland proclaiming the word of life. He was again in Holland in the later years of his life, but his physical infirmities limited his activities.[1]

The same enthusiasm burned in the breasts of Fox's converts, as the extraordinary Quaker missions to the East will show. Mention can be made of only a single case out of a number. One party, consisting of three men and three women, baffled in their attempt to reach Jerusalem, made some wonderful journeys in Mediterranean lands. One of the women even had an interview with Sultan Mohammed IV in his camp at Adrianople. She managed to return safely to England, but two of the men, John Perrot and John Luffe, fell into the hands of the Inquisition at Rome in the spring of 1658. Luffe was hanged, but his companion was deemed insane. After being kept three years in a madhouse, he was released and reached England in safety. We are not surprised to learn that the meetings which this intrepid missionary attended on his return " were much fresher than lately had been known." [2]

---

[1] For the frequent ill-treatment to which Fox was exposed see the *Cambridge Journal*, i. 36, 57–61, 104, 108 ; and for his privations see i. 20, 30 ff., 39 f., 83, 93, 110, 227 ; ii. 224.

[2] I take these details from Braithwaite's *Beginnings of Quakerism*, 418–432 (see also his *Second Period of Quakerism*, 228–231). The docu-

Nor was it otherwise with the converted Cynics and Stoics of the Græco-Roman world. "Benevolent and philanthropic sentiments were regarded," says Gomperz,[1] "as part of the typical Cynic character. Again and again we meet with the picture of the man who mixes with the masses, with the degraded and the despised by choice, strives earnestly after the healing of their souls, and, if reproved for keeping such company, answers in words strangely reminiscent of a passage in the Gospel: ' The physicians also go about among the sick, but are themselves whole.'" Some, like Crates, who won for himself the name of "The Door-opener," intruded into private houses and imparted unsought their words of admonition and advice.[2] After Dio Chrysostom's conversion, "he deemed it a sacred duty to call men to the way of wisdom by persuasion or reproach, and to appeal even to the turbulent masses." [3]

The question whether altruism finds a place in the Buddhist scheme of ethics, or whether, as some have held, it is foreign to the Buddhist ideal, does not concern us here.[4] It finds a place in the lives of the early converts. It manifests itself in Buddha's long ministry of forty years or more spent in loving service of men. His own experience filled him with an intense compassion for the world's sorrow, ignorance and suffering. Soon after his enlightenment he was tempted to leave the masses in their ignorance and folly, and to keep to himself the saving knowledge he had won. But he overcame the temptation to selfishness, and showed his altruism by his missionary zeal. And not only was Buddha himself a missionary, so also were his converts. He gave his followers their marching orders in the following words :

ment printed in the *Cambridge Journal*, ii. 336–338, and headed ' An account of what ffriendes went foorth to preach ye Gospell out of ye North : in ye yeare 1657 : and into what partes : of ye worlde : they travailed : and where they suffered this yeare 1657 : " is well worth study.
[1] *Greek Thinkers*, ii. 166.   [2] Ibid. ii. 152.
[3] Dill, *Roman Society from Nero to Marcus Aurelius*, 340.
[4] Contrast, e.g., Paul Dahlke in his *Buddhist Essays* (E.T.), 132, with Mrs. Rhys Davids's *Buddhism*, 219. Both writers are entirely sympathetic with Buddhism. For a more recent discussion, see Poussin, *The Way to Nirvana*, 74 ff.

The Fruits of Conversion

"Go ye now, O Bhikkhus, and wander, for the gain of the many, out of compassion for the world, for the good, for the gain, and for the welfare of gods and men. . . . And I will go also, O Bhikkhus, . . . in order to preach the doctrine."[1]

With splendid enthusiasm they carried their Master's teaching through the length and breadth of India and beyond. Here they differed absolutely from the self-satisfied Brahmans of their day and also from their kindred, the Jains, who were never filled with the same missionary zeal.[2]

At the same time it is impossible not to feel that the Buddhist system of individualistic self-culture was not the best soil for the growth of altruism. It is by no means a marked feature of the *Thera-theri-gatha*. The following lines are said to have been written by a boy *bhikkhu*, named Sopaka :

> "E'en as she would be very good
> Towards her only child, her well-beloved son,
> So too ye should be very good
> Towards all creatures everywhere and everyone."[3]

The only other passage I have been able to find with a marked altruistic tinge is the following :

> "With all am I a friend, a comrade to all,
> And to all creatures kind and merciful ;
> A heart of amity I cultivate.
> And ever in good will is my delight."[4]

No sooner had Chaitanya returned home after his spiritual awakening at Gaya than he set about winning others to the new faith that had taken possession of him. The opposition he had to face from the intellectuals of Navadipa soon convinced him that he would never be able to carry conviction to the multitude until he had become a *sannyasi* for the sake of his gospel. According to Govinda Das, he thus expressed his intention :

"I shall have my head shaven, cast off the sacred thread, and wander as a *sannyasi* from house to house, preaching the love of

---

[1] *Maha-Vagga*, i. ii. 1.
[2] Cf. J. E. Carpenter, op. cit. 39 and 60
[3] *Theragatha*, 33.
[4] Ibid. 648.

238 Conversion: Christian and Non-Christian

Krishna. Young men, children, old men, worldly men and even the pariahs will stand round me charmed with the name of God. . . . If I do not renounce my home, how can sinners be saved ? My heart feels deep pangs for the sinners of the world, and for those who are stung by the world's woes." [1]

Of the conversion of Debendranath Tagore, Miss Underhill says, it impelled him " to something which closely resembles a missionary career. His was an apostolic nature ; he was forced to share with others the truth he had found. In the hard and definite work of organizing and inspiring the religious movement of the Brahma-Samaj he found that outlet for his enthusiasm and love which Francis found in the life of a preaching friar, Ignatius in the formation of the Society of Jesus, Fox and Wesley in the preaching of the Quaker and Methodist ideals." [2] It is worth pointing out that the altruistic impulse born in his conversion experience sometimes antagonized Debendranath's essentially Hindu temperament. He much preferred the solitary, contemplative life amid the Himalayas. On one occasion, believing that he was now called to a life-long retreat, he spent nearly two years in solitude among the mountains. But one day, as he was gazing at a torrent, a voice told him that he must return to his missionary labours, and, like the torrent, humble his pride and accept the stains of earth in order to fertilize the land. After a struggle he obeyed. He was not a converted man for nought.[3]

Writing of his convert Hazarilal, Debendranath says: " Having obtained release from the tortuous ways of sin by accepting the Brahma Dharma, he tried to bring others also into the path of virtue. He began to point out the way of the highest good, which lies in the Brahma Dharma, to every person in Calcutta, rich and poor and wise and honoured. It was entirely owing to his efforts that so many people then became Brahmas within such a short time." [4] The last time Hazarilal was seen by his master was when he set out on a missionary journey to distant lands.

[1] Sen, H.R.L.L. 450 f.
[2] Introduction to the *Autobiography*, p. xxv.
[3] Ibid. xxxvii. f.   [4] Ibid. 133.

The Fruits of Conversion

Keshab Chandra Sen was full of missionary zeal all his days. He made extensive missionary tours all over India. His enthusiasm for saving fellow-sinners by carrying to them the gospel which had proved so effective in his own life, owed something to Christian influence, but for its primary roots we must go back to his own conversion crisis. How it impressed his contemporaries may be seen from the statement in the *Indian Mirror* of April 15, 1864, that his mission to Bombay of that year was " the first of its kind ever undertaken by a Hindoo." [1]

If further evidence be required of the power of conversion to subdue the egoistic impulses of human personality, while at the same time enlarging and expanding it, we may point to the humility of the converted man. In the case of Paul it is sufficient to refer to passages like 1 Cor. xv. 9 and Eph. iii. 8, though the verse immediately following the former shows that his humility was not inconsistent with a laudable pride in his calling.

After Chaitanya's conversion he showed a new humility that was in striking contrast to his former arrogant manner. He carried burdens for old and sickly people, washed clothes and performed other services usually done only by menial servants. The actual words of the *Chaitanya Bhagabat* are worth quoting:

> "In the morning, when the Master goes to bathe in the Ganges, he comes across the Vaishnavas. . . . He wrings the water out of their clothes with care, and picks up the clothes of others and hands them over to them. In the hands of some he puts Kusa grass and Ganges earth, and sometimes he carries the flower-basket for them to their houses. All the Vaishnavas say: ' Alas! Alas! What are you doing ? ' " [2]

Humility seems to have been a characteristic grace of his converts, whom he commanded to "chant the name of the Lord, becoming humble as grass, as patient as a tree." More than once we read in the *Chaitanya Chari-*

---

[1] There are some good remarks on the missionary activity of the Samaj in P. C. Mozoomdar's *Faith and Progress of the Brahmo Samaj* (Calcutta, 1882), 226–263.
[2] Adi Khanda.

tamrita[1] of converted Vaishnavas taking two blades of grass between their teeth as a sign of their humility. Their humility led them to eschew preaching and to adopt the *sankirtan* as a method of spreading their faith. " Preaching," says Shishir Kumar Ghose,[2] " is almost impossible for a Vaishnava, who is required to be meaner than grass. To preach is to arrogate superiority." The same humility led even Kulin Brahmans among the earlier Bengali Vaishnavas to replace their own family names with that of Das, or servant.[3]

The famous converted Sufi, Abu Saʻid, wrote :

" One day I said to myself: ' Knowledge, works, meditation—I have them all ; now I want to become absent from them.' On consideration I saw that the only way to attain this was by acting as a servant to the Dervishes, for *when God wishes to benefit a man, He shows to him the path of self-abasement.* Accordingly I made it my business to wait upon them, and I used to clean their cells, and privies and lavatories. I persevered in this work for a long time, until it became a habit. Then I resolved to beg for the Dervishes, which seemed to me the hardest thing I could lay upon myself." [4]

Abu Yazid, who, as we have seen, could date his conversion, said: " He whom the Lord loves is known by three distinct signs—his liberality is like the sea, his kindness is like the sun, his humility is like the earth, which allows itself to be trampled on by everyone." [5]

At the risk of prolonging unduly a chapter already lengthy, we may notice another fruit of conversion, namely, the increased physical and spiritual vitality that is attained by the experience.[6] It is difficult for any reader of the New Testament to escape the impression that its converts are conscious of a heightening of all their powers. They have a sense of tremendous enrichment, not only of goodness and joy, but also of both physical and spiritual energy.

---

[1] Sarkar, 232. In India grass is often used as an emblem of humility, because it allows all to walk on it. The tree is so used because it never speaks of the wrongs inflicted on it and shelters even him who cuts it with an axe.
[2] *The Lord Gauranga*, i. 223 n.   [3] Sen, V.L. 173.
[4] Nicholson, *Studies in Islamic Mysticism*, 14.
[5] Field, op. cit. 58.   [6] For James on this point, see 241.

The Fruits of Conversion 241

The fuller evidence available in his case makes this specially apparent in the case of the apostle Paul. His conversion resulted in an enormous dower of physical and spiritual vitality, which manifested itself in a career of ceaseless activity. Though possessed of a weak and ailing body, his energy seems inexhaustible. Deissmann, who has travelled over most of the routes taken by Paul, says: "One of the most lasting impressions derived from these journeys, which are mostly made with modern means of locomotion, is my unspeakable amazement at the purely physical accomplishments of St. Paul the traveller."[1] We may add that there is a remarkable picture of the apostle's tireless energy in Acts xx. 6–12.

Not only does Paul manifest a richer moral and spiritual life and an enhanced physical vitality, he also shows a fuller mental life after conversion. Since he was a fully grown man when his conversion took place, it cannot be maintained that this awakening was, in his case, part of the normal ripening of powers which takes place at adolescence.

How immediate was this mental expansion is seen by the manner in which all the leading features of the apostle's theology came to him at his conversion or immediately after it. At such a creative period in the life of the soul, thought is quicker, feeling deeper, and intuition more penetrating in its insight than at ordinary times. Hence the inclination on the part of many modern theologians to regard the whole of Paulinism as a "systematization of the Christ-vision," and as a generalization of what the apostle had experienced in his own soul, receives a good deal of support from the purely psychological standpoint. "The first condition for any understanding of Paulinism," says H. J. Holtzmann, "is that we should not obscure the volcanic character of its origin by any method which implies the gradual addition of one grain of sand to another. The whole system of doctrine means nothing more or less than the way in which the apostle objectified to himself the

[1] Op. cit. 66. Cf. Delacroix (op. cit. 29, 49 f.) for the great increase of energy that came to St. Teresa when her long conversion process came to an end.

fundamental decisive experience of his life, and theoretically explained its presuppositions and consequences. The doctrine fits the experience with a theory."[1] Speaking of Paul's conversion, Sabatier, who belongs to another school, says: "We find in this event—latent in the spiritual experience and feelings attending it—all the great ideas and the leading antitheses which characterize his doctrinal system."[2] In this country Bruce,[3] Garvie,[4] and H. A. A. Kennedy,[5] and in America McGiffert,[6] hold similar views. They are not blind to the fact that Paul was a living and growing thinker all his days, nor to the fact that apologetic interests in times of controversy shaped the statement of his doctrinal system. But when all allowances have been made they feel that it is impossible to deny that the apostle's theology, as well as his religious life, was the product of the conversion crisis and of subsequent meditation upon it. "The decisive factor in the genesis of St. Paul's theology was experience and his conversion on the road to Damascus."[7]

We have emphasized this point in view of the tendency of writers of the *religionsgeschichte* school to neglect Paul's conversion as a determining factor in the genesis of his theology, and their attempt to make Hellenistic religion and religious philosophy the vital influence on his thought. We contend that it is psychologically much more probable to make the apostle's doctrinal system, in all its essentials, go back to his conversion, and to reflection upon it, than to make him a picker-up of scraps from the multitude of cults and philosophies which surrounded him in the Gentile world. To ignore altogether, as Morgan does in his *Religion and Theology of Paul*, the conversion of the apostle, and to explain all the main features of his thought from the Hellenistic background is simply a *tour de force*.

An even clearer case of intellectual awakening and

---

[1] Quoted by Schweitzer, *Paul and his Interpreters*, 107.
[2] *The Apostle Paul*, 68. Cf. 277 f.
[3] *St. Paul's Conception of Christianity*, 37.
[4] *Studies of Paul and his Gospel*, chap. ii.
[5] *The Theology of the Epistles*, 68–96.
[6] *History of Christianity in the Apostolic Age*, 148.
[7] Wernle, *Beginnings of Christianity*, i. 224.

expansion following upon conversion is seen in the lives of Wesley's early helpers, who, unlike Paul, were men of humble birth, and possessed nothing like the apostle's education and training. After a careful investigation of the effect of conversion upon these men, Professor A. Caldecott states his conclusions as follows:

" Under its influence intellectual activity was quickened for the instrumental purpose for which they required it. In the field which interested them their thinking was vigorous, in some cases notably so, especially considering the limited range of the education they had received. They acquired familiarity with the Bible; they were conversant with human nature on sides which concerned them; they developed oratorical power, sometimes, perhaps, wholly serious, more often not lacking in the seasoning of wit and humour, epigram, and metaphor, and parable. And some of them record considerable wrestlings with fundamental problems, though, as a rule, they accepted the solutions of these which were included in the teachings of Wesley. But it was in the exercise of intellect in preaching and conversation that all were principally engaged, and in these they became, in different degrees, leaders among people of whom even the rank and file were not likely to be the dullards of the towns and villages of England at that time." [1]

What Professor Caldecott has written of Wesley's helpers may stand almost verbatim as equally true of George Fox and his first Publishers of Truth: [2]

I have not been able to collect much evidence from the non-Christian religions for this enhancement of the physical and mental powers at conversion. But here we must remember that in Hindu circles, at any rate, increased physical vitality would not be looked upon as any evidence of the unification of the unhappy, divided soul by religion. One small point may be mentioned. The conversion of Tukaram woke in him the spirit of poetry. The unlettered Sudra grain-seller, who had never composed a line before, set to work to make books of rough paper, and before long had produced a hundred verses.[3] Throughout the rest of his life he continued to produce *abhangs*, of which several

[1] *The Religious Sentiment : Illustrated from the Lives of Wesley's Helpers.* 18 f.
[2] See some good remarks by Prof. Rufus M. Jones in his Introduction to Braithwaite's *Beginnings of Quakerism*, pp. xxxvii f.
[3] Frazer and Edwards, op. cit. 90

244 Conversion : Christian and Non-Christian

thousands are extant to-day; and their quality may be judged by the fact that men like Sir R. G. Bhandarkar and Sir Narayan Chandavarkar turn to them almost daily for spiritual uplift and instruction. In the following *abhang* Tukaram expressly attributes his power of song to the deity he adored :

" 'Tis not I who speak so featly ;
All my words my Lover's are.
Hark, Salunki, singing sweetly,
Taught, as I, by One afar.

" How could I, abject, achieve it ?
'Tis the all-upholding One.
Deep his skill, who can conceive it ?
He can make the lame to run." [1]

[1] Macnicol, P.M.S., 88. Salunki is an Indian bird.

CHAPTER XVII

THE INDIVIDUAL AND THE SOCIAL

WHILE the experiences we have been describing are the subject's own and bear the impress of his own personality, their shape and colour are fixed by the prevailing ideas of the social group to which he belongs. As we shall see, the *milieu* affects the experiences that precede conversion, the form it takes, the feelings that accompany it, its fruits for life, the degree of its incidence, and the terms in which it is interpreted.

Some Christian writers on conversion are apt to assume that there can be no genuine religious conversion without a preceding sense of sin. Investigation, however, shows that the unification of the divided soul may take place in the full religious sense without it. The pantheism of India has always been unfavourable to the emergence of this sense of sin. It is true that we often read in the Upanishads that on the attainment of Brahman all sin is extinguished. "As birds and deer do not approach a burning mountain, so sins never approach those who know Brahman."[1] Similarly, Sankara, commenting on *Vedanta Sutras*, iv. i. 13, says: "It is therefore an established conclusion that on attaining Brahman there results the extinction of all sin."[2] But it would be a complete mistake to assume that sin is here used in anything approaching the Christian sense, as the following prayer of Sankara shows: "O Lord, pardon my three sins: I have in contemplation clothed in form Thee who art formless; I have in praise described Thee who art ineffable; and in visiting shrines I have ignored

---

[1] *Maitr. Up.* vi. 18 (S.B.E. xv. 319). See also *Chh.* iv. 14. 3, v. 24. 3; *Mu.* ii. 2. 8.
[2] S.B.E. xxxviii. 356.

246 Conversion : Christian and Non-Christian

thine omnipresence."[1] As a matter of fact, the idealistic monism of the Vedanta leaves no room for the concept of sin in the Christian sense. Commenting on *Vedanta Sutras*, iii. 2. 29, Sankara concedes that the bondage of the soul is due not to sin, but to nescience only.[2] It is interesting in this connection to compare the conversion of men like Debendranath Tagore and Ramakrishna Paramahamsa with that of Keshab Chandra Sen and his disciple P. C. Mozoomdar. Christian teaching had had little or no influence on the two former, and there is no sense of sin in their conversion experience. The two latter, however, had drunk deeply at the fountain of Christian truth, and their souls were divided by a poignant sense of sin. Ramakrishna, on the contrary, regarded the New Testament, with its stress on sin, as a book fit only for fools, but he was as genuinely converted as his younger contemporaries.

In stifling the sense of sin the pantheism of India has been helped not a little by the karma doctrine. Here we light upon one reason why our analysis of the experiences of the Early Buddhist converts failed to reveal any sense of sin, with its correlative, repentance. In point of fact, any such feelings would have been alien to the spirit of the system. "No one holding the doctrine of karma, in any one of its forms, could accept the doctrine of sin. What the European calls 'sin' he would call 'folly,' a result of ignorance. And there cannot be, in his view, any forgiveness of sin; it must work out to the bitter end, and of itself, its own fruit. This is cosmic law from which there can be no escape—not even with the help of the most powerful deity, for that deity would himself be subject to the law. Again, another implication in the European sense of the word 'sin' is that of an offence against a personal deity. This a Buddhist believer in karma would find difficult even to understand. To him no personal deity ever made the moral law. . . . The Buddhist would equate the abstraction 'sin' by every kind of collision, individual and social, with that cosmic moral law. Such

[1] Quoted by Principal Morrison in his *New Ideas in India*, 244.
[2] S B.E. xxxviii. 174.

collisions he would call evil, wrong, bad, demeritorious, corrupt . . . and he would call them so because as collisions or infractions they threw back the individual in his long and, mainly, painful pilgrimage to higher, happier experience."[1] Thus in Early Buddhism the place taken by conviction of sin in many Christian conversions is occupied by the feeling of misery at the prospect of an unending succession of existences.

If regard be had to the *milieu*, the absence of a sense of sin from the conversion experience of the animistic Battaks of Sumatra is readily explained. As we have already pointed out, they accepted Christ, not as the deliverer from sin, but as the deliverer from the power of evil spirits.[2] The awakening of the consciousness of sin in them was a post-conversion development and " an entirely new psychological experience."[3] The reason for this is that there is nothing in animistic heathenism with which it can be connected, for " that has neither any knowledge of sin against God nor any desire for forgiveness."[4] In circles where to speak the truth and to be honest are regarded as ridiculous, and to live chastely as unmanly, the moral superiority of the Gospel is not at once appreciated.

Time was when the sense of sin was so keen and the fear of hell was so vivid that in Christian circles conversion was sometimes accompanied by paroxysms of fear. Such intense feelings rarely associate themselves with Christian conversion to-day ; not because the sense of sin has entirely been lost, but because it has been modified. As the *milieu* has changed, the feelings have changed, too.

Even the visions and voices reflect the environment and upbringing of him who sees and hears them. Thus the vision of the American Protestant, Finney, was of " the Lord Jesus Christ," but the Catholic Merswin, at the crisis of his career, saw a picture of the crucifix ; and the Japanese Buddhist, Nichiren, saw Kokuzo, the god of wisdom. Nor do these voices and visions, in spite of their appearance of coming from outside sources, embody or convey any

---

[1] Mr. and Mrs. Rhys Davids in E.R.E. xi. 533 f.
[2] Supra, 133.   [3] Warneck. 263.
[4] Op. cit., loc. cit., cf 266 ff.

information beyond the reach of the ordinary processes of reasoning. The same may be said of the new insights and flashes of illumination that accompany conversion. Gotama Buddha's conversion is a case in point. Nor was Dayananda Saraswati's sudden apprehension of the truth of monotheism "a bolt from the blue." He had heard monotheism preached by the Sthanakavasi Jains. The claim sometimes made that in conversion "we see born within us new ideas and perceptions, real revelations that do not come from ourselves,"[1] cannot be seriously sustained.

The prevalence of the self-surrender type of conversion in Protestant Evangelical circles is not independent of the preformed expectations of these circles, in which the dogma of justification by faith and not by works is central. General Booth was not a theologian, but he expressed the pith of the doctrine sufficiently well when he said: " The great plan of salvation is ceasing from making efforts to make yourself a righteous character, and sinking helpless into the arms of Christ and accepting Full Salvation, and a pure heart, and all the blessings of the New Covenant by faith."[2] Similarly the volitional type of conversion finds a congenial home in Early Buddhism, where a central dogma is that every man must be his own saviour. Hence, too, the non-appearance in these circles of the feeling of a divine dynamic impinging on men's lives at conversion. Their agnosticism, as we have seen, completely removed their expectations of it. If many Evangelical Christians have found peace and unity by treading the path of self-surrender, many Early Buddhists discovered them by taking the illuminative way. In each case the form of the conversion was largely determined by the past that each had inherited, and by the influences that had been brought to bear upon their lives up to the time of their conversion.

The fruits of conversion are also affected by the environment within which the convert's development has taken place, and which now presents him with a certain range of possibilities. The convert, who has been brought up

[1] A French Protestant cited by Leuba in his *Psychological Study o Religion*, 222.
[2] Begbie's *Life*, i. 159.

The Individual and the Social 249

and now lives in a Christian land, may be expected to show higher ethical fruits of his conversion than, say, the animist converted to Christianity. The latter's conversion may seem to be ethically incomplete, if we judge by ideal standards. Yet his religious conversion is complete, for he has turned from acknowledged evil to the highest he knows. And no man can do more. Thus we may believe that the conversion of Lucius was real enough, though it did not lead him to expurgate his book. So also was the conversion of Ramakrishna, though he continued to use extremely filthy language. The extreme pantheism of the Hindu saint prevented him seeing any wrong in such language, or in worshipping a prostitute as the Mother Divine, when he met one in the street. As every experienced missionary knows, the moral conduct of some converts to Christianity from heathenism is at times "startlingly out of keeping with their genuine religious life. The heathen Christian Communities of the Apostolic Age had a similar experience."[1]

If, on the other hand, we ask why the Hindu converted to Christianity often excels his Christian brother of the West in the graces of humility and resignation, the answer must be found in the East's characteristic exaltation of the passive virtues and the equally characteristic stress on the active virtues in the West. The convert who belongs to the practical West will find much to commend in the principle laid down by St. Teresa: "Ce mariage spirituel n'est destiné qu'à produire incessamment des œuvres pour sa gloire";[2] but such a principle can hardly be expected to win the approval of him who was won unification of soul by following the *jnana-marga*. The latter holds that all activity, whether good or bad, binds him more firmly to the wheel of rebirth. His release from *samsara* has been won by the destruction of all potentiality of action, whether good or bad.

This is expressly stated in the *Maitrayana Upanishad*:

"Through the serenity of the thought he kills all actions, good or bad; His Self, serene, abiding in the Self, obtains imperishable bliss."[3]

[1] Warneck, 223. Cf. 147, 231, 234.
[2] Delacroix, op. cit. 68.   [3] vi. 20 (S.B.E. xv. 320).

250 Conversion : Christian and Non-Christian

The best emblem of the state of release is a condition of deep and dreamless sleep.[1]

" By obtaining the reward of Brahman his fetters are cut asunder, he knows no hope, no fear from others as little as from himself, he knows no desires ; and having obtained imperishable, infinite happiness, he stands blessed in the true Brahman. . . . Freedom from desires is, as it were, the highest prize to be taken from the best treasure (Brahman). For a man full of all desires, being possessed of will, imagination and belief, is a slave ; but he who is the opposite is free." [2]

This means that he who has won unification by following the *jnana-marga* has at the same time emptied life of all meaning. Here we light upon the reason why in our chapter on the Fruits of Conversion no mention was made of those who were converted by taking the Path of Knowledge. Any outburst of altruistic zeal and missionary fervour on their part would have brought them once again into the fetters of *samsara*. The only possible life for them was that of wandering, homeless, celibate, ascetics. Any other life would have meant the loss of the new-found treasure they had won.

The case was different with the followers of the *bhakti-marga*. They conceived the goal of the religious life, not as absorption in the Absolute, but as union with a personal deity. As we have seen, their conversions were accompanied by an outbreak of altruism and missionary zeal, as was also the conversion of Buddha. But here again we note that the karma doctrine inhibited the full manifestation of those altruistic impulses to which conversion normally gives birth. The outbreak of altruism among the Early Buddhists and the *bhaktas* assumes nothing like the same dimensions that it did in Early Christianity, because the karma doctrine is just as congenial to egoistic complacency as to altruism and missionary zeal. According to the karma doctrine no man can assist his brother in cutting short the round of rebirth, but in Early Christianity the duty of

---

[1] See, for example, *Chhand. Up.* vi. 8. 1 ; *Bri.* iv. 3. 9, and Sankara's Commentary on *Vedanta Sutras*, iv. 4. 16 (S.B.E. xxxviii. 415).
[2] *Maitr. Up.* vi. 30 (S.B.E. xv. 327). Cf. *Bri.* iv. 4. 6 f.

making others better was inculcated as a positive obligation and was deeply grounded in fundamental Christian doctrines.

The feeling of assurance which we find as a characteristic result of many Protestant conversions fits in perfectly with the Protestant theological scheme of justification by faith. The acceptance of the dogma that what God requires of men is not their works, but their trust, at once lifts the cloud off many sin-stricken minds. A Roman Catholic writer on the psychology of religion has pointed out a striking difference between Evangelical and Catholic conversion. "Evangelical conversion," he says,[1] "has in well-marked cases as its normal and expected resultant a state of *assurance*, Catholic conversion a state of *compunction*." This difference in feeling is due to the difference in *milieu*. Evangelicalism "offers the maimed soul a complete, unpurchasable, immediate and unmediated deliverance."[2] But for Catholicism to make such an offer would be tantamount to a denial of the necessity of repeated sacrifices in the Mass and of a mediating priesthood to offer them. From the psychological point of view, we may say that the *raison d'être* of the whole sacramental system is the feeling "you never can be quite sure of your salvation." Thus, the typical Catholic mystic enters into a state of assurance, not at conversion, but after he has trodden the long Purgative Way. The average man may hardly hope to win that state at all. At the end he will still need to be "fortified by all the rites of the Church."

While conversion is a human fact, and found in all religions, its incidence is largely affected by the traditions and expectations of the group and of the period. There are religions and churches in which the forces of social suggestion are so strong, that "the soul that is invited and expected by society to pass through sickness towards strength does so, though in an ideal and moral way, rather than under literal compulsion of the animal nature."[3] Hence the high incidence of conversions among Protestant

---

[1] Howley, *Psychology and Mystical Experience*, 11.
[2] R. H. Coats, *Types of English Piety*, 246.
[3] Marett, *Threshold of Religion*, 197.

252 Conversion : Christian and Non-Christian

Evangelicals. On the other hand, there are great religions and Churches in which there is little or no expectation of conversion. For this reason we find very little " broken earthenware miraculously mended "[1] in later Judaism, Zoroastrianism and the religions of China, and comparatively few abrupt awakenings to the religious life in Churches of the sacramentarian type, though Confirmation and first Communion may bring such an awakening about.

Finally, we notice how the religion in which the convert finds unification for his divided soul always affects the doctrinal terms in which the experience is formulated. In the religion of the Old Testament, in Christianity and in Islam, the doctrinal term used to denote the psychological experience of conversion is repentance. In these religions he who has undergone a true repentance has been converted. This is perfectly natural, for all three place at the centre of their teaching belief in a personal God and in the reality of man's sin against Him. Throughout the prophetic literature of the Old Testament the call rings clear for a definite change of spiritual attitude. The burden of the prophets' preaching was never better put than in Isa. lv. 7 : " Let the wicked forsake his way, and the unrighteous man his thoughts: and let him return unto Yahweh, and he will have mercy upon him ; and unto our God, for he will abundantly pardon " (cf. xxxi. 6 ; Ezek. xiv. 6, xviii. 31 ; Mal. iii. 7, and many other passages). The prophets also made it clear that no repentance is genuine unless it includes a firm resolution to abandon sin as well as sincere sorrow for it. Time and time again they insist that a man's repentance, if genuine, will be followed by a radical change in his life. " Many of the most beautiful passages in the prophets," says Schultz,[2] " insist that deeds, not words, prove a conversion to be true." The Sufi doctrine of conversion is very similar. Their word for repentance was *tawbat*, which etymologically means " return," and at once links their terminology with that of the Old Testament prophets. Moreover, as Nicholson points out,[3] *tawbat* is

---
[1] I borrow the phrase from Moulton's *Treasure of the Magi*, 204.
[2] *Old Testament Theology*, ii. 97.
[3] *Mystics of Islam*, 30.

The Individual and the Social 253

the Moslem term for conversion. Hujwiri says: "It is not permissible that anyone should pretend to conversion without repentance," and he further says that three things are involved in *tawbat*—namely, remorse for disobedience, immediate abandonment of sin, and determination not to sin again.[1] In Islam, as also in the Old Testament, the repentant man is the forgiven man, for forgiveness is the dearest of all things to God.[2]

Throughout His ministry Jesus addressed to all a call to repentance, and it cannot be reasonably doubted that His doctrine of conversion was comprised in that term. It is rather unfortunate that the English term repentance is inadequate as a translation of μετανοία. Repentance in English too often throws the emphasis on sorrow for past sin, but in the teaching of Jesus it also included a definite effort after amendment. For Him repentance was not merely a forsaking of the old life, but a complete change of mind about it and attitude toward it.[3] As His concept of sin was deeper than that of the Old Testament prophets, so also was His concept of repentance. In the parable of the Prodigal Son, Jesus sets forth the relation between repentance and forgiveness. Forgiveness is the immediate response on the part of God to the penitence of man. Here we touch upon the spring of joy of the New Testament converts. Their forgiveness put an end to all those doubts and fears regarding the attitude of God to sin which had lain at the root of their disharmony.

When we turn to the New Testament writings, which reflect the thought of the post-Pentecostal Church, we notice a certain amplification of the doctrinal terms used to interpret the experience of conversion. The tendency early grew up to distinguish between repentance and faith. In Acts conversion is sometimes associated with repentance (ii. 38, iii. 19, viii. 22, etc.) and sometimes with faith (ix. 42, xi. 21, xvi. 31, xvii. 34, xviii. 8, etc.). Repentance is used, apparently, when the stress falls on what the

---
[1] Hujwiri, 181, 294.
[2] Cf. Nicholson, *Studies in Islamic Mysticism*, 54.
[3] Cf. Feine, *Theologie d. N.T.*, 105.

convert turns *from*, and faith when it falls on what he turns *to*, but it is one act of turning (see Acts xx. 21). Repentance, conversion, faith are in essence the same thing.[1] The writings of Paul betray a further tendency to emphasize faith rather than repentance. The references to repentance in his epistles are, at first sight, surprisingly few, though the idea comes out clearly enough in such passages as Rom. vi. 2, Eph. iv. 22, v. 8–14. The apostle's own experience led him to lay more stress on faith than on repentance in his doctrinal statement of the conversion-experience, and, indeed, to make faith the hinge of his whole doctrinal system. For him the moment in which a man is "justified by faith" is also the moment of his conversion.

Religions like Hinduism and Buddhism, in which the doctrine of karma takes the place occupied by the doctrine of sin in Judaism, Christianity and Islam, necessarily formulate the conversion process with an entirely different set of doctrinal terms. The term repentance does not appear, as, for reasons already mentioned in this chapter, there is no conviction of sin in the Christian sense. We have, it is true, found remorse in our analysis of Hindu conversions, but remorse is a very different thing from repentance, and is not a doctrinal term. In the experience of the followers of the *jnana-marga*, conviction of ignorance takes the place of conviction of sin. The maladies of the soul are due, not to alienation from God by sin, but to ignorance; and, when that is removed, happiness is secured. Thus in the *Vedanta* conversion is not a turning by repentance from vice to virtue, but rather the realization by knowledge that neither truly exists. Again, the place taken by forgiveness in Judaism, Christianity and Islam is occupied in Hinduism and Buddhism by release from karmic bonds. This release brings the happiness which in the other religions is secured by the re-establishment of right relations with God. The adjustment brought about by conversion is to the karmic process rather than to a

---

[1] Cf. Feine: " Busse ist der negative Begriff, Bekehrung der positive, der Hinkehrung zu Jesus als Messias und zu Gott. Beide aber sind im Grunde identisch mit dem geforderten Glauben." Op. cit. 212 f.

personal God. It is interesting to notice that the Early Buddhists developed a terminology which appears to reflect the different degrees of unification that were known among them. The man who was truly unified by the discipline of concentrated thought and mental effort laid down by Buddha was the *arahat*, and for him there was no return to the sphere of transmigration. At the opposite end of the scale stood the *sotapanno*, or stream-entrant, whose soul had not yet been unified and made permanently happy, but who was awake to the claims the religious life had upon him. The exact meaning of the term is not quite clear. Some scholars take it to indicate the man who has entered the stream which flows down to the ocean of Nirvana. It is more likely, however, that the reference is to the stream up which a man must forge his way in his fight for character and unification. Even the *sotapanno* will have his reward, for he will attain Nirvana after undergoing seven more births. Midway between the *sotapanno* and the *arahat* stand the "once-returner" (*sakadagami*) and the "never-returner" (*anagami*). The former has overcome desire, hate, and delusion, and will be born only once more in this world before he attains Nirvana. The latter, however, will not be born again in this world, but in the world of the gods, where he will attain Nirvana.[1] Some writers treat these terms as corresponding to four degrees of sanctification, and they make the "stream-entrant" equivalent to the converted man. This has the advantage, as well as the peril, of linking Buddhist and Christian terminology, but it is doubtful whether "entering the stream" means more than a religious "awakening." It seems, therefore, preferable to treat the four terms as indicating not so much stages of sanctification as degrees of unification. If regard be had to the whole tenor of Buddhist teaching, then only the *arahat* can be said to be converted in the full sense of being unified and made happy by his grip on religious realities. The testimony of the authors of the *Thera-theri-gatha* is quite explicit on this point. One woman expressly says she had been a member

---

[1] These technical terms are found in the *Udana*, v. 5 (Strong's trans., 78 f.). See also S.B.E. x. 48 n.

of the Order for twenty-five years without winning self-mastery :

> " Full five-and-twenty years since I came forth !
> But in my troubled heart in no way yet
> Could I discern the calm of victory.
> The peace of mind, the governance of thoughts
> Long sought, I found not ; and with anguish thrilled
> I dwelt in memory on the Conqueror's word.
> To free my path from all that breedeth ill,
> I strove with passionate ardour, and I won !
> Craving is dead, and the Lord's will is done.
> To-day is now the seventh day since first
> Was withered up within that ancient Thirst." [1]

One of the Brethren says that two years elapsed between his becoming a *sotapanno* and his unification. Another puts the period down as five days.[2]

So far as I know, the Hindu *bhaktas* made little attempt to formulate their conversion-experience in terms of doctrine. This is not surprising, for, charming as they are as devotees, as theologians they are disappointing. In their writings they frequently imply that the moment of their conversion was the moment when they turned with loving devotion (*bhakti*) to the feet of the god they adored. Beyond that they rarely go, save to say that their *bhakti* found its correlative in the grace (*prasada*) of the deity.[3] Their main concern is to show the many ways in which *bhakti* can be cultivated, and to indicate by human analogies the different degrees of its intensity.[4] The end secured by *bhakti* is, of course, release from *samsara*. It is true that they lavished their devotion upon a personal god, but they do so, not in order to restore relations with him that have been interrupted by sin, but in order to win *mukti*. The gospel of the *bhaktas* was that loving devotion brings men release as effectively as knowledge.

It is not necessary further to illustrate the effect of the

[1] *Therigatha*, 39–41.
[2] *Theragatha*, 127 f., 222–224. See also 557–562 and *Therigatha*, 37 f., 99–101.
[3] The connection of the doctrine of divine grace and conversion has been dealt with above in Chapter XIII.
[4] See e.g. Sarkar, 284–289.

The Individual and the Social 257

convert's *milieu* upon the doctrinal statement he gives of his experience. It is, however, important to point out that the significance of what has been said is not exhausted by saying that the convert imposes upon his experience the doctrinal terms of the faith in which he finds unification. The doctrinal system also controls to a large extent his expectations, and for this reason he tends to discover in his conversion what he has been led to expect to find. The thesis of this chapter is that the doctrinal system modifies the experience of conversion in all its phases.

PART III

CHAPTER XVIII
CONVERSION IN ITS COMPARATIVE ASPECTS

AMPLE evidence has now been produced to show that conversion is a permanent possibility of man's nature as man, and that it may, therefore, occur in any religion. Is it possible to frame a definition of conversion that will cover all cases, Christian and non-Christian ? In the light of the preceding chapters we may say that conversion in its comparative aspects is a reaction taking the form of a psychological surrender to an ideal, and issuing in moral development. Such a formula obviously covers cases in which the central element of conversion is faith in a divine redeemer. It covers, that is, Christian conversions in which the surrender is made to Christ and those conversions in the *bhakti* faiths of India where the surrender was made to Krishna, or Rama, or Siva. The formula will also include the conversion of the Cynics, Stoics and others in the Græco-Roman world, since they surrendered to an ideal embodied in the philosophico-religious teaching of their respective schools. Similarly, Early Buddhist conversions are included, because the converts surrendered to the ideal embodied in the Four Noble Truths. It is not, however, immediately obvious that the formula will include those who found unification by following the *jnana-marga*. Theirs was, apparently, a purely intellectual process. Deliverance came to them when they apprehended the truth that Brahman was the sole reality, and that each of their souls was the universal Atman whole and undivided. It may be asked what room there was in such an experience for a

Conversion in its Comparative Aspects 259

surrender. Closer examination of the psychology of their experience will show that there was room. Unification of soul and the assurance of deliverance from *samsara* did not come to all who gave intellectual assent to the Upanishadic doctrine of the sole reality of Brahman. Deliverance, it is true, came by knowledge, but not by knowledge of the merely cognitive kind. In other words, their conversion was not brought about merely by intellectual or cognitive processes, otherwise their experiences would not have had so marked an emotional colouring.[1] The knowledge they had won had to be realized by the self—had to be transmuted into belief—before it had the power to bring peace and unification to the soul. And belief is an activity of the self in its emotional and volitional as well as in its cognitive aspects. As William James says,[2] the things we believe we " turn to *with a will.*" Of the followers of the *jnana-marga* those alone were converted who, after they had grasped the truth that their souls and the Universal Atman were one, acted on that belief—in other words, surrendered to it.

In this connection it is of the utmost importance to point out that, when we have come to understand the psychological mechanism of conversion (see Chapter XIV), we have not dealt fully with its psychology.[3] Men and women are not converted by a rearrangement of their complexes. For example, Paul's conversion, as we have seen, turned on his acceptance of the proposition that Jesus of Nazareth, though crucified, was the Messiah. When his Christian complex rose from the unconscious, where it had been buried by repression, into his consciousness, he was able to give his assent to the proposition. He would, however, have remained unconverted if he had done no more than give his intellectual assent. In point of fact, he did much more than admit the proposition to a place among the cognitive elements of his mind. He transformed intellectual assent into the white heat of belief by surrendering himself

---

[1] See above, 49 f.
[2] *Principles of Psychology*, ii. 297. Italics his.
[3] For this reason Chapter XIV was headed " The Psychological Mechanism of Conversion " and not " The Psychology of Conversion."

to all that the proposition implied. He resolved to organize his life around a new centre, and to put forth all his energy in the pursuit of a new goal.

Again, Gotama Buddha was not converted when a complex long incubating in the unconscious suddenly became clear-cut and closely knit. During the long years of his spiritual travail it is not improbable that other schemes of salvation than that which brought him unification presented themselves to his mind with equal clearness, but they had failed to bring about his conversion. They had all been rejected by him. At last there came one which he could accept—in other words, to which he could surrender. Only when he had thus surrendered did all things become new.

Other cases might be examined, but sufficient has been said to show that, whatever the psychological mechanism of conversion, the self has to make a conscious surrender to the ideal before conversion can take place.

At this point another question may be conveniently discussed: What is the relation of the surrender, which we find in all conversions, to what we have called the psychological mechanism of conversion? The answer seems to be that the psychological mechanism makes the surrender possible. Quite obviously Paul could not surrender to Christ so long as his Christian complex remained buried in the unconscious. Nor, again, could Augustine surrender to the higher ideal of the Christian life while an acute conflict was going on between his sexual and religious complexes. His surrender was a psychological impossibility until a rearrangement of the complexes had taken place. Nor, moreover, could Gotama Buddha surrender to the new ideal so long as his conception of it was blurred and dim. As soon as it was sufficiently clear-cut, surrender was possible. And, to take one other example, the victim of some vice, whose conversion occurs the moment he abandons his own strivings and flings himself upon some higher power, cannot surrender so long as he is obsessed with the fear of falling into his besetting sin. His morbid complex needs to be reassociated with thoughts of power and ability.[1]

[1] Cf. above, 185 f.

Conversion in its Comparative Aspects 261

This attempt to correlate the psychological mechanism of conversion with the surrender factor in it is not inconsistent with a belief in human freedom. It does, of course, rule out the old libertarianism, which held that the will has absolute freedom to determine all mental activities. Room, however, is left for the view of the will as "character in action,"[1] which view is by no means committed to the notion that determinism reigns absolutely in the psychical as in the physical realm. Nor does our correlation rule out the possibility of the bestowal of divine grace. As we have said above,[2] in speaking of the psychological mechanism of conversion, God is a God of order even in the affairs of the spirit, and it is not the less He who has done a thing when we have come to understand how He has done it. Moreover, our exposition is distinctly favourable to the view that what divine grace does in conversion is to come to the will with healing and enabling power so as to make surrender to God possible.

Into the further problem as to how much of the surrender is of God and how much of man we cannot enter here. The attempt to divide the ground between God and man, and to assign to each his exact share in conversion, is one of the most baffling problems that has tempted the theological mind. We reject equally the view which holds that man can be converted without divine grace and that which denies that he makes any contribution. We must hold that God and man co-operate, but the precise terms of their co-operation are hid from our eyes. All we can say is that the operations of divine grace are psychologically and ethically conditioned. We cannot, however, say where the work of either God or man begins and ends. In actual experience the subjective life of man and the objective grace of God so interpenetrate that to separate them exactly is impossible even for abstract thought.

We turn now to the moral development which always follows conversion. How real it is we have seen in a previous chapter, and we are safe in saying that it always finds a place wherever there is a conscious surrender to

[1] McDougall, *Outline of Psychology*, 446 f.
[2] P. 194.

the ideal. The only dubious cases are those in which the subject is unified by following the *jnana-marga*. No outbreak of the active virtues followed these conversions. It would, however, be a mistake to assume that no moral development ensued. We may safely say that entry into the path resulted in freedom from passion (*vairagya*).[1] This virtue, on which Hindu ethics lays so much stress, meant freedom from all selfish passions. But we have also seen that the moral fruits of conversion are always conditioned as to their extent and quality by the environment within which the subject's development to the time of his conversion has taken place, and also by the nature of the ideal to which he surrenders. If the ideal be imperfectly moralized, the ensuing moral development will be impoverished, for men inevitably become like that which they most admire. That being so, it follows that the most important factor in conversion is that to which a turning or surrender is made. We are thus led to the question whether our survey of conversion in the different religions has put us in a position to say what characteristics an ideal should possess if surrender to it is to be facilitated and some guarantee be forthcoming that the moral development will take the highest form.

In the first place, we notice that the influence of an ideal embodied in a person is always greater than that of an ideal considered merely as a body of ideas or precepts. This was never better put than by Martineau in a well-known passage, which we quote here in full, because it is impossible not to hear in it the echoes of his own experience of conversion:[2] "Loving wonder at some impersonated goodness is the sole attraction to which we rise: this it is that sprinkles us with a wave of true regeneration. . . . Among those who have had any deep moral history at all there are probably few who, on looking back to the sources of their first faith, do not see the sainted image of some companion or guide, whose like they never think to meet again, and through whose spirit, to the end, they will not cease to gaze at life. To others, less happy in their living

[1] On this virtue see Max Müller, *Six Systems of Indian Philosophy*, 339.
[2] See above, 122.

friendship, the new birth may have come from some image of ideal excellence in the pages of biography or fiction ; for though here the voices and stir of reality do not beat upon the ear, conception does the work of the eye, and the story tells upon the heart, like scenery still speaking, though silent, to the deaf."[1]

Now, in religion, as distinct from morals, the source and seat of the ideal are always found in the highest order of religious reality. Indeed, only when the ideal is religious is it able, in the vast majority of cases, to lay claim to man's surrender with an authority that is above him. In religious conversion, therefore, surrender to the ideal means surrender to the highest order of religious reality the subject knows. And it follows that surrender to that religious reality will be greatly facilitated, if it is conceived as personal, as well as the source and ground of the ideal.

This truth is written large over the religious history of man, and not least over the story of India's remarkable religious quest. Man is more than intellect and will. His psychic structure gives him the capacity to feel emotion, and confers on him the power to love. His religion, moreover, must appeal to his whole personality and provide an outlet for his emotions and his love, as well as afford material on which to exercise his intellect and will. We cannot, however, love the impersonal. Tulsi Das speaks for the whole race of mankind when in his *Ramayana* he says : " The worship of the impersonal laid no hold on my heart."[2] There were those, it is true, who found unification for their divided souls by surrendering themselves to the impersonal, all-comprehending Brahman, or, more strictly speaking, by realizing their unity with it. *Jnana-marga*, however, is a way attractive only to the select few. The multitudes of India have sought unification by way of loving devotion to a personal deity. The same principle emerges from our study of conversion in Early Buddhism. Nothing is more striking than the way in which, in defiance of his system, Buddha's own personality drew men to him in the bonds of personal affection. " The Buddha's new

[1] *A Study of Religion*, ii. 29 f.
[2] Cited by Cave in his *Redemption, Hindu and Christian*, 218.

264 Conversion : Christian and Non-Christian

method of salvation," write Rhys Davids and Oldenberg,[1] "his new doctrine of what salvation was, did not present itself to the consciousness of the Early Buddhist community as an idea, as a doctrine, standing alone, and merely on its own merits. In their minds it was indissolubly bound up with the memory of the revered and striking personality of him who had proclaimed it." To his early followers he was their ideal, summing up in his own life and character all that they hoped to be. He was the captain of their salvation and their leader in the upward path that leads to character. He was the living embodiment of his own teaching, presenting to the world a life of purity and a life of love. Gracious, kindly, winsome, patient, courageous, sympathetic, calm, tolerant, he was bound to win the hearts of men in a land like India, where the ideal man is he who, amid all provocations and in all situations, is gentle and patient.

In theory, however, attachment to the person of Buddha was a mistake, because the task Buddhism set itself was to deliver men from all attachment, and, therefore, from attachment to Buddha as from all else. When the new convert made his confession, "I take refuge in the Buddha, the Dhamma, and the Sangha," it did not mean that personal relationship to the founder was an integral part of Buddhism. Faith in Buddha was not attachment to or faith in his person, but reliance on his teaching, acceptance of his system of deliverance. "One takes refuge in the Buddha in order to take refuge in himself, as the Master has done," says one who is himself a Buddhist ;[2] and nothing could be clearer. At this point, however, Buddhism maltreated one of the fundamental human instincts, for all men are hero-worshippers and lovers. To this instinct Mahayana Buddhism paid regard when it deified the Buddha and made faith in him one of its fundamental doctrines. Our brief survey, which might be indefinitely extended, leads us, then, to the conclusion that the ideal to whom surrender is made in conversion needs to present itself to man in a living personal God.

[1] S.B.E. xiii., p. xvii. See also 150 f. above.
[2] Prof. Anesaki in E.R.E. v. 448.

Conversion in its Comparative Aspects 265

Again, the surrender is made still easier if this personal deity is also a God of grace, drawing near to his worshippers in redemptive love. The hearts of men crave for a God who condescends to share their lot and their need, and who is actively at work on their behalf in their fight for the higher life. Such a God can hardly fail to evoke a response from the heart of man; and the surrender will be no lifeless, flaccid thing, but will take the form of warm, personal love. Time and time again the history of religion reveals the pull, so to speak, of a redemptive idea. For vast numbers of Hindus the most moving verse in the Gita is the following, which is put into the mouth of Krishna: " Whensoever the Law fails and lawlessness uprises . . . then do I bring myself to bodied birth. To guard the righteous, to destroy evil-doers, to establish the Law, I come into birth age after age." [1]

Association with a redemptive idea has transformed even the dread and terrible Siva into a god of grace, who, as we have seen, is able to call forth from his worshippers a most fervent surrender. The motive which is said to underlie all his appearances as Sat-guru is his boundless love and grace to his suffering children. Manikkar Vachakar and the other Tamil poets often speak of him as the " blue-throated one." " It is an emblem of the suffering he graciously endured to save the world. The gods at one time were in sore distress and came to Siva for assistance. He descended from Mount Kailasa and churned the sea of milk, and from thence there issued an ambrosial food of undying joy. But first there came a stream of black halahala poison, and this Siva drank up. His neck, thus dark and swollen, is the perpetual witness of his mighty grace. So to the gods he gave ambrosia; for himself he took the deadly poison." [2]

Even Buddhism made room for the redemptive idea by picturing its founder as passing through many previous lives, in one of the earlier of which he solemnly resolved not to attain his own immediate deliverance, but to become a Buddha, and guide men to the other side of the ocean of *samsara*. He then passed, in face of many trials, through

[1] iv. 6 f. Barnett's trans. 103.   [2] Cave, op. cit. 132.

a round of births, refusing to enter final peace alone, but intent upon the salvation of all men, upon whom he bestows his grace. Here, again, we see later Buddhism trying to make good one of the deficiencies of its Founder's teaching. Beneath the varying idioms our witnesses use we can trace a common cry that the God to whom they surrender shall be One who comes to their help, and who shall invade their souls with a triumphant power they do not themselves possess.

Thirdly, in this connection, we need not do more than again point out, what needs no detailed proof, that the ideal needs to be conceived in stringently ethical terms, if guarantees are to be had of the nature of the moral development that follows conversion.

At this point we are naturally led to ask : In what living religion is the highest form of conversion facilitated and found ? A full discussion of this question might seem to lead us into the extensive field of comparative theology, since the prevailing ideas of the religious group to which the convert belongs affect the conversion-experience to such a large extent. Such an extensive study is not, however, necessary. We can confine attention to two crucial points : the character of the ideal to which surrender is made, and the quality and extent of the ensuing moral development.

Judaism, Zoroastrianism and the indigenous religions of China may be put aside, for in them we find very little " broken earthenware miraculously mended." For the scientific student of religion Islam also is excluded, if only on account of the character of Muhammad. Though the Prophet repeatedly declared that he was an ordinary man, specially chosen by Allah as the organ of his revelation, it soon became one of the fundamental dogmas of Islam that the Sunnah (the " way " pointed out by the Prophet's word and example) was the necessary and indispensable completion of the Koran. A thing was right because the Prophet had said or done it. Thus arose the idea that the life of the Prophet was the revealed norm of conduct for all the faithful. Surely it is no exaggeration, but sober judgment, to say that Islam " has preserved, in the life and character of its Founder, an enduring principle of degradation."[1]

The claims of Hinayana Buddhism have already been considered, at least implicitly. In it the ideal to which surrender is to be made is neither personal nor redemptive. Devotion to the person of Gotama is, in theory, forbidden; and every man is to be his own saviour by his own unaided efforts. How really Early Buddhism failed to meet the religious needs and cravings of the human spirit is seen by the modifications it underwent before it became the faith of millions in its Mahayana form. Unfortunately, however, these changes were not always carried out in the lofty ethical spirit of its founder. The teaching of Gotama was more often degraded than elevated by association with crude animistic beliefs, magic and priestcraft. The Mahayanist doctrine of divine grace is everywhere encumbered with the karma doctrine, and it is mediated to men, not through the historical Gotama, but through the mythical Amida, Kwanyin and Avalokiteswara.

Turning now to Hinduism, we may first of all consider the claims the *jnana-marga* can put forward as offering to men the highest form of unification for the divided soul. Whatever value it may otherwise possess, it will be rejected by most men, because it results in a form of life of no value save to him who lives it. Thus many educated Indians to-day reject it decisively because it empties life of all meaning, and deprives those who follow it of all incentives to a life of unselfish activity and service.[2] The *jivan-mukta*, as Deussen says,[3] "is deprived of every incitement to action or initiation of any kind; he is lifted out of the whole circle of illusory individual existence, his body is no longer his, his works no longer his; everything which he may henceforth do or leave undone belongs to the sphere of the great illusion which he has penetrated, and is therefore of no account.... When knowledge of the Atman has been gained, every action, and therefore

---

[1] W. St. Clair Tisdall, *The Religion of the Crescent*, 122.
[2] See, e.g., the passionate protest of Rabindranath Tagore in his *Sadhana*, 129 f.
[3] *Philosophy of the Upanishads*, 362.

every moral action also, has been deprived of meaning." How the doctrine works out in practice may be seen from the following incident : During the epidemic in the autumn of 1918, Mrs. Sinclair Stevenson, of the Irish Presbyterian Mission in Gujarat, found a dying man abandoned on the verandah of an empty house. It was impossible to get food or medicine between his clenched teeth, nor could men be found strong enough to carry him to the hospital. On a bridge near by two sturdy, powerful ascetics were sitting, intoning sacred verses. She asked them to help her to carry the unknown sufferer to the hospital. With astonishment and blazing anger they cried : "We! we are *sannyasi*; we never do anything for anyone else."[1] In a word, *jnana-marga* can never hope to win acceptance as the highest form of conversion because it fails utterly when put to that test which the unsophisticated mind will always regard as the most acid of all tests. The plain man naturally feels that in the fruits of conversion for life he has a perfect touchstone by which he can estimate its value. But he who has won unification of soul by following the *jnana-marga* is condemned to a life of no value to any save himself.

Much more can be said in support of the claims of the *bhakti* cults of Hinduism. Rama, Krishna and Siva are personal gods of grace, who respond to the need of their worshippers. As we have seen, Saivite and Vaishnava *bhaktas* alike ascribe their wonderful experiences of spiritual illumination and moral renewal to the dynamic grace of the god they adored. This is a very remarkable fact when we remember that the all-pervading karma doctrine made it difficult for the Hindu to find a place in his scheme of things for the grace of God. " The Indian theist, for whom the karma doctrine was an axiom, found himself in a sore dilemma. If God had His hand upon the world at all, if He was engaged in its concerns, then He was no God, but a fettered soul, needing to be freed from *samsara* as much as man himself. If, on the other hand, He was conceived as free, then it was a condition of His freedom that He have no connection with the world and no influence upon it.

[1] Mrs. Sinclair Stevenson's *Rites of the Twice-born*, 426 f.

Conversion in its Comparative Aspects 269

It was the logic of this argument that made atheists of the Buddhist and the Samkhyan and the Jain."[1] But the *bhakti* saints were not so logical. Their experience of divine grace, especially at conversion, was such that they celebrated it in song, and sought to find room for it in their systems in spite of all difficulties. " It is in the Saiva Siddhanta alone that we find this conception of God's gracious energy realized in some measure as a higher law, transcending and taking up into itself the lower. It comprehends within the sweep of its doctrine of grace the whole of the world-process, teaching that the purpose of the Lord from first to last is gracious, and that the end in view throughout is the soul's emancipation and his entrance into blissful union with his Lord."[2] Yet even in the Saiva Siddhanta, as Dr. Macnicol points out, the operations of Siva's grace are limited and hindered in various ways, and the god has to divide his empire with his rival, karma.

But it is not enough for the ideal to be conceived as personal and redemptive; it must also be construed in stringently ethical terms if it is to produce the highest type of conversion. Can we, then, say that in Krishna, or Rama, or Siva we have presented to men the highest ideal of moral goodness? The present writer has never heard such a claim made on behalf of the dread and terrible Siva. There are, however, many Hindus who are prepared to make this claim on behalf of the Krishna of the *Gita*, whom they regard as worthy of a place alongside Christ. Unfortunately, Hindus, with few exceptions, regard the picture of Krishna in the *Bhagavata Purana* as every bit as authentic as the picture of him in the *Gita*. To say the least, this means that those who surrendered themselves in loving devotion to Krishna surrendered to a god whose character was conceived along immoral lines. Hence the marked tendency of the sects founded on the *Bhagavata Purana* to slide into the morass of eroticism. Chaitanya bade his followers contemplate the love of Krishna and his mistress Radha. It requires no great psychological insight to see how detrimental this must be to the moral imagination of the *bhakta*. " The veriest tyro," says

[1] Macnicol, *Indian Theism*, 225.   [2] Ibid. 228.

Jogendranath Bhattacharyya, himself a Hindu, " ought to be able to foresee what the fruits of a tree must be that owes its existence to seeds supplied by the *Bhagvat* and the *Brahma-Vaivarta*."[1] Nothing is more suggestive, in this connection, than the way in which the leaders of the Neo-Krishnaite movement in Bengal to-day have rewritten the life of their hero-god, purging the stories about him of their grosser features in order to make him a more worthy object of their *bhakti*. A few Hindus go further, and fearlessly denounce all the immoral features of the old legends.[2] Others, again, seek to explain away the discreditable features by finding a spiritual meaning beneath the literal one. The device is an old one, and has found a place more than once in the history of religion. We may, however, safely say that the method of allegory will ultimately satisfy none. The followers of Krishna will be compelled by the march of thought to leave the method behind and to give full play to their moral judgment on these matters. In any case, the condition of affairs in India to-day makes it clear that the higher conscience of India has already rejected Krishna as the ideal of moral conduct.

Bhaktas like Ramananda and Tulsi Das, who rendered their devotion to Rama, were more happily placed, for, unlike Krishna, Rama was an exemplary husband, and his story everywhere makes for chastity and manly effort. But the influence of the moral ideal he embodies is sadly hampered by many gross superstitions that stand in connection with it ; and, without dispute, it may be said that it is not the highest concrete realization of the moral ideal known to the history of religion. Above all, the Ramaite *bhakta* is expressly warned not to copy the gods. Says Tulsi Das in his Ramayana : " The fool who in the pride of knowledge presumes to copy the gods, saying it is the same for a man as for a god, shall be cast into hell for as long as this world lasts."[3] That such a warning should need to be given is in itself a most significant fact.

---

[1] *Hindu Castes and Sects*, 463.
[2] See, e.g., Barnett's *Heart of India*, 6.
[3] Cited by Cave, op. cit. 222;

Conversion in its Comparative Aspects

We may next apply the pragmatic test, and ask whether the fruits of conversion among the Hindu *bhaktas* were pure and elevating in character and broad in their range. In the preceding chapter we have pointed out how limited these fruits were, and how the altruistic impulses to which conversion gave birth languished in the chilling atmosphere of the karma doctrine. Men, it is true, are often better than their logic and creed; but, in the long run, they cannot give themselves whole-heartedly to the cultivation of virtues with which the governing principles of their creed are inconsistent. Nothing could be more magnificent than the protest made by the *bhakti* saints against caste, and nothing is more suggestive than their failure to break its iron regime. How unusual a phenomenon missionary zeal was in India may be seen from the statement of the *Indian Mirror*[1] that Keshab Chandra Sen's missionary tours were the first of their kind ever undertaken by a Hindu.

Again, the fruits of conversion among the *bhaktas* were always liable to degenerate, if not into eroticism, into mere transports of unethical emotion, which were of little or no value either to the individual or the community. The ideal to which they surrendered lacked just that ethical content that would ensure enduring ethical fruits. They exposed themselves to all the dangers of an unethical emotionalism in religion because they were too often content to begin and end in a tempest of love and joy. When the wave of emotion had passed, it left little spiritual residuum. No provision was made for the continuous moral development of the convert. All he was bidden to do was to continue to meditate upon and praise the Adored One and to keep company with his fellow-devotees. If he did this, he would again experience that rush of emotion which chokes the speech and thrills both mind and body with pleasurable feeling.

Turning now to consider the claims of Christianity, we find that Jesus began His ministry with a call to repentance, as the Baptist had done before Him. He took sin seriously, and in His concept of it included not only external acts of

[1] Quoted above, p. 239.

272 Conversion : Christian and Non-Christian

wrongdoing, but also any failure in love. He was not, however, content to din a summons to repentance in the ears of men. No message of mere denunciation sufficed Him. He mixed with sinners, ate with them, and sought to touch their hearts in different ways. Some He rebuked, others He encouraged, others, again, He consoled. Thus He evoked their love and gratitude. He made His whole ministry a picture of the divine love—an embodiment of the truth that the Heavenly Father " desireth not the death of a sinner, but rather that he should turn from his wickedness and live," and, inferentially, that the divine aid is at the disposal of all who seek the higher life. His personal influence was the great force which moulded men into a new life. Indeed, He often stated His call to repentance (conversion) in terms of a personal relation to Himself. " His summons to enter the Kingdom took the form of a personal invitation, ' Follow me.' Ever and again He declared that men's attitude to Him would determine their attitude to the Kingdom of God. They were to see in Him its living embodiment, and according as they welcomed or rejected Him they would be judged." [1] In brief, He invited men to an act of moral trust in Himself. Those who responded found themselves not only able to forsake their sinful life, but to change their mind about it and their attitude toward it. What He succeeded in inducing in the lives of those who obeyed His call was nothing less than a complete change of the whole mind, dispositions and standards.

Further, the moral development which followed their conversion was guaranteed by the character of Him to Whom they had surrendered. Those who came into daily contact with Him were led in various ways to see the depth and subtlety of their sin, till one of them could cry in his moral agony, " Depart from me, for I am a sinful man, O Lord " (Luke v. 8). They never felt inclined to judge Him by their own ethical standards. On the contrary, it was He who was constantly refining and criticizing theirs. As their companionship with Him continued, they saw that He had no share in their moral failings ; and they found

[1] E. F. Scott, *The Kingdom and the Messiah*, 153.

themselves constrained to treat Him as more than human, for He did for them "what the moral insight of the penitent would ask from God."[1] They also found that the more they revised their standards and values, the deeper their penitence and the clearer their spiritual insight became. He was increasingly and continuously to them a living sacrament of divine grace. So although He never dictated to men the needs of which they should be conscious in coming to Him, His character always determined the nature and quality of the moral development that followed upon surrender to Him. One of the wonderful features of their experience was that they always found more in Him than they had sought.

Our all too brief survey of the experience of those converts who knew Jesus in the days of His flesh, shows that they discovered in Him an ideal that was at once personal, redemptive and perfectly moralized, and which, therefore, guaranteed the nature of the moral development that followed upon surrender to Him. And such, we may fairly claim, has been the discovery of all Christian converts since the withdrawal of His bodily presence. The central factor in their conversion has always been an act of self-surrender to His personal influence. Indeed, it was not until after the Resurrection and Pentecost that His followers came to realize all that was involved in their experience of Him, and they were led to give His person a centrality they had not accorded Him before. The unique experience and the dialectical ability of a convert like Paul enabled him to unfold this experience and to give it expression in theological terms. But the apostle was only continuing a line of development already marked out. His connection of faith in Christ with the attitude of personal devotion to Him was not really new. It went back to that affection which Jesus awoke in the breasts of His disciples, and is the explication in theological terms of that "expulsive power of a new affection" which had transformed their lives as well as the apostle's. Again, all that the Pauline doctrine of sanctification does is to give fuller doctrinal expression to that experience of moral

[1] Principal Douglas Mackenzie in E.R.E. vii. 52.

renewal which followed conversion. Paul's aim is to insist that the new life in Christ, begun at conversion, cannot be otherwise than moral, or it would be out of accord with Him Who is its origin and source (Rom. vi. 2, 11 f.). The modification of character which begins at conversion must always be in the direction of Christ-likeness. Moreover, it was not until after the death of Jesus that the full import of His redemptive work was seen as an overpowering disclosure of the love of God in the sacrifice and death of His Son. After the Crucifixion the surrender of Christian conversion was made, not only to the Jesus Who lived on earth amongst men, but also to the Christ, the Son of God, Who rose from the dead after dying on the cross a vicarious death for men and out of love for them.

It is just at this point that Christianity possesses in its doctrine of atonement, through the vicarious suffering of Christ, a depth of appeal that is not to be found in other religions. In Hinduism, for example, there is no cross, no revelation of vicarious suffering in the heart of God. A suffering deity is unknown. No one of its many incarnations fails to be triumphant, and not one of them is represented as seriously suffering for men. The love of the Adored One, which drew the Hindu *bhaktas* to him, lacks, therefore, something that would make its appeal most poignant. Again, the life and death of Christ rest on a basis of historic fact. But the stories of the grace of Krishna, Rama and Siva have no such basis. This is a line of argument that at present impresses few Hindus. To them, as to some extreme Christian Modernists, an idea is as good as a fact. Some go farther and assert that Christianity's dependence upon an historic Founder is one of its weaknesses. They quote with approval the statement of Swami Vivekananda that Hinduism alone escapes shipwreck on what he calls "the rock of historicality." It seems, however, a safe prediction that the demand for historicity will grow rather than diminish. Ultimately the Hindu will not be able to rest his faith upon a legend.

At this point an interesting question arises which we can treat only briefly and parenthetically. How far is a conceptual knowledge of Christ's life and work necessary to Christian conversion? James and Leuba contend that it is non-essential, "although so often efficacious and antecedent."[1] Here, surely, they go too far. Yet there is an element of truth behind the position they take up. A complete dogmatic presentation of Christ is not necessary to Christian conversion. One of the standing wonders in the experience of most ministers and missionaries is that converts, who know so little about Christ, nevertheless manifest very remarkable changes in their lives at conversion.[2] But in every conversion that can rightly be called Christian some knowledge of Christ is present. It may be slight; it may lie at the periphery of consciousness; but it is always there. If the question be raised as to how much of Christ needs to be known before Christian conversion is possible, the answer seems to be that sufficient must be known for the ideal He embodies to make its appeal to the soul.

This leads naturally to another point. The appeal of Christ is not only to reason and emotion, but to conscience; indeed, He is most truly apprehended when He speaks to the conscience of man. The grace He bestows on all who surrender to Him enlightens the mind, but it also speaks to the conscience, and, above all, it comes with enabling power to the will. In the Christian doctrine and experience of grace the central emphasis falls upon grace as a divine power conferring moral ability on sinful man. In the greatest of all Indian systems of divine grace, the Saiva Siddhanta, the emphasis falls on enlightenment.[3] The difference is not accidental. It runs back to different conceptions of the nature of man's greatest need. Christianity claims that it is deliverance from the guilt and power of sin; Indian thought asserts that it is deliverance from karmic bonds. The divergence between the two systems is fundamental, and comparison is difficult, because

---

[1] James, 246.
[2] For detailed proof of this statement, see Harnack, *Mission and Expansion of Christianity*, i. 87, and Campbell N. Moody, *The Heathen Heart*, 90 f., 119, 140, 156. The former is dealing with conversions to Christianity in the post-apostolic age, the latter with conversions from heathenism in Formosa to-day.
[3] Cf. Schomerus, *Der Saiva Siddhanta*, 289.

276 Conversion : Christian and Non-Christian

we are dealing with disparate ideas. All we can do at this juncture is to reaffirm the conviction that the position adopted by Christianity is the much more adequate analysis of the moral life of man.

We may now apply the pragmatic test to Christian conversion and ask whether it is followed by moral fruits, abundant and elevating, and also of value both to the convert himself and to the society to which he belongs. The history of the Christian Church as a moral agency in the world is the answer, for through the men and women within it, who have consciously surrendered themselves to Christ, it has been the greatest and most elevating ethical force known to men. It is not denied that other religions have exercised a noble influence on the race, but it is surely beyond dispute that their contribution has been less extensive and less elevating. They have never been the equal of Christianity in producing enthusiasm for philanthropic effort and in supplying inspiration to social service. How true this is may be seen from the earnest efforts now being made by many educated Indians to copy the active philanthropy of Christianity by dedicating themselves to the work of social amelioration among the degraded and despised classes of their land. Such work was hitherto unknown in Hinduism. There have, of course, been times in the history of the Christian Church when she has failed to do her rightful work. But she possesses what no other religion has, " an enduring principle of regeneration " [1] in the character of her Founder. Further, in Christianity the altruistic impulses to which conversion gives birth are never inhibited by its doctrinal system. On the contrary, the converted Christian is instigated both by the teaching and the personal example of his Lord to an unappeasable desire to heal, uplift and save his fellows. He can say with conviction what no believer in the karma doctrine can say of his Master :

> " I knew that Christ had given me birth
> To brother all the souls on earth."

Thus in our search for the highest form of conversion

[1] The phrase is Lecky's. See his *History of Morals*, ii. 9.

we are led to Christianity. With justice it claims to possess the promise and potency of the highest type of conversion, because Christian conversion is a reaction in which Christ is central. The history of religions reveals no other person, historical or legendary, who can be placed beside Him as so entirely worthy an object of the soul's surrender, and who presents the same guarantees of the kind of conduct and character that such surrender will produce. In His moral perfection He stands alone, unique and peerless, the Master of every man's conscience and the Judge of all. And, further, in the ideal He embodies there are no provincialisms. Buddha, Krishna and Rama cannot be other than Indian; Muhammad other than Arabian; Confucius other than Chinese. But the character of Jesus has no racial peculiarities and limitations. He is a Son of man, the ideal of all human conduct and the crown of all human strivings after the good and true. Both East and West may find in Him the highest and fullest expression of their characteristic virtues. He thus possesses a universality of appeal which is the promise of His sway over men of every race and land. But He is much more than the ideal of all human conduct. Men confront in Him the redemptive grace and energy of God in a degree that transcends all their hopes and prayers.

INDEX AND GLOSSARY

Abnormal phenomena, 211
Abu Bakr, 81
Abu Sa'id, 86ff., 233, 240
Abu Yazid, 83, 240
Adolescence, 116f., 190
Akbar the Great, 127f.
Akhnaton, 96, 130
Alexander (revivalist), 205, 208, 213, 220
Altruism, 230ff., 250, 271, 276
Amos, 18f.
Anesaki, 98f., 131, 165, 174, 264
Antisthenes, 91
Apollonius of Tyana, 93, 123
Arahat, one who has reached Nirvana
Ardigo, Roberto, 192f.
Arnold, T. W., 80ff.
Arya Samaj, 63
Asavas, a Pali term for the four intoxicants: sensuality, individuality, delusion, ignorance
Assurance, feeling of, 187, 251
Atman, the self or soul; a name for the Absolute
Atonement, 274
Auditions, *see* Voices
Augustine, 16, 147, 151, 165, 180ff.
Australian Bushmen, 105f.
Automatisms, 168, 211f., 215

Babism, 89
Babylonian religion, 95
Backsliders, 221
Baptism, 104ff., 109ff.
Barclay, Robert, 120
Barnett, 46, 58
Battaks of Sumatra, 133, 247
Baudouin, 185
Belief, 259
Benedict, St., 117
Benson, Mr. A. C., 208

Bernard, St., 117
Beza, Theodore, 135
Bhakta, he who shows *bhakti*, i.e. loving devotion
Bhakti, 47, 50ff., 250, 256, 268ff., 271
Bhikku (*bhikshu*), Buddhist monk
Bhikkuni, feminine form of *bhikku*
Blindness, 167
Bodhi, wisdom, knowledge
Bois, chap. xv., *passim*, 201, 205, 210, 213ff., 219f., 225
Booth, General, 136, 183, 189, 190, 206
Brahma Samaj, 63ff., 197, 206, 229, 234
Brahman, a name of the Absolute
Brainerd, 187
Brother Lawrence, 118f.
Brotherly love, 230f.
Buddha, the, 15, 67ff., 144f., 155, 189, 226, 236, 248, 260, 264
Buddhism, 67ff., 124ff., 144f., 149ff., 155ff., 164, 172ff., 226f., 236f., 248, 250, 254ff., 263f., 265f., 267
Bunyan, John, 14, 187, 189

Caldecott, 154, 243
Carpenter, J. E., 51, 144, 160, 237
Caste, polemic against, 232, 271
Catherine of Genoa, 119, 191
Cave, S., 263, 265, 270
Cellini, Benvenuto, 168
Chaitanya, 56, 127, 139, 149, 159, 164, 191, 201, 204, 206f., 212, 216ff., 219, 227, 232f., 237f., 239, 269
Chandidas, 209
Chela, disciple
China, religions of, 97, 252, 266
Chrysostom, 135

279

Coats, R. H., 251
Coe, 13, 116, 179
Communism, 230, 232
Complex, 178, 259 f.
Compunction, 251
Confirmation, 131
Confucius, 97
Copleston, 70, 73
Cornelius, 36, 189
"Counter Conversion," 192
Crates, 91 f., 236
Crowd, psychology of, 198 ff., 202 ff., 205 ff.
Cumont, 94, 104 f., 107
Cutten, 206
Cybele, see Magna Mater
Cynics, 91 ff., 236

Davenport, 197, 221
Dayananda Saraswati, 63, 129 f., 145, 179, 248
Definition of conversion, 13 f., 258
Deissmann, 45, 177, 188, 241
Demons, fear of, 133, 136 f., 247
Dengyo, 131
Deussen, 267
Devadasis, temple-women, often prostitutes
Dhamma, Pali for *dharma*
Dhanurdasa, 53
Dharma, religion, the Hindu law of conduct
Dill, 107, 236
Dio Chrysostom, 236
Diogenes, 91
Doctrinal formulation of conversion, 252 ff.
Durkheim, 105
Dynamic, feeling of, 168 ff.

Egyptian religion, 95 f.
Eleusinia, 106, 108
Eliezer b. Durdaiya, 21 f.
Ellwood, Thos., 121
Euripides, 90
Expansion of intellectual powers at conversion, 240 ff.
Ezekiel, 18 f.

Faith, 253 f., 273
Fariduddin Attar, 88
Fear as a motive to conversion, 134 ff., 207

Feine, 169, 177, 253 f.
Finney, C. G., 147, 165, 184, 189, 202 f., 208, 229, 247
Forgiveness, 252 f.
Fox, George, 119 f., 198 f., 203 f., 218, 224 f., 235, 243
Francis of Assisi, 117 f., 148
Freedom, 261
Fruits of conversion, 223 ff., 248 f., 252, 261 ff., 271 ff., 276
Fudayl, 83
Fursac, 174, 195, 225

Generosity, 230
Gennrich, 114, 169
Ghat, river-side steps
Ghazali, 14, 89, 134
Gita, 50, 265
Glossolalia (speaking in a tongue), 34, 211
"God-fearers," 200, 224
Gore, Bishop, 186
Govinda Das, 139, 207
Grace, 170 ff., 194 f., 256, 261, 265, 268 f., 275
Granger, F. S., 151, 168, 174
Grief as a motive to conversion, 139
Grierson, 51 f.
Guru, spiritual guide
Guyon, Madame, 119, 191

Hadfield, 186, 195
Hallaj, 233
Harnack, 153, 230, 275
Hazarilal, 64, 238
Hilprecht, Professor, 194
Honen, 98
Hopkins, 226
Howley, 226, 251
Hujwiri, 83
Humility, 239 ff., 249
Hypnotism and revivalist methods, 220

Incidence of conversion, 251 f.
Inge, Dean, 222
Initiation, chap. ix., *passim*.
Isaiah, 18 f., 165
Isis, 104, 107

Jackson, H. W. V., 96
Jacoponi da Todi, 139
Jalaluddin Rumi, 88, 149

Index and Glossary

James, Wm., 11, 14, 116, 153, 163, 165, 168, 179, 182, 184, 223, 230, 240, 259
Jami, 89
Japan, religions of, 97, 131
Jeremiah, 18 f.
Jesus Christ, 24–33, 109, 253, 271 ff., 276 f.
Jhana, Pali for *jnana*
Jivan-mukta (delivered while on earth), 49, 267
Jnana, knowledge.
Jnana-marga (Way of Knowledge), 47 ff., 249 f., 254, 258 f., 262, 267 f.
John the Baptist, 23 ff., 109
Jonah, 20
Jones, Rufus M., 166, 195
Jones, Sir Henry, 193 f.
Joy, 153 ff.
Judaism, 20 f., 252, 266
Jung, 167
Justin Martyr, 224

Kabir, 55, 126 f., 161 f., 228
Karma, 46, 246, 250, 254, 268 ff., 275
Kennedy, H. A. A., 111
Kirtan, shortened form of *sankirtan*
Kobo, 97 f., 131, n. 1
Krishna, 51, 265, 269 f., 274

Lao-tse, 97
Le Bon, 210
Love as a motive to conversion, 138
Lucius, 107, 109, 249
Lucretius, 94
Lull, Raymond, 137, 147
Luther, Martin, 135, 189
Lydia, 39, 189

Macnicol, 57, 133, 145, 269
Madhva, 51, 53
Magna Mater, 103 f., 107
Manikka Vachakar, 58 ff., 160 f., 169 f., 227 f.
Mantra, a religious phrase or formula
Marett, 105, 251
Marga, path or way
Margoliouth, 82, 84

Martineau, James, 122 f., 262 f.
Mecca, pilgrimage to, 197
Mira Bai, 52, 127, 149
Missionary zeal, 234 ff., 250, 271
Mithraism, 104, 107
Mogallana, 71
Moksa (release from karmic bonds), 46
Montefiore, 21, 25 f., 27 ff.
Moody, Campbell N., 230, 275
Moody, D. L., 138, 163 f., 208
Moral ability, 223 ff., 275
Morgan, W., 242
Moses, 19, 166
Motives of conversion, 133 ff.
Mozoomdar, P. C., 63 f., 246
Muhammad, 80, 266 f.
Mukti, release from karmic bonds
Mus'ab b. 'Umayr, 81
Mystery religions, 93 f., 103 ff., 108 ff., 136, 171, 197

Namdev, 54, 138, 159 f., 228
Name, change of, 101 f., 103
Newness, feeling of, 162 ff.
Nibbana, Pali form of Nirvana
Nichiren, 99, 164 f., 247
Nicholson, R. A., 86, 134
Nimbarka, 51

Oaksmith, 92
Oldenberg, 77 f., 124
Omar, 81, 138, n. 3
"Once-born," 190
Onesimus, 43

Pandas, temple ministrants
Pantheism, 245
Parenti, John, 183
Parsis, *see* Zoroastrianism
Pascal, 166
Paul, the apostle, 14, 35, 37–44, 110 f., 135, 145, 151 f., 153 f., 163, 165, 167 ff., 177 ff., 182, 187 ff., 199, 222, 224, 234, 239, 241 f., 259, 273 f.
Pauline theology, genesis of, 241 f.
Penn, Wm., 120
Pentecost, 33 f., 200, 230
Peter, Simon, 26, 34, 117
Philip, the evangelist, 35
Photisms, 164 ff.

Pindas, balls of rice offered to ancestors
Plan of salvation, 147, 248
Plutarch, 107
Polemon, 123
Pratt, 11, 116, 143, 187
Preaching, 240
Prophets of Old Testament, 18 ff., 252
Psychotherapy, 186, 195

Quakers, 119 ff., 198 f., 224 f., 229, 231 f., 235

Rabi'a, 85
Rahula, 125
Ram Mohan Roy, 63
Rama, 270 f., 274
Ramakrishna, 65 f., 246, 249
Ramananda, 51, 53, 270
Ramanuja, 51, 53
Re-association, 186
Rebirth, *see* Regeneration
Regeneration, 100 ff., 112 ff.
Remorse as a motive to conversion, 138
Repentance, 113, 246, 252 ff., 272
Repression, 178 ff., 190
Restitution, 229 f.
Reversed effort, law of, 185 n.
Revivals, 174, 197 ff.
Rhys Davids, Mr. and Mrs., 67, 74, 78, 125, 150, 236, 246
Roberts, Evan, 201, 204, 210
Robinson, H. W., 15, 169
Rolle, Richard, 118, 166

Sacred thread, investiture with, 102 f.
Sadhu, religious mendicant
Saiva-Siddhanta, a Tamil school of Hindu philosophy, 269, 275
Salvation Army, 206, 210, 223 n.
Samadhi, a state of intense concentration of mind
Samana, a mendicant ascetic
Samsara, the process of transmigration
Samuel, 17
Sanctification, 273 f.
Sangha, the Buddhist order of monks
Sankara, 48, 51, 245 f.

Sankirtan, 206 ff., 209, 217
Sannyasi, a wandering ascetic
Sariputta, 71
Sat-guru, real *guru*
Schultz, 252
Schweitzer, 30, 136, 242
Scoffers converted, 218 ff.
Scott, E. F., 24, 112, 272
Self-surrender, 143, 184 ff., 248, 258 f.
Sen, Keshab Chandra, 63, 128 f., 197, 204, 239, 246
Seneca, 123 n., 171
Sergius Paulus, 37
Sex libido, 191
Shradda, post-funeral rites
Simon Magus, 35
Sin, 132 f., 245 ff., 271 f.
Singing, effect of, 205 ff., 214 f.
Siva, 57, 265, 269, 274
Socrates, 91
Stalker, 135, 141
Starbuck, 12 f., 116, 132, 141, 147, 153, 163, 184, 221, 230
Stead, W. T., 122
Stevenson, Mrs. Sinclair, 47, 102 f., 268
Stoics, 91 ff., 236
Subconsciousness, 176 f.
Subhadda, 72 ff.
Sublimation, 190 ff.
Sudden conversions, 177 ff.
Sudra, the lowest Hindu caste
Sufiism, 82 ff., 148 f., 172, 233, 252 f.
Suggestion, suggestibility, 195, 202 f., 218 ff., 221
Sundaramurti, 62
Suso, Henry, 118, 191

Tagore, Debendranath, 63 f., 128, 162, 170 f., 238, 246
Tagore, Rabindranath, 129, 163, 267
Tayumanavar, 62
Tennyson, 180
Teresa, St., 118, 249
Testimony, 210 f.
Thera-theri-gatha, 74 ff. and *passim*
Thouless, 131, 151, 181 f., 184, 190
Tilak, N. V., 132 f.
Timothy, 39, 117
Tirunavukkarasu, 62, 161

Index and Glossary 283

Tol, school
Torrey, 205, 210, 213 f., 220
Tukaram, 54 f., 139, 149, 160, 170, 232 f., 243 f.
Tulsi, a plant sacred to Krishna
Tulsi Das, 47, 56 f., 263, 270

Upanishads, 47 f., 167, 249 f.

Vane, Sir Harry, 121 f.
Varamukhi, 191, 227
Vedanta, a monistic system of Hindu philosophy
Vedas, 46
Vidyapati, 209
Vimala, 78
Visions, 164 ff., 247 f.
Visnuswamin, 51
Vitality, 240 ff.
Voices, 164 ff., 247 f.

Volitional type of conversion, 143, 248

Warneck, 133, 138, 155, 224, 230, 234, 247, 249
Weinel, 234
Wellhausen, 26, 224
Welsh Revival, 138, 174 f., 201, 205 f., 209, 214 f., 218 f., 221 f., 225 f.
Wesley, John, 14 f., 122, 135, 189, 218, 243
Will, in conversion, 143, 248, 259 f.

Yama, the Hindu god of death
Yasa, 70, 124
Yoga, 49 f., 166 f.

Zacchæus, 29 f., 138, 224, 229
Zeno, 92
Zoroastrianism, 96 f., 103, 252, 266

GEORGE ALLEN & UNWIN LTD.
LONDON: 40 MUSEUM STREET, W.C.1
CAPE TOWN: 73 ST. GEORGE'S STREET
SYDNEY, N.S.W.: 46 CARRINGTON STREET
WELLINGTON, N.Z.: 4 WILLIS STREET

A Jewish Portrait of Jesus
His Times, His Life, and His Teaching
By JOSEPH KLAUSNER
Translated by the Rev. Canon H. DANBY

Demy 8vo.   18*s.*

Though Jesus was a Jew, His followers are not Jews. This "great contradiction" constitutes the difficult and complicated problem in every attempt to portray the life of Jesus. The present book is an attempt to solve this problem. It first presents a rather full account of the times of Jesus and of His Jewish environment, and then seeks to discover what there was in Him of earlier and contemporary Judaism, and likewise what there was in Him which was opposed to the Judaism of His own time as well as to that of the past and the future generations of Israel.

What Jesus Read :
His Dependence and Independence
By Rev. THOMAS WALKER, D.D. (Lond.).

Cr. 8vo.   4*s.* 6*d.*

An ever-increasing number of people are becoming interested in the relationship between Judaism and Christianity. Adherents of both faiths are more interested in one another than they have been. The centre of this interest tends more and more to be Jesus. This little book seeks to answer three questions concerning Jesus, namely : What, and where, did Jesus read ? What was the extent of His dependence on the teaching of His own synagogue ? In what respects does He reveal His own independence of mind ? Dr. Walker here seeks to serve two classes of readers, namely, those who desire to get at once at the results of independent research without the toil which the reading of larger works would involve, and those who, having read these, would like to have by them a handy statement of results. The discerning treatment of Judaism, which is a characteristic of Dr. Walker's earlier work, characterizes as much this more popular work. His chapter on reading facilities, most readers will find, will lead them to consider an aspect of the life of Jesus that had not as much as occurred to many.

The Unwritten Gospel:
Ana and Agrapha of Jesus
By Rev. RODERIC DUNKERLEY, B.A., B.D.

La. Cr. 8vo.   7*s.* 6*d.*

The closing words of the Fourth Gospel remind us that Jesus said and did " many other things " which for various reasons were not included in the canonical records. The study of the sayings ascribed to Him elsewhere than in the Bible and of other extra-canonical matter relating to the Gospel story is a fascinating one. In the present work—the largest on this subject in English—nearly 250 passages are gathered and commented upon, which either are possibly authentic or at least appear to express some Christian truth happily. It represents in a measure the sort of " extra " Gospel that was not written, but might well have been.

Christian Monasticism
By IAN C. HANNAH, F.S.A.
Professor of Church History, Oberlin College

Sm. Demy 8vo.   10s. 6d.

An account of monasticism, from the early Egyptian movement on, which is not only historically well-balanced, but makes interesting reading. Particular attention is given to Cluny, St. Francis, and St. Bernard. The especial contribution which the general reader would get from the way that Professor Hannah treats his subject is the share which the monks had in the work of social transformation, in the building up of agriculture, the welfare of the state, and the extension of missions. There is also a chapter full of surprises on the part played by the monks in military affairs. Profound respect for the great monastic movement is the final impression which the book will leave with the reader.

The Historical Jesus
By C. PIEPENBRING
TRANSLATED BY L. A. CLARE

Cr. 8vo.   7s. 6d.

"The book meets a long need. Especially will it be valuable to the reader who has little or no time to study the larger and more technical treatises."—*Yorkshire Post.*

The Message about the Cross:
A Fresh Study of the Doctrine of the Atonement
By REV. C. J. CADOUX, M.A., D.D.

Cr. 8vo.   3s. 6d.

This book restates in modern terms what is generally known as the "moral theory" of the Atonement. It tries to do full justice to aspects of the truth represented by older theories, and also emphasizes the bearing which any adequate understanding of the death of Jesus must have on Christian Ethics.

Quaker Thought and History:
A Volume of Essays
By EDWARD GRUBB, M.A.

Cr. 8vo.   5s.

The history of the little Quaker body repeats, on a smaller scale, many aspects of the history of the Church at large, and throws light on some of its problems. In this volume the author, a Quaker modernist who has made a life study of the subject, has gathered together a number of essays and addresses, most of which deal, from his own point of view, with matters of general interest and pressing importance. Such are "The Use of the Mind in Religion," "Christ and the World Problem," "Creed and Life," "Christian Reunion," and "Spiritual Healing." The relations between Mystical and Evangelical thought and experience are illustrated in the essay on the impact of the Evangelical revival on the Society of Friends; and the modern attempt to recover for Christianity its old power of spiritual healing is shown to have been made, with some success, by the early Quakers. The guiding thought throughout is that Christianity is essentially not a fabric of beliefs but a new experience of God, and a life of whole-hearted following of Jesus Christ.

THE CHRISTIAN REVOLUTION SERIES

Edited by NATHANIEL MICKLEM, M.A.

The Christian Revolution
By Dr. HENRY T. HODGKIN   Cr. 8vo, 7s. 6d.

The Constructive Revolution of Jesus
By Professor SAMUEL DICKEY   Cr. 8vo, 6s.; Paper, 3s. 6d.

Religion and Biology
By ERNEST E. UNWIN, M.Sc.   Cr. 8vo, 6s.

Essays in Christian Thinking
By A. T. CADOUX, B.A., D.D.   Cr. 8vo, 6s. 6d.

Christian Justice
By NORMAN L. ROBINSON, M.A.   Cr. 8vo, 6s. 6d.

Christ and Cæsar
By N. MICKLEM AND HERBERT MORGAN   Cr. 8vo, 6s. 6d.

The Meaning of Paul for To-day   By Professor
C. H. DODD, M.A. *Second Impression.*   Cr. 8vo, 6s. 6d.

The Remnant By RUFUS M. JONES   Cr. 8vo, 5s. 6d.

The Christ of Revolution
By JOHN R. COATES, B.A.   Cr. 8vo, Cloth, 5s.; Paper, 3s.

The Way to Personality By GEORGE B. ROBSON
Third Edition.   Cr. 8vo, Cloth, 5s.; Paper, 3s

The Christian Ideal By W. E. WILSON   Cr. 8vo, 5s. 6d.

The Open Light By NATHANIEL MICKLEM   Cr. 8vo, 5s.

Reconciliation and Reality
By W. FEARON HALLIDAY   *Second Impression.*   Cr. 8vo, 5s.

The Early Christian Attitude to War
By C. J. CADOUX, M.A., D.D.   Cr. 8vo, 10s. 6d.

Lay Religion By HENRY T. HODGKIN, M.A.   Cr. 8vo, 4s.

Man and His Buildings
By T. S. ATLEE, A.R.I.B.A.   *Illustrated.* Cr. 8vo, 6s.

The Kingship of God
By GEORGE B. ROBSON   Cr. 8vo, Cloth, 5s.; Paper, 3s.

Economic Justice
By GERARD COLLIER, M.A.   Cr. 8vo, Cloth, 7s. 6d.; Paper, 5s.

The Mystical Quest of Christ
By REV. R. F. HORTON, D.D. *Cheaper Edition.* La. Cr. 8vo, 5s.
"A book packed with good things."—*British Weekly.*

Living Issues in Religious Thought
From George Fox to Bertrand Russell
By PROF. H. G. WOOD.
(*Selly Oak Colleges Publications*, No. 6) Cr. 8vo, 6s.

Ideas of God in Israel Their Content and Development
By REV. EDWARD PACE, D.D. Demy 8vo, 10s. 6d.
"A notable book."—*Spectator.*

The Teaching of Jesus and the Jewish Teaching of His Age
By REV. THOMAS WALKER, D.D. Demy 8vo, 12s. 6d.
"This scholarly and illuminating treatise."—*Spectator.*

The Pharisees
By REV. R. TRAVERS HERFORD, B.A. Demy 8vo, 10s. 6d.
"The spirit in which the book is written is as admirable as the learning manifest on every page."—*Manchester Guardian.*

The Legends of Israel Essays in interpretation of some famous stories from the Old Testament
By REV. LEWIS JOHNSON. Cr. 8vo, 7s. 6d.
"The preacher will find real help in this book."—*Church Times.*

Christianity and the Religions of the World
By DR. ALBERT SCHWEITZER.
(*Selly Oak Colleges Publications*, No. 3) Cr. 8vo, 3s. 6d.
"Everything from Dr. Schweitzer's pen carries with it the flavour of his heroic mind."—*British Weekly.*

All prices are net.
LONDON: GEORGE ALLEN & UNWIN LTD.
RUSKIN HOUSE, 40 MUSEUM STREET, W.C.1

For Product Safety Concerns and Information please contact our EU representative GPSR@taylorandfrancis.com
Taylor & Francis Verlag GmbH, Kaufingerstraße 24, 80331 München, Germany

www.ingramcontent.com/pod-product-compliance
Lightning Source LLC
Chambersburg PA
CBHW071808300426
44116CB00009B/1242